Contents

Acknowledgments

It's sort of miraculous how we meet the right people in this world who inspire and encourage us to open up and become who we are meant to be. Michael Foster Stewart asked me to form a band with him while I was still a classical violinist in music school. Poi dog Pondering, Alejandro Escovedo, Charlie Sexton, and Giant Sand took me on tour and showed me the world. My mom wanted to travel more than she did and always asked me what it was like on the road—the land, the architecture, the accents, the flavor of a local meal. I wrote it all down. Years later I pulled boxes of journals from the closet shelf to refer back to while writing this book. I thank the entire Cast of Characters for their friendship and each memorable quote of perfection uttered during those colorful tours.

The book would have been incomplete without the help of everyone who kindly agreed to be interviewed. You've given the reader a depth of insight that only your knowledge and experience can provide. Also, I thank everyone I pestered into sending tour forms and documents. These are golden. I'm grateful to the photographers who capture an impossible subject and offered many, many photos to choose from.

And finally, I thank Frank Q. Orrall, my good friend and musical compadre, for taking me on my first tour and showing me, with his elegance and extravagance, not only how to tour well but how to live well.

THE
MUSICIAN'S GUIDE
TO THE ROAD

A SURVIVAL HANDBOOK &
ALL ACCESS BACKSTAGE PASS
TO TOURING

Susan Voelz

BILLBOARD BOOKS
an imprint of Watson-Guptill Publications
New York

Executive Editor: Bob Nirkind
Project Editor: Ross Plotkin
Production Manager: Salvatore Destro
Interior Designer: Meryl Levavi
Cover Design by Steven Cooley, Cooley Design Lab

The principal typefaces used in the composition of this book were Caslon
BookBQ and Memphis.

First published in 2007 by Billboard Books,
an imprint of Watson-Guptill Publications,
Nielsen Business Media,
a division of The Nielsen Company
770 Broadway, New York, NY 10003
www.watsonguptill.com

Library of Congress Control Number: 2007920285
ISBN-13: 978-0-8230-7776-2
ISBN-10: 0-8230-7776-4

Printed in the United States
First printing, 2007
1 2 3 4 5 6 7 8 9 / 14 13 12 11 10 09 08 07

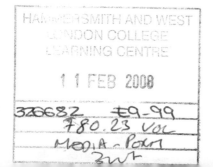

Photo Credits:

Melissa d'Attilio (The author at the Double Door in Chicago)

Rob Meyers (Matt Morrison unloading gear from the box truck)

Miko (Poi dog Pondering, circa 1988)

S. M. V. (Jared having morning coffee, front lounge of the bus in the Canadian Rockies)

Matt Carmichael (Guitar in silhouette and Frank Orrall swinging the "light bulb of death" overhead at the Metro in Chicago)

Tour forms and documents provided by:

Ben Richardson, Tour Manager and Sound Engineer for Alejandro Escovedo–Stage Plot, Input List, Day Sheet, Itinerary Page, Grady Rider

Gil Gastelum, Cosmica Artists–Weekly Income Report, Weekly Tour Report, Backline List, Performance Settlement Sheet, Merchandise Settlement Sheet

Jackson Haring, High Road Touring–Performance Contract, Deal Memo

Matt Morrison, Stage Manager PdP and Thievery Corporation–Show Advance Form

Frank Snowden, Snowden Custom Coach–Bus Lease Agreement

Poi Dog Pondering–Technical Rider

Additional thank you:

Dag Juhlin penned the back-cover text and seasoned the intro

Brigid Murphy performed the second editing of the introduction and epilogue

Jeff Voelz scanned and prepared photos and documents printed herein

Introduction

A rock tour is one long kiss on the lips of excess.

It starts simply with a song you love. Then there's a melody in your head you coax onto a four track tape recorder set up in your bedroom. You'd love to hear your music coming out of a car radio. You imagine performing on *Saturday Night Live*. So you form a band with some friends, record a CD and go out on tour. Somewhere out on that road, you flip on a radio and there you are.

My journey as a touring creative musician began one rainy night in Austin, Texas, playing at the Continental Club with Ronnie Lane, Alejandro Escovedo, and the Seven Samurai. We'd first met the night before, rehearsing in front of a fireplace drinking rum in coffee cups. I was a classical violinist and had recently arrived in town with my Fostex four track, not sure what I was searching for but sensing I'd stumbled into something. Opening the show at the Continental that night was a young band, Poi dog Pondering, who were about to record their first record and asked if I'd come play some "fiddle" on it.

Poi dog Pondering and Alejandro Escovedo came to be the musicians with whom I'd spend the majority of my musical touring life—first in a cargo van with a mattress in the back and later traveling on two tour buses; from driving miles to play at a run-down club with more people on stage than in the audience to storming the stage of a sold-out Red Rocks Amphitheatre in Colorado, opening for the Dave Matthews Band; from Austin, Texas to the U. S., Canada, and Europe.

A friend asked me "Why rock? Why go out on the road for two hours of rock?" Because rock says I am and I can. It's every moment of your life that you held back finally set free, ablaze with both fury and delight. It's reckless and raw and selfish and truthful. You don't have to sell your soul for rock 'n' roll, but you will have to risk revealing your soul to find it.

The idea for this book came in pieces. My friend was going on tour with Bob Dylan and asked, "What's it going to be like on a tour bus?" I told her to sleep with her feet toward the front of the bus (see: Estefan, Gloria), liquids only in the bus bathroom, and never open a bunk curtain if it's closed. At the same time, a new version of Poi dog Pondering was planning an East Coast tour and one of the new members asked, "How many suitcases should I bring?" I thought "How many?" It was clear that we needed a handbook. We were about to take seventeen people on a tour bus meant for twelve and only three had been on the road before. I wrote a short "pocket handbook." Along with rules and tips, I included journal entries and "Quotes of the Day" (nuggets of accidental wisdom or droll non sequiturs uttered by sleep-deprived, anxious, or wine-filled tourmates) I had stealthily collected in a notebook on previous tours.

The pocket handbook may have remained a ten-page document but every time I came home from tour I'd add more information, freshly minted revelations, and of course more quotes of the day. Soon it was a messy, bulging manuscript; a teetering, overgrown pile of data begging to be groomed.

The late Timothy White, former editor of *Billboard* magazine, read an early version. "It's a remedy for the road," he said. "You've done a wonderful job. Add more serious, credible tips, fix the typos and send it back to me." Encouraged, I asked myself: "What do I wish I had known? How could I have avoided all those unnecessary heartbreaks and headaches?" So I broadened my scope to include other perspectives besides the musicians', to include the decidedly non-rock realities that ride shotgun on every rock tour.

In your hands is a comprehensive touring guidebook. The information will prepare you for a five-week tour. Chapters are arranged chronologically, covering everything from tour preparation to day-to-day life on the road, and finally the shock of re-entry when the tour ends. You may be a musician about to go on the road for the first time. You may be a manager or tour manager wanting your upcoming tour to run smoothly, or perhaps you used to tour and are curious now to read an account of it from the ease of your home. Maybe you'll never travel the world in a rock band but secretly always wanted to and you just wonder what it's like. This is your all access backstage pass.

Every tour is different yet every tour is the same. It's a layered journey: personal, musical, familial, financial, and fanciful. You go out on the road to support your record, happy to be playing in front of an audience night after night, but something unexpected happens: As a tour bangs you up, it shines you up. It begins to show you who you are.

Whether you're in an indie rock band or traveling as a solo artist, a touring veteran or virgin, we all meet the same road and some days we all could use a map. May this handbook in some way serve as your roadmap.

Cast of Characters

- Joey Burns–Calexico founder
- Matt Carmichael–Concert photographer
- Bill Carter–Filmmaker and author
- Ted Cho–Guitarist and mandolin player with Poi dog, record producer
- John Convertino–Most amazing drummer of Calexico and Giant Sand
- Robert Cornelius–"Roberto Cornelioso," actor, singer, PdP member during the *Pomegranate* era
- Max (Dave Max) Crawford–Trumpet, Mellotron, keyboards, set-list maker, king of segues, Austin and Chicago PdP
- Jody Denberg–Program director and DJ, KGSR in Austin, Texas
- El John (John Nelson)–Percussionist, drummer, PdP and Thievery Corporation
- Alejandro Escovedo–Writer, singer, rocker
- Peggy Firestone–Psychotherapist
- Matt Fish–Cellist with the Alejandro Escovedo Orchestra
- Keith Fletcher–PdP's first tour manager and sound engineer
- Deanne Franklin–PdP's sound woman during the Austin years, later front-of-house sound for Tom Waits, Sonic Youth, the Breeders, David Byrne
- Jimmy "G" Galocy–Stage manager, Chicago PdP, Smash Mouth
- Gil Gastelum–Tour manager for Alejandro Escovedo and David Garza
- Heinz Geissler–Alejandro Escovedo's manager
- Howe Gelb–Founder of Giant Sand, poet, cowboy
- Steve Goulding–Acclaimed English drummer, PdP member during the *Pomegranate* and *Natural Thing* eras
- Jon Dee Graham–Songwriter, singer, blazing guitarist
- Howard Greynolds–Thrill Jockey Records
- Kornell Hargrove–PdP singer, fireman, paramedic

- Jackson Haring–Austin PdP tour manager, now with High Road Touring
- Daren Hess–Drummer, Austin PdP
- Chris Houda–"Twin," PdP stage tech
- Josh Houda–"Tokyo," PdP stage tech and monitor engineer
- Bruce Hughes–Bassist, Austin PdP
- Jelle–Calexico sound engineer from Amsterdam
- Dag Juhlin–Guitarist, rocker, writer, member of Poi dog Pondering
- Greg Kott–Music critic, *Chicago Tribune*
- Brad Madison–Booking agent, Mongrel Music
- Yvonne Matsell–Director, North by Northeast; talent buyer for El Mocambo
- Abra Moore–Singer, songwriter, Hawaii PdP
- Matt Morrison–PdP stage manager and monitor engineer, Thievery Corporation stage tech
- Frank Quimby Orrall–Founder of Poi dog Pondering, 8fatfat8, singer, writer, and drummer/percussionist; also performs with Thievery Corporation
- Dr. Andy Pasminski–Chiropractic physician, naprapathic specialist
- Laureline Prud'homme–Singer, Giant Sand
- David Pulkingham III–Guitarist with Alejandro Escovedo Orchestra
- Mike Reed–Lighting director and owner of Reed Rigging
- Ben Richardson–Tour manager, bass player
- Mike Santucci–Audiologist, Sensaphonics
- Luke Savisky–Film-loop artist and projectionist
- Billy Schmidt–PdP's first monitor man, later front-of-house sound for Aimee Mann and Beth Orton
- Charlie Sexton–Singer, songwriter, guitarist with Bob Dylan, record producer
- Martin Stebbing–PdP's longtime front-of-house English sound and recording engineer
- Mark Stevens–Chicago PdP monitor engineer, now in Minneapolis
- Patrice Sullivan–Masseuse, acupuncturist, nutritionist, sang on the first Poi dog Pondering record
- Adam Sultan–Guitarist, Austin PdP
- Chris Von Thies–Head talent buyer for Direct Events, Inc.
- Ken Wagner–PdP tour manager during the *Natural Thing* era, now with Wilco
- Gloria Winter–Musicians' personal assistant
- Maggie Wrigley–Self-described "door bitch" at Mercury Lounge

1. Preparing Yourself to Tour

I just flew to Tucson to begin the Giant Sand tour, and no one is here at the airport to pick me up. I call Howe. "Am I not there to get you?" he asks. And so tour begins.

A rock tour is a bit like Shackleton's valiant voyage to the South Pole, without the ice (*usually* no ice) and no arctic sea. You leave home for a long stretch of time. Pay is low. You've got to pack lightly and wisely. You'll be cold. You'll be hot. If you get sick, you can't go home. There are usually more guys than girls. Food is local and can be surprisingly good or just awful. Sleep is hard to come by. You'll daydream of the faraway land where you live. You'll see some amazing things and meet some great characters. It's good to get off the ship. It's good to return to the ship. You don't want to get left behind. You might overdrink to relax. You will love your mates. You probably shouldn't sleep with them. You'll be amazed how weird they can be when you thought you knew them. Some days you won't even recognize yourself. If the expedition is successful, fame and fortune might be yours, although a successful expedition is doubtful.

How can you prepare yourself for the unpreparable journey? First and foremost, you need to make sure you want to go out on tour in the first place. It's a complete immersion in another life. If you're going to fight it, forget it. You'll pull against yourself, you'll be unhappy, you'll be a complainer. You've got to feel strongly enough about yourself or your band and what you offer it to live the life of a touring musician.

Perhaps you're on back-to-back tours and really want some time off. Perhaps home life is pulling you to stay. Perhaps there's something else you'd really rather be doing. Sometimes you won't actually know that you want to go on tour until you're in the van or on the bus on your way out of town.

> Dag was asked to be one of two openers for a solo songwriter tour. He's not so sure about going out. "Am I just gonna be the third guy in the backseat who pumps the gas while they sit up front telling stories of Michael Stipe?"

You may need to ask yourself at some point whether this is your dream or whether you're simply supporting someone else's. Perhaps seeing the world and performing and partying are enough. Perhaps you're getting your shot at the music business that everyone said was impossible. Perhaps you're being paid a lot of money.

But be forewarned: if you go out as the drummer and you're really a writer or a singer, you'll henceforth be known as a drummer (unless you were in Nirvana, which you were not). If you go out as a tech, and you're a creative musician, you'll be an arm's length (or stage width) from your dream, but not living it. You may become so frustrated that you become the problem drinker or the difficult tech who's not a tech and calls himself "talent." Worse yet, you may give up and become resigned to the improbability of your own heart's desire.

> "Because there is only one of you in all of time, this expression is unique and if you block it, it will never exist through any other medium and be lost. The world will not have it. It is not your business to determine how good it is or how valuable nor how it compares with other expressions."–Martha Graham

Ideally you'll begin your tour healthy and well rested. The night before leaving, you intend to have a good dinner and go to bed early, but that rarely happens. You'll be up late, pack until dawn, and then be unable to fall asleep.

You need to make some practical preparations before you leave town. You need to make a budget. You'll need to make a stage plot and input list. You'll call and "advance" your show with the club, going over contract details. (See "Advancing Your Show," page 29.) You need to rent a van or lease a tour bus. You'll buy a big road atlas if you don't already have one. You need to map out the best route to each gig and know the distance in miles and hours. You may need to get some new guitar cables and maybe a new effects pedal so you aren't the big technical problem being sorted out mid-show each night.

Author Tour Tip: Please don't use the tour to begin your rehab, your sobriety, or your divorce. It may seem like a great time to change your habits—"I won't drink. I'll quit heroin. I'll break up with my girlfriend. I'll drink a lot of water and get healthy. I'll lose weight, read my books, write my book, record songs on my laptop."—but it probably won't happen, because mainly what happens on tour is the tour.

> "Let go. You're not in control of a tour. If you let go of control then you're more in control."—Jelle

Finally, enjoy your tour for exactly what it is. It is its own reward. Don't expect a big payoff of millions of dollars and *Rolling Stone* recognition. Maybe. Maybe not. Then again, quite possibly, maybe.

> "Yes, it's as fun as it looks."—from the Hideout stage in Chicago.

PACKING FOR YOUR TOUR

> If you don't wear it at home, you're not going to wear it on the road.

If your red boots don't fit and you don't choose to wear them at home, they aren't going to suddenly fit and be your favorite boots on tour. How do you decide what and how much comes with you on tour? There are three things to consider: What are you going to do on your tour? What climates will you encounter? How long will you be out?

> "You don't want to ruin your best stuff, but you want to bring something you feel at home in."—Howe

What Are You Going to Do on Tour, and How Will You Dress for It?

You don't want to look like you just rolled off your couch when you make your entrance onstage or when you get recognized at breakfast the morning after your show, unless that's your particular style. You might want to create some mystique. These are the main events of your novice rock star day:

- Out walking around a college town or the downtown (or run-down) section of a major city (daywear)
- Traveling in the van or on the bus (daywear, but more comfortable)
- Radio station or in-store performance (daywear, but foxier)
- Stage getup (foxiest, even if completely casual)
- Fitness room or pool (You'll feel really sorry for yourself when

everyone is sneaking into the hot tub at 3 AM and you don't have a suit or a foxy substitute.)

- Sleep (At some point, sort of, you will sleep, so bring what's cozy.)

What Climates or Seasons or Altitudes Will You Encounter?

On tour, you're outside and affected by weather a lot more than when you're at home. Once you arrive at the venue, you walk to find food or coffee. You don't drive. It's too much of a bother to maneuver and park a van and a trailer. And if you're traveling by bus, once it's parked by the venue the driver is off the clock. The bus doesn't move until the end of the night, so you often walk from the venue to the café to the hotel and back.

These places are not always as close together as we might wish, so you'll be outside and need things like a hat, umbrella, or a rain jacket–things you'd rarely use at home, where as a musician you probably wouldn't take a long walk in an icy rain or under a hot noon sun.

It was 107 degrees here yesterday, like a disease.

It's also important to keep in mind that seasons start and end at different times in different latitudes. If you're on tour in April and the snow is just melting up north, it'll already be steamy warm in the south. Check out weatherunderground.com for current weather conditions and temperature wherever you are headed.

"Leather and layers."–John Convertino packing tip

SUMMER IN THE SOUTHEAST AND SOUTHWEST. In the Deep South, dress for the really well-air-conditioned buildings, not the street temperature. You may want to wear jeans or long pants and bring your jacket or sweater with you into restaurants, movie theaters, and malls. However, the venue may have sketchy air-conditioning that is turned on only when doors are opened. ("Doors" means the time the audience is let in, usually an hour before showtime.)

We are under an awning that keeps misting us to cool down this 106-degree heat. But it's still way too hot to be out here pretending that it's not.–Phoenix

In the Southwest, many older buildings use something called swamp cooling. It's sort of cool and sort of wet.

Allergy Note: If you travel south in the spring you may discover that you have an allergy to some weed or bloom that you've never had before. Take some Claritin and Visine and skip the dairy food. Know you will be leaving this place tomorrow.

SUMMER IN THE NORTH. The North in the summer gets incredibly humid and hot. The brick and cement buildings in big cities like New York, Chicago, Detroit, and Toronto retain and radiate heat like a sauna. The clubs will have inadequate air-conditioning, if any, so be ready onstage with towels and iced drinks. Wear loose clothing so the sweat can roll down your belly and legs and not just soak your whole outfit. Fortunately, the heat waves usually break with a line of thunderstorms after a few days. (Hopefully these roll into the region while you're sleeping, not driving.)

SUMMER AT A MOUNTAIN FESTIVAL. Telluride, Colorado, is warm in the daytime but by sundown it'll be cool enough for that very heavy sweater you don't have with you. Festival artisans will be selling these near the toe rings. If they "love your band" they may offer to loan you a hand-knit sweater to perform in. It's not your usual stage wear, but you're at a festival, there's a starry night, and you need to be warm.

> Bliss, Idaho. It's windy and dust is flowing like snow. I'm loading my things in the van when a tumbleweed rolls by. Walking to the café, my mouth is full of grit and my skin is filmed with fine dust. I understand why cowboys wore kerchiefs over their faces.

You'll walk more at a festival than in a town. In the West, generally, you'll walk or hike more than in the East. There's more land, fewer buildings. You mean to bring comfortable walking shoes but you won't really know your shoes until you've walked around a festival. They may be heavier or more slippery than you ever knew.

WINTER IN THE SOUTH. When it gets cold in the South, it's uncomfortable because the South isn't used to it. Older homes and cheaper hotels have inadequate heat. Clubs may have strange heat-coil contraptions suspended overhead to heat the room. Fortunately, onstage during the show, the heat from the lights and the crowd will warm you up. Backstage you'll want your jacket, and in your hotel room your leather coat will double as a blanket.

WINTER IN THE NORTH. On one tour, we left Austin on a temperate morning in February heading north to Chicago. Every time we stopped for gas it was 20 degrees colder. Finally we had to unlock the trailer to get out the suitcases to retrieve sweaters and hats. Don't become alarmed by the memory of your Southern newspaper calling 32-degree weather "Killer Cold!" Your face will be okay. Your fingers won't turn black from frostbite. At 25 degrees, though, you'll want to wear mittens and a hat or your hands and ears will ache. Mom said, "Eighty percent of your body heat escapes through the top of your head," so wear your hat.

Author Note: Bulky winter clothes and boots take up more room than summer clothes. You may need a larger suitcase. (See "What Size Suitcase Should You Bring?" below.)

> "Cold today, quite cold tonight, continued very cold but not quite as cold tomorrow," the weatherman just informed us.

THE PACIFIC NORTHWEST. Early in the year in San Francisco or Seattle it will rain and rain and rain. I never bring an umbrella. If you need one on a very rainy day, then buy one.

THE EAST COAST. Bring something to dress up if you are going to the East Coast. Someone may want to take you to dinner, and your jeans and T-shirt look like you just came out of a van with Texas plates. I know you did, but you can express your soul now; you're in a touring rock band.

How Long Is Your Tour?

Tours vary a lot in length, from one week to two months. I'm sorry, a weekend out of town is not a tour. Basically, pack for a week of fairly temperate weather. The longer the tour, the more options you'll need for your mood. You'll do laundry, or better yet have it done for you, about every eight days, so on a five-week tour you don't need to bring thirty-five pairs of socks.

What Size Suitcase Should You Bring?

Now that you've thought about what you're going to do on your tour, where you're going to go, and how long you'll be on the road, you need to think about what size suitcase to take. Here are some suggestions:

- One-week U.S. temperate tour = One 22-×-14-inch expandable suitcase
- One-week U.S. winter tour = One 24-×-18-inch expandable suitcase
- More than two weeks U.S. tour = One 22-×-14-inch or one 24-×-18-inch expandable suitcase
- Any length European tour = One 22-×-14-inch expandable suitcase. A small suitcase is infinitely easier to maneuver if you're traveling on and off trains, staying in hotels with small European elevators or perhaps with no elevators, walking with your luggage on cobblestone streets, or being picked up in smaller European vehicles by promoters.

Every tour I've been on, there's a macho "looking over of the bags." If you have a huge and heavy bag, be ready to be teased about it. "Whose bag is *that?*" You'll be glad it isn't yours, because it implies you don't know how to tour, can't make clothing decisions, and in essence don't rock. However, if every day you wear one of three outfits and every night you've got the same sweaty show clothes on, you should have brought more. You won't think you've internalized your bandmates' complete wardrobes, but as soon as someone wears a newly purchased shirt, you'll know and you'll be happy to see them in it.

Hint: The zippers always break, so choose luggage with strong zippers. A lifetime guarantee would be good, too. Swiss Army suitcases have both.

What about Suitcase Weight?

Can you carry your stuff from your front door to the curb to get in a taxi? Can you roll it six blocks and still be in a good mood if the key to your hotel room doesn't work and you have to roll it back six blocks to the front desk? If not, leave something home. The airlines have a weight limit of fifty pounds per bag. You probably don't want to lift any more than that yourself.

> I pack too much again–options for each and every mood, comfort, and weather condition.

Less is more, but more is even more. You be the judge of how much weight you want to deal with day after day after day. If you overpack or overpurchase, you can always mail things home in a box. Find a UPS Store or a FedEx connected to a Kinko's and send extra shoes, books, and those wrong pants home.

Gender Tip: If you are a woman, *be* a woman. Don't feel you need to bring fewer hair products, skin lotions, coats, or boot choices. But remember, if you bring it, you carry it. DO NOT ask anyone to carry your heavy suitcase for you unless he's wearing a red cap and soldier coat and you're paying him a dollar or two a bag.

What to Walk Out of Your Home With

Here are the essentials:

- One suitcase
- A day bag. This could be a backpack, computer bag, or shoulder bag that holds the stuff you'll want during the day, with enough space to store rolled-up clothes for that evening's show.
- An optional smaller purse or bag so you don't always have to carry the very heavy day bag everywhere you go
- Your instrument
- Your gig bag with cables and effects pedals

- Your amp with some sort of cover or case around it
- Perhaps a pillow, and maybe a blanket

The Big Tour Checklist

The day before I leave on tour, I print out a big checklist stored on my computer. Then I list every day we'll be out of town. This helps me visualize just how long this tour is and adjust what I want to bring with me. Making a checklist is helpful because it's so easy to remember everything but the most obvious, important things, like your belt.

BIG TOUR CHECKLIST

- Toiletries
- Makeup
- Socks and underwear
- Pajamas
- Swimsuit and workout clothes
- Shoes and boots
- Pants, belt, skirts, or dresses
- Shirts and tops
- Show clothes
- Jacket and sweater
- Jewelry
- Hat and hair ties
- Cell phone and charger
- Cash and your own personal credit card
- First-aid kit: herbs and medicines
- Entertainment
- Extras

TOILETRIES. Bring the items you actually use every day. Except, use real deodorant on tour. The nonaluminum, naturally fresh deodorant crystal, or Tom's of Maine All Natural, might work just fine for you at home. On the road, on the stage, you're probably going to need a more powerful deodorant. Toiletry items are heavy, so take only what you truly use, and remember that one day something will leak all over everything. You might want to keep bottles of liquids separate in a waterproof bag.

Something else you may not use at home but you might want to use after being in a smoky club each night is face wash. Put some on a wet washcloth, draw it across your face, and look at all the dirt on it. Do you want to sleep with sweat, smoke, and breath stuck to your face all night?

Author's picky editorial regarding hygiene: Why does personal hygiene suffer so on the road? I've seen the great unwashed, and it's not pretty. It may be pretty from a distance, but not sitting next to me for hours. Depending on your tour budget, the bathtub in your hotel may be clean and you can soak in Kneipp bath oils that come in little two-ounce bottles or some bath salts.

Extra Tip: Travel and trial sizes work well. Don't even think of bringing a bar of soap. You could bring a little bottle of Dr. Bronner's Miracle Soap. These days, I just use the soap provided by the hotel.

MAKEUP. Being onstage is theater. If you wear makeup at home, bring it and then play around with more or weirder makeup if you feel like it. If you're doing any TV shows or photo shoots, you might be asked to apply your own makeup (men and women). It helps you show up under bright lights. Bring your own concealer to dab under your eyes (it'll sort of cover the dark circles that appear from lack of sleep and drinking alcohol) and gloss for your lips. If applying some eyeliner or blush feels strange to you, remember that the ancient Greeks wore makeup to simulate the flush of sex. Not a bad thing.

SOCKS AND UNDERWEAR. It's time to do laundry when you run out of clean socks. I bring nine days worth of socks because laundry day is always a few days later than you think. You've still got clean socks while you wait for that day with a laundromat nearby.

PAJAMAS. Maybe you sleep naked at home, but hotel blankets are thin and hotels can be cold. Bring some warm pajamas. Riding the bus overnight, you're going to be seen in your pajamas. When you get up to pee and the late late nighters are still watching a movie or partying, or in the morning as you stumble to the front lounge to see where you are and if anyone else is up, you'll be in your pajamas. You might even stay in your PJs during an all-day drive. So bring some comfortable, sort of foxy pajamas.

Alejandro's up early, walking into the front lounge wearing pajama bottoms and red cowboy boots.

SWIMSUIT AND WORKOUT CLOTHES. You'll have to decide if you want sleep or to have a quick run or a workout. Give yourself the option: bring your workout stuff. You may be absolutely sure there won't be a pool on your budget tour. There will be one. Bring a swim suit. You want to use the hot tub, don't you?

SHOES AND BOOTS. You'll need your everyday shoes, your good-looking boots, your running shoes. You'll want your best, most worked in, comfortable shoes you own. You'll walk more on a tour than you ever do at home. Really? Yes. There's no car. The van with trailer is a bother to park, so it stays put. If you're traveling by bus, once it's parked at the venue, the bus driver disappears until after the show. You probably don't know your way around this town to take a city bus or subway (although you might try). And taxis are either expensive or rare in many cities. So you walk.

And, of course, the people who give you directions always think the recommended restaurant or movie theater is closer than it is. I think they must only drive to these places. The Indian restaurant that's "just around the bend" is actually in the next county. The movie theater "just down the hill" is about eight blocks away. And we're talking country blocks, not city blocks, or even suburban blocks.

Once you're onstage or at the in-store, you might want your red shoes or your Fluevog boots that aren't broken in yet. You want to look good onstage just as much as you want to be comfortable during the day. Fox factor and comfort. You've got to have both. This dichotomy of your day is why suitcases get so heavy.

> "I'll have you know I have on my Elvis T-shirt *and* my blue suede shoes."
> –Robert, before the in-store

PANTS, BELT, SKIRTS, AND DRESSES. Take four pairs of pants. You can wear a pair of pants three or four days before needing to wash them. Bring two skirts or dresses you wear at home. Maybe here is where we have to admit there are both men and women traveling in the band. Suitcases will pack differently. There's a lot of androgyny and levels of male and female in all of us, but women will pack differently than men. Rather than divide the specifics out like this is the employment section of a newspaper in the Fifties, we'll just put it all together.

SHIRTS AND TOPS. Pack five shirts, two T-shirts, and maybe two more show tops. Pack so that most every top goes with every bottom. Black is, of course, always right. White shows up best onstage but is too bright for television shows.

SHOW CLOTHES. Whatever "rock clothes" mean to you, you have the excuse of being onstage to wear them. Whether it's jeans, fur, big hats, scarves, glitter, color, or not, choose the costume for whatever your band and music is expressing. (See "Selecting Your Stage Wear," page 149.) I bring three or four show outfits.

"She's wearing the Liberty Bell and it's a little tight."–Robert, during some awards show we're watching.

If you don't know how to dress, find a stylist. Why not?

JACKET AND SWEATER. Even if you're touring in the summer, bring a jacket, a hoodie, or a sweater. A cold front may come in. Air-conditioning may be refrigerator cold. You may be out in the rain. It's good to have something to put on to keep the cold or wet out.

"I'm telling you, leather is not so much a fabric but a form of defense." –Billy's leather jacket was stolen off the stage during load-out tonight.

JEWELRY. Take nothing you can't bear to lose. This is true of every item. If you remove rings and your watch at night, put them in your boot, not on the nightstand. When you get the wake-up call from hell, you won't leave without your five silver rings and Swatch watch as you scramble out of bed. Instead, you'll pull on your boot and wonder why there seems to be a paper clip under your toe.

HAT AND HAIR TIES. You may not wear a hat so much at home. On tour, it's great to have one. Hats keep the sun out of your eyes and your hair out of your face. If you've been on the bus all night and haven't had a shower as you walk into the radio station or the in-store performance, you can put on your hat to hide your flat hair. In a windy van, you may want a hair tie. It keeps your hair out of your face, and you don't wind up with flat hair from wearing a hat.

CELL PHONE AND CHARGER. Cell phones changed everything about touring. If you're running late and can't find the club, you simply call them and they'll direct your van on into town. You can also keep track of band members. We spent a morning looking for a band member who had gone home with a fan, driving up and down a street another band member sort of remembered the house was on. A cell phone gives you freedom on a day off to take your time and tell your bandmates to go ahead on without you. "I'll call your cell and find you all later."

CASH AND YOUR OWN PERSONAL CREDIT CARD. This is your emotional insurance. If you need to fly home for an emergency, if you must have your own hotel room or you'll kill yourself (or the bass player), if you've found the perfect Kenneth Cole leather jacket on sale, you need your own cash or personal credit card. Plus, there's the slight possibility that the club or promoter won't pay in full, and you'll need to be able to take care of yourself if there's no money from the tour for food or a bed.

Consider very carefully whether you want to put the band hotel rooms on your credit card as a backup if the band card doesn't work. There should be a second card available, and it probably shouldn't be your own personal card.

First-Aid Kit: Herbs and Medicines

Most medicines you need on the road will be pretty basic: tablets or tinctures to avoid pain or to prevent illness. Think of Elvis: pills to wake up, to go to sleep, to aid digestion, and to avoid constipation. Bring some basics, then purchase others as you fall apart. There's no time and no money to be dropping you off at the emergency outpatient clinic after sound check. Take care of yourself. If you've got a spider bite that has swollen your hand and turned it black, your bandmates will probably go to the hospital with you. But for everyday illnesses, you're on your own. I don't pack all of these herbs and medicines listed below every time I go out on tour, but it's a good reference list.

FOR PAIN

"It's not a hangover, it's a hang-in-there."–Deanne, load-in.

- *Advil:* My acupuncturist clearly said, "Sometimes just take drugs." You'll hear someone ask for aspirin probably every single day. Supply them and they'll owe you a favor somewhere in your frayed future. It's best to stop a headache as it's beginning and not let it take hold. There's so many potential headache triggers–a bad phone conversation, tension between bandmates or with management, or the quantity of alcohol enjoyed last night.

  This is the "let's have champagne hangovers tomorrow" tomorrow.

  Band members have been known to become addicted to Advil before a show.
- *White Flower or Tiger Balm or BioFreeze:* Bring some liquid heat or gel for strained muscles. Someone always hurts their back. First, apply ice to keep the swelling down. Later, add heat with a sweet little massage. There's a theory that pain is unexpressed emotion. So, unless you were hurt when a random guitar amp rolled into you during load out, rock hard, express yourself, and your neck and shoulders muscles may not ache so much.
- *Kanka:* This is weird stuff, but it's the only thing I've found for a split lip or canker sore. Just don't get it in your hair.

- *Maker's Mark:* Oh, it's just a joke, right?

FOR FLUS AND COLDS: Prevention and Treatment

- *Emergen-C:* The champagne of nutritional drinks. Lots of C and B, super energy booster. Tastes like fizzy lemonade. Comes in single packets that you can pour into a bottle of water.
- *Food-based vitamin and mineral daily supplement:* Take with food or you'll get really nauseous and the families at the after-church brunch may think you're pregnant as you cut in line looking for some saltine crackers.
- *Ester-C:* Time-released vitamin C capsules.
- *Ginger root:* For colds, fever, upset stomach. Find a grocery store to purchase fresh ginger root. Slice coins of ginger into a cup of hot water with lemon.
- *Advil Cold and Sinus:* You can buy individual doses at convenience stores. These will clear up your runny nose and watery eyes so you can sort of perform.
- *Oscillococcinum:* (Just sound it out, okay?) If someone in your little party comes down with the flu, chances are you're all fair game. Oscillococcinum can be purchased at any health food store. Purchase this before you're achy and pukey.

TO GET UP

"I'm so unwound, I can't wind."

- *Coffee:* Find good quality coffee or you'll feel weird. Better yet, bring it with you. We used to bring an espresso machine, plug it in outside a truck stop, and nine people would stand around waiting for their little drop.

"Coffee. It's a guaranteed good mood."

- *Tea:* Get some good black tea (Yorkshire Gold, Barry's, PG Tips) and there you are at your truck stop having a diner breakfast and your own English or Irish caffeine.
- *Siberian Ginseng:* It comes in a tincture. If you're anxious it'll even you out; if you're dead tired it'll give you a little support.
- *Ginkgo:* If you must stay awake and perform or do a radio interview and you're not thinking well, take some ginkgo.

It'll help with the ringing in your ears and the stress of a love triangle. If you're in the midst of a three-show, in-town run and you haven't slept for days and both of your lovers are backstage and there's a tour in front of you, I'd suggest ginkgo. Then get on the bus, listen to Erykah Badu's "See You Next Lifetime," and drive overnight to New York.

To Get to Sleep

- *Rescue Remedy:* It's a Bach Flower Remedy. If I'm still full of adrenaline from a show and need to sleep it slows me down. It's also good for anxiety. I had to pull a call button on a Southwest Airlines flight while we were taxiing out to the runway. "I'm sorry I have to get off the plane now." It was my first and only panic attack, brought on by lack of sleep, mild claustrophobia, and a slippery fear of flying. Now I take Rescue Remedy as I board the plane.
- *Deep sleep:* Found at Whole Foods Market, it's my favorite sleep aid. The first ingredient listed is poppy.
- *Coffea cruda:* Okay, it's a weird name. It's homeopathic. It very gently stops your brain from chattering so you can fall asleep.
- *Benadryl:* Some supermodels recommend Benadryl for sleeping on buses and international flights, and don't they know about looking good?
- *Valerian:* For me, way too much like a narcotic the next day. It's a root and comes in a tincture. Use just a few drops.

   We had a batch of valerian in water as a cocktail (the bar was closed). I gave everyone a little too much. We are still valerian-delirious today. Alejandro tells the audience he thinks I tried to kill him and the cellist.

For the Stomach

- *Tums:* They just work.
- *Acidophilus:* Chewables that contain billions of bacteria that eat all the bad stuff in your digestive tract.
- *Catnip/fennel:* Tummy soother. I order this tincture from Winter/Sun in Flagstaff, Arizona, and I always carry it with me.
- *Red or white wine:* My herbalist said wine is good for digestion. Your ability to think clearly may be impaired, but this may or may not matter to you.
- *Spirulina:* It's algae in a big pill or powder. It'll stop you from being so ravenously hungry that you get impatient and spacey. Take six to eight spirulina tablets if you're starving and there's no food to be had. Then you won't just inhale your late lunch and have to find your Tums to soothe your belly later.
- *Ginger, chamomile, or mint tea:* A cup of warm tea with honey helps the belly. You can buy dried crystallized ginger and suck on it if your tummy hurts.

- *Psyllium husks or psyllium seeds:* Just about every first-time-on-the-road traveler gets constipated. You sit all curled up in a van and the hours are screwy. Most bathrooms on tour–the truck-stop bathroom, the port-a-potty, the club bathroom–are not like home. Take a teaspoon of psyllium in an eight-ounce glass of water before bed for good poop. Be sure to drink the whole glass of water. You could also do fifty sit-ups a day.

Warning: If you're traveling on a tour bus, stay away from Smooth Move tea or anything like Ex-Lax. The timing is unpredictable, and you cannot poop in the bus bathroom. Why? Because it'll travel with you in the bus bay under your bunk. The bus driver could fine you $500. (See "The Bus Bathroom," page 77.)

- *The Greatest Herb of All:* "Be discreet, be respectful, be happy. Do not give strangers money who promise to return with herbs. About two hours after they are supposed to return, you'll understand why." (Ken Wagner's advice.) Also rumored to help with every single ailment above.

EXTRAS IN YOUR FIRST-AID KIT

Items you should probably bring include Band-Aids, Neosporin, Clearasil, and Burt's Bees' Green Clay Mask. Way past adolescence, your skin will break out from smoke, stress, bad food, and for no reason at all.

Entertainment

So much of what you'll do is preceded by tediously waiting. Often there's not a whole lot going on. Waiting for the city nine hours in your future. Waiting for sound check to start or end. Waiting for food to be served. Waiting for the show to start. Waiting for the vans or tour bus to drive you to your hotel room. You wait a lot on tour. You practically loiter.

> "Nothing's changed except the sun's in a different spot."–Mark, on a drive from Nashville to Hoboken

MUSIC. Bring your iPod, ear buds or noise-canceling headphones, and power supply. Climb into your bunk. Press play.

BOOKS. Short stories are good. Children's books are great because BIG PRINT IS HELPFUL. Also, you become a bit dim-witted sitting for ten hours in a vehicle. The whole *Wrinkle in Time* series is cool, *A Moveable Feast* by Hemingway, any Harlan Coben mystery. You might want to read about performers that inspire you: *Miles: The Autobiography, Bono on Bono,*

Dylan's *Chronicles*, *Rock Lives* by Timothy White, *Scar Tissue* by Anthony Kiedes.

> Traveling to Little Rock, he reads aloud to me from *Kiss of a Vampire*. Then we read Kerouac's *On the Road* with a thin strip of red on the horizon.

JOURNALS. Document your travels to entertain family and friends upon your return. Write down a "quote of the day" when someone says something that crystallizes a moment, as though it's from a movie–your tour movie. If you write a lot, go ahead and invest in the perfect pen.

> "There is no need to ever use a pen you don't like."

CAMERA. My new plan is to take one picture of each city I visit on tour. I always break this rule. I take too many photos of the band outside Sun Studios in Memphis. Or I take none, asking the guitar player to "send me a copy of that one." He agrees but I never get a copy.

Sometimes you can just take pictures in your head. Too many actual pictures can take up too little free time to actually go see the Buddhist temples, to walk on the glacier, or to swim in the river in Montana.

> "Do I look like I have a camera? I write haiku, bitch."–El John *(He was not talking to me when he said this.)*

There's also something I call camera mayhem. Camera mayhem occurs when so many pictures are being taken that you're stuck in one place. Imagine you're all at the five-way intersection in Tokyo. You take a picture of everybody. Then you ask the bass player to take your picture with everybody. Then the keyboardist asks if someone will take a picture of him with his camera. You've entered camera mayhem. It's a sinkhole. It's a whirlpool. It's a vortex that sucks time and direction out of the little adventure you're on.

There's also camera tedium. Camera tedium is a series of photos of nothing; photos taken while you all wait for the vans to arrive, for example. Here's the band standing with the luggage inside the airport in Honolulu. Here's the band standing with the luggage *outside* the airport in Honolulu. Nothing going on here.

That said, good photos are priceless souvenirs. I love having the grainy picture of a guitar player sitting in front of Peter Buck's house the morning after the party where the tour manager was busted stealing a bottle of vodka out of the house *twice*. Or the black-and-white train tracks out the window of the last car leaving Vienna on the way to Budapest. Or the photo of Howe Gelb reading *On the Road* out loud to us as we drive overnight. And of course, the picture of *me* at the five-way intersection in Tokyo.

Author's picky editorial: Take a picture of the audience every night if you want to have a picture of them—if you sincerely want to remember your view from the stage at the Metro in Chicago, for instance. But if you're just trying to rile up ten people in the front, this has been overdone and over-done.

MOVIES. There will be a DVD and VCR in the front and back lounge of your bus. Bring concert DVDs of musicians who inspire you (*Spinal Tap*, of course), anything about the supernatural or dead people, and action adventure.

> "We spent an hour and a half in a Wal-Mart trying on sunglasses and going through a big box of sale DVDs."–Travel-day rest stop

Don't bring anything subtitled unless it's the *Count of Monte Cristo* with Gerard Depardieu. Do bring movies to laugh, to cry, to be very scared, to travel far, far away, like outer space or to the middle of the ocean or another time.

CARDS. Poker. You can double your per diems. Or you can have no dou-ble latte money for the rest of the week or tour . . . just like that.

> "It's not the money. It's the camaraderie."–Bruce after nearly thirty minutes without winning a pound. Poker on the bus in England.

GAMES. Scrabble is amusing yet messy unless someone brings the travel edition. Charlie Sexton would play dominoes in his room at night after the show, but he never drank and always won. You could use the road atlas to guess which state goes with which state bird or slogan. This seems like fun only late at night to those who may have been drinking Maker's Mark pur-chased at the 7-Eleven three miles from the distillery.

EXTRAS. Bring things to help you stay in touch with home—your address book, postcard stamps, and a Sharpie. If you don't keep in touch with home, it won't be the same when you return. Write two sentences on a postcard and *mail it*.

Bring things as if you were camping: your own watch that will light up to see the time in a darkened club or bunk, a travel alarm, a mini flashlight on a key chain, a tiny sewing kit, safety pins, and Swiss Army knife with scissors, corkscrew, and tweezers. If you're flying, pack the Swiss Army knife in your suitcase, not your carry-on. The airlines already have two of mine. You can bring a pocket road atlas if you care to know where you are and don't want to make everyone look around the van for the Big Laminated Road Atlas.

Bring things to help you sleep: squishy earplugs and an eye shade. You want it quiet and dark inside your head. The sun is up by 7 AM, and hopefully you will not be.

Author's endorsement: Brookstone has the Cadillac of eye shades made with Tempur-Pedic foam and velvet and shaped to not squish your eyeballs.

You might want to bring your pillow, especially if you're on a van tour. You'll try to talk yourself out of it as you leave home, thinking it's just one more thing to carry. But if you don't bring it, you'll be sleeping with your head resting on your folded-up leather jacket against the side window pane. In a bus, your pillow will remind you of home, and you have a chance to sleep more deeply.

Organizing Your Pack

Now that you've got your checklist, how do you organize your bags? What goes in what bag and where? Yes, you do care about this. You'll lose stuff the first days on tour. At some frustrated moment you'll dump everything on the floor, looking for the matching sock or your travel alarm. You've just moved into your new home–your suitcase. "I think I lost my notebook." "I think I forgot my lotion." You didn't lose it; you didn't forget it. You just can't find it. There are many pockets and places to look into and return things to. You just don't know your way around yet.

Place shoes on the outer edges of your suitcase as an extra wall to protect any breakable items. Keep clean socks and underthings zipped in a pocket or placed together in a mesh bag.

I try to keep pants together on the left and shirts together on the right. This never lasts, but it's a good way to start. You might want to roll up your jeans, your pajamas, your pretty little tops or black T-shirts, instead of laying them flat. It makes it easier to find specific items without having to unearth everything. It keeps clothes from getting wrinkled (sort of) and somehow takes up less space, although I'm not sure how.

Items I'll need in the morning, like toiletries, I place on the left edge of my suitcase. Things I'll be looking for at night–alarm clock, squishy earplugs–I put on the right side. This is tedious, I know, but it helps me find things when I'm thinking below my IQ late at night or early in the morning.

Your Instruments

Never bring an invaluable, irreplaceable instrument on the road unless you can bear its loss or demise, which pretty much means it wasn't invaluable and irreplaceable to begin with. Touring and playing clubs are rough on them. There's heat, cold and humidity, beer and inebriated fans, loading and unloading. Gear can be stolen. (See "Load-Out Robbery," page 177.) Guitars can fall over and the neck can break. Cellos have been smashed by airlines. Keyboards have been rained on.

But do you buy an instrument because "it'll be just fine onstage?" No. You have to play an instrument you love. If you don't love it, don't buy it. Take care of your instrument the best you can and buy some insurance. (See "Purchasing Insurance for Your Instruments and Gear," page 35.)

Your Gig Bag and Pedal Board

Inside your gig bag are your effects pedals attached with Velcro or twist ties to your pedal board. Each pedal lets you change the sound of your instrument—delay, phase, distortion, chorus, compression, etc. You'll start with one or two pedals but then keep trying out and adding more. Musicians are always in search of the tone and effect that expresses them. We go through different eras and seasons of sounds.

> "I left all my pedals and tricks with wires at the last minute, back home... my security blanket, and it has been a fine buoyancy doing without them."–Howe e-mails.

Setting up for your first gigs you'll probably just lay your pedals out on the floor in front of you and toss them in a bag at the end of the night. Then you hear from a tech with another band that if these pedals were attached to a board they wouldn't break as easily. Plus they are much easier to move on and off the stage if they are affixed to one board.

Your Amp

If you load your unprotected amp into a trailer night after night it's going to get scratched up, knobs will break off, tubes may break. If you can't afford an anvil case, look up TukiCovers.com. They make padded covers that will fit over your amp for around seventy or eighty dollars. If you can't afford that or need a cover in a hurry, make an amp cover with a cardboard box and duct tape. It's better than traveling with no cover on your amp at all.

YOUR BOOKING AGENT

How has it happened that you're leaving home tomorrow for a month of rock? You've made your CD. Your record label (which might be you) has released it and sent promotional copies to radio stations, newspapers, and magazines. Your job now is to travel to clubs around the country playing shows in support of the record.

You'll hire a booking agent who should know the appropriate club in each city for you to play—performance places, established, reputable clubs. He probably already has a business relationship with the owners. Your booking agent is the person who negotiates your performance contract with the clubs, and you'll pay him 10 to 15 percent of your gross income each night for this. With luck, you'll be on a bill with compatible bands, playing gigs not more than 250 miles apart each night.

> I have a new plan. I'm calling up [booking agent's name here] when we go to sleep and I'm calling him up when the wake-up calls scream us awake four hours later to make it to the next gig he booked. He should feel some of this ache, he should know how tired feels, he should pay. Has he forgotten we are not merchandise? We are live human musicians, and we're beat.

When I asked Brad Madison, booking agent with Mongrel Music, how he books gigs, here's what he said:

"Here's how it works. We confirm a date with the club and issue a contract to the buyer. We send them three copies and the rider [additional specific technical items the band requires]. The club reviews the contract and rider terms, ticket price, hospitality. The club's supposed to read it and sign it. Any changes should be discussed. They sign all three copies and send them all back. We sign all three, agreeing to changes if there are any. We send one copy back to the buyer, one to the artist, and we keep one.

"We request a deposit in most cases—between 10 and 50 percent. The deposit insures the date."

Terminology Note: Often you'll hear the word *promoter*. The promoter is whoever organizes the show. At smaller shows, the club is the promoter. Sometimes the local radio station is the promoter, or it could be an independent person. This person is taking the financial risk putting on the show.

YOUR PERFORMANCE CONTRACT

A responsible band member or your tour manager will bring the signed contracts out on the road. If there's a disagreement between the band and the club you are playing, refer to your contract (Figure 1). The most serious problem is not being paid or being underpaid. Other problems can include your sound needs not being fulfilled, or catering being ignored, or perhaps two bands both thinking they'll be headlining. The tour manager may need to call the booking agent if what the club says and what the contract says don't agree. It's rare that a phone call needs to be made. A good tour manager or your sound person will call the club a week before your show to advance the date (see "Advancing Your Show," page 29) and review the contract and rider with them.

Mongrel Music

THIS CONTRACT for the personal services of musicians on the engagement described below is made this

Name of Artist: Number of Musicians:

1. Name and Address of Place of Engagement:

2. Date(s) of Engagement: Type of Engagement: **Club**

3. Starting Time of Engagement:

4. Compensation Agreed Upon:

5. Purchaser Will Make Payments As Follows:

Contracts due IMMEDIATELY.

NOTE: Support act, if any, must be approved by Artist.

NOTE: Any attached riders are herein made a part of this contract.

6. Ticket/Capacity: Ticket Price(s): Capacity: X

No. of Shows:

Total GP:

Net GP:

Total Capacity:

DEPOSIT IF BY BANK WIRE TO:
Mongrel Music, Account # at

Tel:

DEPOSIT
$
REC
BY

IN WITNESS WHEREOF, the parties hereto have hereunto set their names and seals on the day and year first above written.

Print Purchaser's Full & Correct Name (If Purchaser is Corporation, Full & Correct Corporate name)

Print Name of Signatory Musician

X____________________

X____________________
c/o

Phone: Fax:

Promoter Email:
Promoter Website:
Venue Phone:
Venue Website:

Phone: Fax:
Artist Co.:
Fed ID #:
Artist Website:

FIGURE 1

The main considerations and information of the performance contract are listed below:

1. *Artist.* There should be no doubt when you arrive in the club that your band is the headliner if on the contract next to your name it says "100 percent headliner."

2. *Venue.* The name and address of the club or place of engagement is listed here, as is the phone and fax number and the name of the production person you'll be dealing with at the club.

3. *Date.* Obvious and important. Yes, I've heard stories of the band arriving on the wrong day.

4. *Tickets.* The contract states the capacity of the club (the number of tickets that can be sold) and the ticket price–decided by the booking agent, the club, and the manager–arriving at the gross potential for the night. Tax and Ticketmaster percentage deductions are listed.

   I asked booking agent Brad Madison how ticket price is determined: "You want to be in the right realm with the ticket price. Check out what other comparable artists are charging. Maybe the ticket price should go up after you've played at this club a couple of times and things are strong. Chicago prices aren't the same prices as Austin. Here's what people are used to paying here. The promoter and the club have a better feel for the right ticket price than the agent."

5. *Schedule.* Your contract will state the time doors are opened (audience let in), showtime for both the opener and the headliner, and curfew if any. Load-in and sound-check time might be left blank for the tour manager and production manager to decide on later (during that advancing call). It will also set forth whether it's an all-ages show (18+) or 21 and over.

6. *Merchandise.* The club usually takes a percentage of your merchandise income. The contract will state the percentage and whether a member of your crew or the club is doing the selling. Typically the club will take between 15 and 20 percent of your merch, although I've seen clubs ask for as much as 35 percent. If you've got a solid, longstanding personal relationship with the owner of the club, they might waive their merch percentage on recorded materials but still take a percentage of T-shirt sales.

7. *Terms.* Probably the most important part of your contract is how you'll be paid. There are three basic payment structures: a straight guarantee, a guarantee with a percentage, and a percentage only.

   Straight guarantee: A straight guarantee is an exact fee you are guaranteed. "Opening band slots and festivals are typically, most of the time, a flat deal [a guarantee]," Brad Madison told me.

Guarantee with a percentage: The band is guaranteed an exact fee plus a percentage of the door–money earned in ticket sales that night–after expenses are met. The percentage varies but is typically 85 percent. The remaining percent goes to the club. "Percentages are for situations where you're the headliner. After the club has recovered their cost, if there's extra money, the lion's share should go to the artist. People are there for the artist. These costs should be written in the contract and agreed to," Brad Madison advised.

The bigger the venue, the more expenses deducted. (See "Contract Expenses" page 168.)

Percentage only: A percentage-only situation is when you are paid an agreed-upon percentage of tickets sold. The contract will state there is a "$0 guarantee." The band will be paid an agreed-upon percentage of the door and the club will keep the rest. There is no money guaranteed the band. If you know you'll sell a good amount of tickets in this town, you might accept a percentage only deal.

Brad Madison adds: "A straight percentage minimizes the risk to the promoter. But it's nerve-racking for a band on the road. You have to look at your history in this town and at this club and think about it."

8. *Sound and Lights.* Usually the club will agree to provide and pay for sound and lights.

9. *Payments.* The agreed method of payment is listed and if a deposit has been sent to the booking agent. At the end of the night when you're getting paid you'll want to know if you can expect your full guarantee or if half has already been sent to the booking agent.

10. *Taping and Recording.* This provision says that the show can't be recorded, reproduced, or transmitted without a specific written agreement with the artist.

11. *Cancellation.* The phrase "the show must go on" probably has as much to do with money as it does with a show-biz pride. Despite difficulties, shows do go on. And then a few get cancelled. There is a provision in your performance contract regarding cancellations: "The agreement of the artist to perform is subject to proven detention by sickness, accidents, riots, strikes, epidemics, acts of God, or any other legitimate conditions beyond their control."

YOUR TECHNICAL RIDER

A technical rider (sometimes called a production rider) is a document attached to your contract detailing your additional needs that aren't spelled out in the performance contract. After touring a bit you learn you can ask the club for some of these extras that will make the day run more smoothly for everyone. Below are some basic rider provisions taken from a Poi dog Pondering technical rider:

1. *Parking.* "We will be transporting our equipment in one fifteen-foot box truck or two cargo vans, and require safe, secure, well-lit parking for these vehicles with easy access to the venue."

2. *Loaders.* "We must have a minimum of four competent, able-bodied, and sober loaders for both the load-in and -out. These loaders should be available throughout setup, sound check, and our performance to assist with the set up and tear down of our equipment and stage."

3. *Stage Requirements.* "The stage must be a minimum of twenty-four feet deep by thirty-six feet wide and a minimum of four feet in height, with a minimum overhead clearance of twenty feet."

   "All sound, lights, and power should be in place and entirely functional prior to artist's arrival on day of show. Sound system should be fully EQed and rung out prior to artist's arrival." This request that the sound system be all ready to go when the artist arrives rarely happens, but it's nice to ask for it anyway.

   > This is one venue that is set up ahead of time and is ready for us when we arrive at sound check—only everything is set to the wrong stage plot. Sadly, we can never get the current stage plot sent out. The sound guy who tells us he's been out with a lot of famous people, including Prince, keeps saying, "This is a nightmare, this is a nightmare," when he has to swap some cables and move a monitor. Oh, it's not a nightmare. It's an inconvenience.

4. *Sound System.* "We use forty inputs on the console. We require enough microphones and direct boxes per the attached input list. Please provide a variety of professional quality microphones and direct boxes solely for our use." (See "Stage Plot and Input List," page 31.)

5. *Monitor Requirements.* "If possible we need eight monitor wedges with eight separate mixes." Monitor wedges or monitors are speakers facing the band. Your monitor mix is the mix of instruments or vocals you specifically ask to hear coming out of your monitor. It's

helpful if each mix is separate, because what the lead singer needs to hear in his monitor mix and what the drummer wants to hear in his will be very, very different. (See "Sound Check," page 124.)

6. *Runner.* "Please provide a knowledgeable, responsible individual with a reliable car and good driving record to work as a runner to run errands our behalf." You might need a runner to go to the guitar store for emergency strings or to pick up some Thai food for dinner if the Thai restaurant is not within walking distance.

7. *Production Office.* "Please provide one large production office for our staff to use from the time of our arrival until our departure. This office should be private, well lit, secure with a lockable door, and quiet, with desks, lights, outlets, and direct access to the backstage area."

   If your tour manager has access to a production office, it makes it easier for him to print out day sheets, (see "Day Sheet," page 84), continue advancing shows, check in with management, do tour accounting, etc.

8. *Security.* "Please provide professional, competent, and courteous security capable of protecting your venue, our people, and your customers in a way that will be satisfactory to all parties involved. This should include:
   • One security guard to protect artist's vehicles from time of arrival until departure.
   • One person to guard each entrance to backstage to ensure that the stage, dressing room, and production areas are kept safe and secure from thirty minutes before doors open until venue is closed to the public.
   • Two people to work stage security during artist's performance. No unnecessary or excessive force by any security personnel will be acceptable. Please ensure this."

9. *Backstage Access.* "Backstage access shall be expressly limited to artist and tour personnel, working crew, and venue staff. No one should be admitted backstage for a period of twenty minutes prior to, or twenty minutes after, artist's performance, except working personnel. No one except artist's entourage, or individuals accompanied by artist's personnel, shall be admitted into artist's dressing rooms at any time."

Author Note: On occasion I have tried to walk a friend who did not have an all-access pass backstage after the show. Security stopped me and said since she didn't have a pass she'd have to wait in the weird meet-and-greet balcony area set aside for fans. But it clearly says in the rider that if she's accompanied by the artist or the artist's personnel she can come with me to the dressing rooms. With this provision, you know it's in your contract that you can escort a friend backstage past security.

YOUR HOSPITALITY RIDER

Also attached to your performance contract will be your hospitality rider. This is your food and drink request for the night. If you're a brand new band playing at this club, you might be given eight complimentary drink tickets and a twelve-pack of water. If you draw a fairly good crowd, you can ask for more. Take some time to consider what you'd like. You'll be seeing the bagels and cream cheese you asked for every single night. If nobody is eating them, take this request off your rider.

The club will charge you for these items and probably charge you more than they paid for them. Chris Von Thies, head talent buyer for Direct Events Inc. told me, "Anything outside of beer, soda, and water is a show expense. If the show doesn't make enough money the promoter pays for hospitality. If the show goes into points then the tickets pay for it." But ultimately that's still money coming from the pool of cash you and the club are dividing at the end of the night. So, be reasonable about your hospitality requests.

The hospitality rider also may include dinner. It might be a buy-out (cash given to the band to go buy dinner on your own) or be provided in-house by the club. (See "Dinner Provided by the Club," page 136.) Below are two actual hospitality riders that are pretty basic and easy for the club to fulfill.

Hospitality Rider #1

24 cold bottles of spring water

14 bottles of spring water at room temperature (for stage)

24 bottles of imported beer

2 six packs of Bitburger nonalcoholic beer

Organic apple juice

1 box of throat coat tea–hot water for tea

Brewed coffee (organic free-trade coffee), coffee maker set-up with cups, spoons, napkins

Sugar, honey, milk, lemon wedges

Assorted fresh organic fruits–washed, with knife, paper plates

Assorted sandwiches: turkey/cheese, ham/cheese, cheese only

8 clean towels

Hospitality Rider #2

A small fruit tray (apples, oranges, bananas, pears, grapes, whatever you feel like)

Fresh vegetable platter

Water crackers

TECHNICAL AND HOSPITALITY RIDER

2007
(Any rider dated before Feb. 6, 2007 is no longer valid)

Contact: Big Ben Richardson
Tel: --- --- - ----
Email: ----@-----.---

FIGURE 2

Humus

Chocolate

1 gallon of fresh-squeezed orange juice (Odwalla preferred)

Chips & salsa

Six 16–20-ounce bottles of spring water for the stage

Some ice

1 pack of black Sharpies

VERY IMPORTANT: 2 clean hand towels (don't need bath towels, but not facecloth)

Two 9-volt batteries

Purchaser will also provide a hot meal to feed three (3) hungry adults. In lieu of providing a meal, a cash buyout of $15 per person ($45) is acceptable.

Please make sure that all drinks are well iced throughout the evening. All items should be in the dressing room at least two (2) hours prior to performance. Thank you!

Author Note: Items that you will need that the club often forgets to provide: a corkscrew, a bottle opener, half-and-half, hot water for tea, heat in the dressing room.

Author's Deli Tray Suggestion: If you are on a long tour, may I suggest asking for even- and odd-day deli trays. That way you could have English water crackers, brie, and grapes on the 11th and a little Mideast feast on the 12th.

"Monday, Wednesday, and Friday they asked for Sake. Tuesday, Thursday, and weekends they wanted tequila and imported beer."

CONTEMPLATING YOUR TOUR BUDGET

The safest way to budget your tour is to add up your guarantees and subtract your projected expenses—booking agent percentage, van rental, gas, tolls, oil, taxis, hotels, and tips. You could add an extra 5 percent to your expenses to cover unexpected costs. If you have a guarantee plus a percentage deal, all you can really count on is your guarantee, especially the first few times you go out on tour. If you have a show with no guarantee and only a percentage of the door, you'll have to make a guess at what you might earn. That's your budget. Will you break even? Do you have any money left to pay yourselves? If you answer no to either question, there are two other income sources.

Merchandise Income

Your merch income can significantly help your tour budget. It's your bonus money. Your merchandise table is a little business inside the rock show business, offering CDs, T-shirts, posters, hats, and even underwear. When people enjoy your show, they want to take something home with them, and it probably shouldn't be you.

If 10 percent of your audience buys merch, that would be considered a good merch night. Sometimes it's as high as 50 percent. Heinz Geissler, Alejandro Escovedo's manager, told me, "There are some nights when a small number of people might come to the show and yet half the audience—50 percent—will want merchandise."

Author Note: Your record label may sell you CDs for $8 each that you then sell at the show for $15 or $20. They may ship you several boxes with an invoice enclosed. Put the $8 per CD you owe them aside—in a separate envelope even. Trust me, you don't want a big unpaid CD bill looming larger and larger. The label can even decide they won't send you any more CDs until you've paid them back in full.

Tour Support

Your record label (assuming you have one) may be able to give you a bit of tour support—money to help cover tour expenses. When you signed your record deal, you'll have negotiated how much tour support the label will give you. Do you have to pay this money back? One manager told me, "Unfortunately, yes." Another tour manager who worked at a major label said the opposite. So it varies.

Author Note: If the band breaks up, you aren't personally responsible to pay the label back. Your records are responsible. Income from your CDs will keep paying off what you owe the record label. Even if the CD stops selling, the label doesn't sue you for the money still owed it.

Bring a Bank with You

The band needs to have a little extra money as it begins its tour. The first gig may be preceded by two days of driving. The first few gigs may not be big money makers. You'll still have to fill up the gas tank, pay tolls, buy food, and pay for your hotel rooms. Bring a zip bag with $1,000 of "float"—money to float you to the next bit of income.

Where does this float come from? Well, it could be tour support from your label. It could be advanced from your manager. It could be from a well-paying, in-town gig before your tour. No band member should be personally paying for these initial expenses, unless that seems the best way for your band to begin. Everyone will feel more confident about the tour if there's a bank to draw from.

ADVANCING YOUR SHOW

Before you leave town, your tour manager will call the production manager at each of the clubs you'll be playing to agree on some of the basics about the show. Much of this information is already in your performance contract, but he calls to introduce himself to the production manager and to verify or update the information. This is called *advancing*. Club owner Yvonne Matsell told me: "The person advancing your show is the first contact the club has with you. If he's too hard or too demanding during the phone call, then the band arrives at the club and wonders why everyone there is so mean to them right off the bat." When he makes these calls, it's helpful to write the information down on a Show Advance form, one for each gig. Figure 3 is a blank Show Advance form.

SHOW ADVANCE FORM

SHOW DATE _____

VENUE NAME _____

VENUE ADDRESS _____

(Exact Location)   _____

PROMOTER NAME _____

PROMOTER PHONE/FAX _____

PROMOTER E-MAIL _____

VENUE CONTACT NAME _____

LOAD IN TIME _____

SOUND CHECK _____

SUPPORT ONE _____

SUPPORT TWO _____

SET TIME _____

SET LENGTH _____

GUESTS _____

MEALS (BUYOUT OR IN-HOUSE) _____

RIDER/STAGE PLOT RECEIVED _____

HOTEL SUGGESTION _____

ADVANCE SALES _____

NOTES/ADDITIONAL INFO _____

_____

FIGURE 3

Basic Advancing Questions

- What's the *load-in* time?
- Where does the band load in? Is there an alley, side door or a loading dock?
- What's the *sound check* time?
- What's the *show* time?
- What's the *length of the set* (and the curfews, if any)?
- Did the club receive the *stage plot* and *input list* the tour manager just sent?
- What are the *directions* to the club from the main highway?
- Will the club arrange to *save a parking space* for the van or bus outside the club?
- Will there be *loaders* to help load in AND load out?
- Is *dinner* included? You can request vegetarian, which may mean they'll take out the meat and serve you noodles and tomato soup unless you get specific.
- Is there a *buy-out?*
- Has the club seen and agreed to your *hospitality rider?*
- Does the club have a deal with a *nearby hotel?*
- What are the *directions* to the hotel from both the highway and from the club?

Attempt to finish advancing before you leave home. It's easier to phone from your couch or home office than when sitting on a curb somewhere during a dinner stop. Much of the advancing information will be printed into the tour itinerary that each band member will receive at the beginning of the tour. (See "Your Tour Itinerary," page 89.) If advancing is incomplete, you either leave that portion of the itinerary blank or make a guess. This is why later in the tour the itinerary is wrong and is fondly called the "book of lies."

Stage Plot and Input List

Part of advancing is to fax or e-mail the stage plot and input list to the club. Figure 4 is the Alejandro Escovedo 8-Piece Band stage plot. It's a diagram of where things go on the stage.

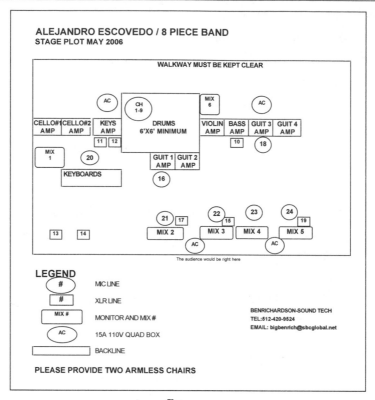

FIGURE 4

The legend in the lower-left corner identifies the shapes on the stage plot.

1. A circle indicates microphones and microphone lines for vocals and amps.

2. A small box signals where a type of cable called an XLR cable connects to an instrument DI. DI stands for direct input, usually used for acoustic instruments, keyboards, and computers.

3. A larger box with "Mix #" on it indicates where the monitors should be placed and which monitor mix is placed in each. (See "Sound Check," page 124.)

4. A circle with the symbol "AC" in it is where the band will need power onstage.

5. The long rectangular box indicates the row of seven amps back by the drums, called backline.

Although there are similarities in the way bands set up (drums in the back, bass near the drums, singers up front), there are distinct differences, so a drawing is helpful for the house sound guys to wire up the stage.

Sometimes a stage plot will include the names of the musicians on the stage. This helps the sound guys because what they refer to as "cello" we might refer to as "Matt Fish" (the cellist's name), and the sound guy will be clueless about what you are asking for.

On the reverse side of the stage plot is the input list. An input list is just that–a list of DI and microphone lines being sent to the soundboard. Figure 5 is the Alejandro Escovedo 8-Piece Band input list. One by one it lists which instrument or vocal is being sent to the soundboard, what channel is being used, whether it's a mic or DI line, and what kind of mic stand is needed onstage. From the soundboard, the sound engineer has the ability to adjust each channel's volume, or EQ (highs and lows), or add effects (delay or echo), creating the desired mix and mood in the room.

ALEJANDRO ESCOVEDO   8 PIECE BAND
INPUT LIST MAY 2006

CH	INPUTS	MIC/DI	48V	STAND	PATCH	NOTES	CH
1	KICK	AKG D112		SB	GATE 1		1
2	SNARE	SM 57		SB			2
3	HI-HAT	CONDENSER	X	SB			3
4	DJEMBE	SM 57		SB			4
5	TOM-1	SENN 604		CLIP	GATE 2		5
6	TOM-2	SENN 604		CLIP	GATE 3		6
7	TOM-3	SENN 604		CLIP	GATE 4		7
8	OVERHEAD-L	CONDENSER	X	TB			8
9	OVERHEAD-R	CONDENSER	X	TB			9
10	BASS (SL)	XLR		NO	COMP 1		10
11	KEYBOARD-1 (SR)	XLR		NO			11
12	KEYBOARD-2 (SR)	XLR		NO			12
13	CELLO #1 (SR)	XLR	X	NO			13
14	CELLO #2 (SR)	XLR	X	NO			14
15	VIOLIN (SL)	XLR	X	NO			15
16	AL ELECT GUIT (CENTRE)	SM 57		SB			16
17	AL ACOUSTIC (CENTRE)	XLR		NO			17
18	DAVID ELECT GUIT (SL)	SM 57		SB			18
19	DAVID GUIT-ACOUSTIC (SL)	XLR		NO			19
20	KEYBOARD VOX (SR)	SM 58		TB			20
21	AL VOX (CENTER)	AUDIX OM6		TB	COMP 2	MIC SUPPLIED	21
22	VIOLIN VOX (SL)	SM 58		TB			22
23	BASS VOX (SL)	SM 58		TB			23
24	GUIT VOX (SL)	SM 58		TB			24
25							25
26							26

MIC STAND LEGEND
SB   SHORT BOOM
TB   TALL BOOM
NO   NO STAND

BEN RICHARDSON
TEL: 512-420-9524
EMAIL: bigbenrich@sbcglobal.net

PLEASE PROVIDE TWO ARMLESS CHAIRS

MONITOR MIXES
1   KEYBOARDS (SR)
2   ALEJANDRO (CENTRE)
3   VIOLIN (SL)
4   BASS (SL)
5   GUITAR (SL)
6   DRUMS

FIGURE 5

ADVANCE PUBLICITY

Sometimes you'll show up at the club and there's no mention of your gig in the local paper and not a poster on the wall or in the windows advertising the band. If no one knows about your show, who will come?

Howard Greynolds, of Thrill Jockey Records, suggests the following to whoever is doing the band's publicity: "Do some homework. Go on-line, find what the alternative weekly papers are in the area and send them a copy of your record. Most papers have to fill their paper up, and if you get them something three to five weeks in advance you have a decent chance of them running a show preview, record review, photo, or more."

You want to interest the writer/music critic in your band. Your first press kit should include a bio, a photo, your tour dates (i.e., you're on a thirty-date tour, including five dates with a very famous band) and your MySpace page where anyone interested can go to hear some of your songs. As part of the bio, include something that makes your band unique— an interesting angle or background story. Maybe your band used to be a street band from Hawaii, maybe you are all art students or fallen classical musicians, or the lead singer survived a serious illness or a spectacular car wreck and the songs from this record reflect the experience. Give the writer the good stuff to write an intriguing article.

BOOKING HOTEL ROOMS

To keep expenses down on your first tour, you may seek lodging other than hotels (see "Finding Inexpensive Lodging," page 66), but eventually you'll be booking hotel rooms. It's possible but not recommended to book rooms as your tour rolls along. You play your gig and then all pile in the van and look for a hotel. You drive to one and it seems too expensive. You drive to another and it's full. You continue down the highway and realize there's a NASCAR convention in town and there are no hotel rooms for sixty miles.

> Last night we couldn't stay in the city of Richmond because the Mary Kay convention had overrun the city.

Preferably, you'll book a hotel in advance, in town, *within walking distance to the club* rather than out by the Cracker Barrel on the highway. You'll waste a lot of time trying to locate the distant hotel after sound check, then driving back for the show and then driving back to the hotel again at the end of the night. If you're cabbing it, you may have a long wait for a cab, and then you've got to pay the fare. You may see nothing of this city you're in. People you meet at your gig will say things like "Why aren't you staying at the rock hotel? Everyone stays there. They've got a great café next door."

During your advancing phone call with the club, you'll ask the production manager for a hotel recommendation. I asked Heinz Geissler how to get the best hotel rate. "Number one is ask if the club has a deal with a hotel. The club rate will often be better than a corporate rate. I never take anything for granted. When they tell me the rate I say, 'Let's talk. I need six rooms. Can you do better?' If the hotel is full, the club rate may not be available because the hotel knows they'll be able to sell the room at a higher rate. Mainly, by moaning, groaning, bitching, and being friendly is how I get the best hotel rate."

If the club doesn't have a deal with a hotel, they probably know the hotel most bands stay at, so the price will be right and it'll be fairly close. It may be a run-down hotel, but night after night you may appreciate some uniqueness in choice of lodging. Driving into San Luis Obispo and staying at an old downtown motel run by two older women with no telephones in the rooms and a plank across the front door at midnight is charming. It is not necessarily efficient for your tour manager.

> I'm in the deer-head room about to have Sunday brunch. We stayed at this hotel last night that used to be a hunting lodge. I've just counted eighteen taxidermy heads on the wall.

Alejandro Escovedo Tip: "Get the confirmation numbers for the hotel and for flights. I never did. You might think, 'Oh, they've got it,' but it comes in handy—especially at hotels when they lose the reservation."

Author Note: When budgeting for hotels, be aware that there may be a city tax and a hotel tax that bump up the price of each room by an additional $20.

If you need to keep hotel costs down, you could put four musicians in one room. The mattress can be taken off any bed and suddenly you have two beds (box spring and mattress). Call to get extra blankets and pillows. Or for an additional $10 or $20, housekeeping will deliver a rollaway or fold-up bed.

Some bands use Priceline.com or Hotwire.com to secure hotel rooms. On the plus side, you'll be staying at a nice hotel at a fairly low price. Unfortunately, at a fancier hotel you may have to pay extra to park in the parking garage and for Internet service. Occasionally with Priceline the hotel may be far from the venue and you may be surprised with one king bed instead of two doubles.

PURCHASING INSURANCE FOR YOUR INSTRUMENTS AND GEAR

Before you leave home you may want to insure your gear. While on tour, the instruments are not always going to be in your sight. Yes, everything will be in a locked trailer or locked van, but these can be broken into. Tour buses seem like fortresses, but they can be broken into as well. Dressing rooms at the club should be locked or have a security person posted by the door, but money, jewelry, and instruments still disappear. It seems there is an unwritten rule that the stage is respected and nothing will be stolen off of it, but things do get stolen. One time, two Poi dog Pondering fans stole a brake drum from the front of the stage and left a note on our van:

> GREAT SHOW POI DOG! WE HAVE YOUR METAL HUBCAP PERCUSSION THANG—
> THANX LOADS. IT WILL BE AN X-CELLENT B-DAY GIFT FOR MY DAD! LOVE
> ADAMS & HEATHER. DROP US A LINE. WE'RE COLLEGE KIDS!

Ask your musician friends if they have insurance and what company they use. The Musician's Union offers insurance if you're a member. There are several insurance agencies that an ex–band manager recommends for touring bands: MusicPro.com, Clarion.com, UnitedAgencies.com. Your annual premium may be anywhere from $250 for $10,000 replacement coverage to $750 for $40,000 replacement coverage. Be sure to ask whether your instruments and gear will be covered not only while they are onstage but in the van or bus, at the hotel, or in the belly of an airplane.

PREPARING TO LEAVE HOME

Who dates or marries a touring musician, a road manager, a sound guy, a filmmaker, a traveling salesman, or a circus performer? They're here. They're gone. Some bands tour all the time. Some only tour to support a record. Some tour for a few weeks. Some tour for months. All travelers face the same question, though: "How do I leave home?"

> I'm packed and ready to go, but not ready to leave.

What to Do Two Days Before Your Tour

You could try to run all your errands the day you leave, or you can start a few days earlier. There will be so many little petty things to do—buy stamps to mail your bills, buy razors, get a battery for your travel alarm, pick up an extra power supply for your pedals, buy shampoo, get a haircut. Be calm. If you can't get everything done, you can do these errands while on the road.

That said, it's usually much easier to take thirty minutes while at home to go to the Osco to buy some Clearasil than to walk twelve blocks in the heat looking for a drugstore in Columbia, Missouri.

Two nights before you leave is the official last night to spend with your sweet one. The actual night before you leave, you're just too weird and scatterbrained.

> "We just take each tour separation one at a time. We don't take on all tours to come. We handle one at a time."–Abra

What to Do the Day before Your Tour

Okay. The tour starts tomorrow. You're going to be gone five weeks. You have to pack. And you have to separate from your things in a way that when you return, your friends still like you, the lights are still on, your plants are alive, and the house isn't full of rotting garbage you forgot to take out.

PACK. Make a list of what you want to bring. Then pack. (See "Packing for Your Tour," page 3.) Once you're finished, it's very important to zip up the suitcase, because once it's zipped, you can forget about it and think about other things. Until then, you'll be adding another pair of pants, taking out a shirt, wondering if you did indeed pack the brown belt. You'll justify not zipping it all up because you'll need some of these things in the morning. Yes, you will. Zip it all up. Open it again in the morning to pull out your shampoo.

PAY YOUR BILLS. It may seem when you're gone that bills do not exist, but do you want to come home to a place with no electricity and no phone service? Your stuff needs a home and so do you, so pay your rent and your bills. If you live with roommates, give them rent and bill money. Yes, ahead of time. If you don't, when you get home they won't be pleased. They may even evict you.

If you live alone, it's possible to pay your utilities before the bill even arrives. Or you can call your electric or gas company from the road and they'll gladly tell you what to pay them. You could also set up on-line bill paying.

SECURE YOUR STUFF. Hide valuables. Choose your hiding places well. I heard a story where some musicians went on vacation and hid their instruments in the shower. Somehow the water turned on and ruined the instruments. You can store jewelry in winter coat pockets or shoes you won't be bringing on tour. I imagine burglars might be in a hurry. Hide valuables far from the front door. Use cheaper instruments as decoys for a thief to see and take first.

If you live alone, empty out your refrigerator. If you have plants, give a friend your house keys so he or she can come over and water the plants and bring in your mail. Bring this person a present from the road.

DECIDE WHAT TO DO WITH YOUR CAR. Maybe you can park your car in a garage. Maybe you have to park on the street and there's random street cleaning and if you don't move the car (and how can you when you're somewhere across the country?) you'll get a $50 ticket. You could ask a roommate or neighbor to keep an eye on it for you and move it as needed. Or you could loan it to a friend and cross your fingers that he'll keep it safe.

> I loaned him my car while I was on tour. When I returned, he picked me up at the airport, announcing he has accidentally cracked my radiator while overheating the car.

AVOID THE LEAVING-ON-TOUR FIGHT. It seems there's always a relationship fight before you leave town. There are theories as to why couples fight just before a tour. You may fight to make it easier to separate. You may fight to make sure you are loved. Sigh.

> "It's always about sex or money."

Be wise. Be kind. Be the bigger (wo)man. Declare that there will be no leaving-on-tour fight and back down, lie down, apologize, and attempt to consider your lover's point of view.

> "We were on our way to the airport at 7 AM and I said to her, 'Why do you always have to be such a bitch about everything?' I got to thinking about it. What if the plane goes down and that's the last thing I said to her? So I had to call and say, "I'm still right and I'm still mad at you, but about that thing I said, it's not true."–El John

Most important, do not assess the relationship the night before your tour starts. Really. This is a good time to only remind one another how fascinating and interesting and irreplaceable you are to each other.

What to Do the Day You Leave

The only thing you really have to do the day you leave is to make sure you're packed and that you've got your instrument and your gear. The last thing I do before leaving the house is to shut off my home computer, close and lock the windows, and take out the trash. Most errands you haven't finished you can do while you're on the road. Nonetheless, you'll get wound up trying to do way too many last-minute things. It's just how it is.

> I'm scattered and tense trying to wrap up everything in my life before leaving. There is never a time in my life when everything is wrapped up and

finished. Why would I expect it to be so before I leave on tour?

There's such joy in leaving town. There are great shows coming up, unexpected adventures, and you get to leave your normal life behind. But it's also awkward and stressful separating from what and who you love. It's the beginning of the conflicting pull of "frontier and home."

ZIP UP YOUR SUITCASE, IF YOU HAVEN'T ALREADY. Declare yourself packed and zip up that suitcase. You're going to forget something. Just resign yourself to it. Unless you're going to Europe, whatever you forget you can probably purchase at any truck stop. Zip up your suitcase.

SEPARATING FROM YOUR LOVER. If you go out for breakfast or lunch with your girl/boyfriend, be ready for inattentive conversation. The one leaving is thinking of a million details that need to be remembered. The one staying feels left out.

Before you actually rendezvous with the van or bus, leave a little note or present for your mate to find in the house when he or she goes to bed that first night. Maybe under a pillow. Maybe in the refrigerator. The one staying home could secretly place a note in your wallet or journal to find later that evening. A picture of the two of you on a happy occasion might ward off potential road romance three weeks from today.

As you say goodbye, agree on a time you will call each other. It's important for the one staying at home to have a plan to occupy him- or herself the first night. It sets a precedent. It begins a pattern for the next five weeks. The one at home does not want to become the longing, empty, whining, difficult relationship the musician complains about and avoids. There's an art to this long-distance relationship, and it's not easy. But at its core is keeping yourself full while he or she is gone. And developing the art of conversation to bring these separate full lives to each other.

WHAT TO DO WITH YOUR HOUSE KEYS. Once you leave home, put your keys in a zipper pocket that you rarely open. It will be very important to you weeks from now, standing on your doorstep at 6 AM, that you know where your house keys are.

ALMOST LEAVING TOWN

You meet at the appointed place and time with suitcases and amps and instruments. Everyone decided it was a good idea to leave "before traffic," but it always takes longer to load everything and everybody. No matter how great your tour manager is, no matter how well laid out your plans are, your scheduled leave time is never true. Something will always happen to change your departure time. Unfortunately, you still need to be there, ready to go.

> "I'm not gonna get annoyed. I'm just gonna let it play itself out."–Mark's tour left late.

The delay could be your van or bus not arriving as scheduled, or the keyboard being locked in someone's rehearsal space, someone's car not starting, or someone leaving to get food but saying that they'll "be right back."

> Everyone was in the van. Everything was loaded. And still we waited for the missing musician.

2. Touring by Van

"Everything in a van tour is about keeping the peace."–Peggy Firestone

Most musicians begin their touring days traveling in a van towing a trailer of gear behind them. It's not a bad way to travel. You'll drive yourselves across the country day after day to play your gigs night after night. (You might have a peripheral memory of seeing these gypsy musician vans and trailers on the highway or stopped at the gas pump next to you, but you never knew that it was a band on tour.) Each morning, you'll attempt to map out the best route to the next city, avoiding rush hours, taking into consideration time zones and bad weather. You'll be sitting close to each other from four to six hours a day for weeks at a time. A kind of van etiquette begins to reveal itself, and a need to entertain yourself soon becomes apparent.

GETTING YOUR VAN AND TRAILER

Will the band and its gear fit in your Honda Civic? Probably not. You're going to need to get some kind of van–most likely a fifteen-passenger van–but if you're a small band with little gear, a minivan. Your options are to rent from a reliable national company, rent from a friend, or purchase a van yourself.

Commercial Van Rental

The most effective way to rent a van is to ask your touring musician friends for a recommendation. They probably already know the place in town that has the best rates and has a fleet of vans that are in good condition with low mileage–25,000 miles or less. You might even be handed the keys to a brand new van with an odometer reading of twenty-eight miles. A newer vehicle will have excellent heat, air-conditioning, and defrost. The windshield wipers will do their job well and the seats will be fairly comfortable. The brakes may be much better than in your own car. The van interior will have been professionally cleaned since the last person rented it. Commercial rental rates vary a lot depending on the company you call, the type of van you need, and the availability of vans in the area. Also, additional drivers may cost an additional $5 each per day.

Author Note about Unlimited Mileage: You want to have unlimited mileage because your tour is going to rack up a lot of miles. Sometimes the rental place will give you 150 miles a day free, but each additional mile costs 22–25 cents. If your tour is on the East Coast where cities are closer to each other and you're driving shorter distances, this may work for your budget. But consider this: not only do you have to add up the distance between cities, but there are also hidden miles–between the venue and the hotel and the breakfast place and missing turns and getting lost. You'll have to get out your atlas to calculate what works best for your tour, but usually a van with unlimited mileage is what you want.

RENTING A FIFTEEN-PASSENGER VAN. On your first tours you'll most likely be in a rented fifteen-passenger van. It's comfortable for about six or seven people. Ideally everyone will get a bench to themselves, and that's important on long drives. It gives you room to straighten your legs and have a modicum of privacy. The claim of a fifteen-passenger van being for fifteen people is true only if you are driving in from the airport. Traveling with three people to a bench for up to five hours a day for a month is not realistic. It is lunacy. Fire your tour manager immediately if this is his or her plan.

Rates: The cost to rent a passenger van is between $500 and $600 a week. In some places the rates are highest during the summer (June, July, and August), when demand is higher.

RENTING A MINIVAN. If you have a four-piece band with a small amount of gear, you may choose to rent a minivan and take out the back seat to store your amps and guitars. A minivan costs less to rent than a passenger van and is more fuel efficient. It also handles more like a car than a passenger van, so you might feel safer driving it and find it easier to park. But the smallness may feel confining after a few weeks of travel.

Rates: A minivan costs between $300 and $400 a week to rent.

PURCHASING INSURANCE. The rental place will ask if you want to purchase insurance. If you can afford it, buy it. It will raise the rental fee quoted that sounded so reasonable, but get it anyway. To keep tour expenses down, you could call your auto insurance company to check if your insurance covers you while driving a rented van. You may already be covered, but do you want your rates to go up if you have a fender bender on the way to a gig? Touring is a business. The more your business is in place, the better your creative life can thrive.

I've heard stories of bands who didn't purchase insurance on their rented van, but they had a friend on the inside who, after a small wreck, would change the rental agreement to reflect that of course full insurance coverage was in place when the van was rented. This is good luck, which is not a good method of insuring your van.

> "Ever since the police-car incident, I've been instructed that you guys always choose to take the insurance."–Rental place informed us today

Evidently, there was a minor incident with our rental truck and the bumper of an unmarked police car outside of the Metro. Matt Morrison, our monitor engineer, was standing on the bumper trying to disengage the two vehicles when the man with the gun came around the corner. We hadn't purchased the insurance. I think the rental place helped us out on that one.

If you purchase the insurance offered, take a moment to understand it. It's a language we never use unless we're buying car insurance, and even then we barely understand what we're agreeing to. And then we promptly forget what it all means. If you're in an accident and it's your fault, *collision coverage* will pay to repair any damage to your vehicle (the van). It costs about $20 to $25 a day. *Liability insurance* covers "bodily injury" to people in the other car and damage to their vehicle. It may cost between $10 and $35 per day depending on the type of van rented and the state it is rented in. *Comprehensive insurance* covers things like vandalism, acts of nature, glass claims. (You begin to see how nice it will be to have a manager take care of all this calling and cost comparing for you one day.)

USING A CREDIT CARD. You'll be told that you must have a credit card to rent a van. This means your card can't be maxed out. You need to have some money left on it even if you intend to pay the bill in cash upon your return. You can't rent a van with cash and a prayer and a maxed out card.

WHAT HAPPENS IF THE VAN BREAKS DOWN? Breakdowns are less probable and easier to overcome if you're touring in a fairly new, well-maintained commercial rental van.

"Raise a yellow flag and yell for help?" Paragon Van Rental in Chicago joked when I asked him what a band should do. Ask your van rental agency what you should do if your van breaks down. Paragon's policy is if the breakdown is minor just go ahead and fix it, get a receipt, and they'll reimburse you when you return the van. If it's a major breakdown, they'll help find a repair shop that will come get the van and fix it.

Capps, a popular van rental place in Austin, told me: "We offer a 1-800 number for you to call if you break down. All our vehicles are covered under warranty and can be taken to any Chevrolet dealership in the U.S. Chevrolet also offers a roadside assistance number. They'll tow you and open locked doors as well."

RETURNING THE VAN. If you need to keep the van longer than originally intended, just call the rental place and let them know. This is usually no problem. As far as filling the gas tank when you return the van, the policy varies. Budget has a sign that says you have to fill up within three miles of the return drop off, insuring that the tank will truly be full. If you return the van with a less than full gas tank, they'll fill it up for you and charge you twice the actual cost of gasoline. Capps, on the other hand, has a new system: When you pick up the vehicle, you start with a quarter of a tank of gas. When you return it, the tank can be empty. They call it a "complimentary quarter tank of gas." Enterprise offers you the convenience of returning the van with an empty gas tank, but you have prepaid for them to fill it for you.

As far as cleaning the van when you return it, all you have to do is get all of your stuff from under the benches. They'll clean it for the next band. There's not a separate cleaning fee.

Renting a Van from a Friend

The only reason to rent a van from a friend and not a commercial operation is to save the rental and insurance costs. Your friend may be willing to rent you his old rusted cargo van or overheating passenger van if you get the oil changed and pay him the cost of registering it at the Department of Motor Vehicles before you leave town. A van rented from a friend is likely to be uncomfortable and not in the best working condition. The seats may be hard or too springy. The heat, air-conditioning, and defrost may not be working. You may need to buy new windshield wipers. But this van may be the only affordable way for you to travel to your gigs.

If you take this route, call your car insurance company to see if your insurance covers you driving someone else's van. But, then again, if there's a wreck and you are using your own insurance, your personal rates will go up.

There's a very real possibility that the van will break down while you're out on the road, and you should probably work out a deal with your friend regarding who pays for what. You'll be on your own to figure out where to repair it and how to get it towed there. Somebody could join AAA. It's like having your mom and dad come to your rescue without suggesting you go back to school or choose another career.

Purchasing a Van

By your third tour you may have received an advance from your record label. This is a sum of money given to you to make the record or buy gear or pay rent while you write and record your CD. You might consider using some of it to buy a new or used van. If you are touring a lot, it will be less expensive to own a van than rent it week after week, and you won't have to go pick it up and drop it off. Buying a van with band money can be messy. Be in clear agreement what the band will and won't pay for, where the van will be parked, and who can drive it when you're off the road. Also, when you decide to sell the van, how will the money be divided?

Besides saving money, you can renovate your own van however you like. You may want to install captain's chairs and a DVD player. This helps to pass the time tremendously for everyone but the driver and the co-pilot sitting shotgun. You can also build a "coffin," a loft made of two-by-fours and plywood, in the back. Underneath, you pack your instruments and suitcases. On top, somebody's extra futon is laid over the plywood with maybe two feet of stretching room to the ceiling. It'll fit two people lying down. There might be room to lean on your elbows and read. Despite its name, it is not the most unsafe spot to be.

Getting a Trailer

Now that you've got your van, you've got to decide whether you can fit all of the band members, amps, instruments, gig bags, and luggage into it comfortably. Probably not. You'll need to rent or buy a trailer. You can rent a five-foot-by-eight-foot trailer for about $20 a week plus insurance of $5 a day. Trailers are usually waterproof, but you might want to ask to be sure. The rental place will hook it up for you so the lights work properly.

After several tours you may realize you could have purchased your own trailer instead of renting one all this time. It costs about $1,000 to buy a trailer, and you need to register it at the Department of Motor Vehicles. Perhaps someone you know has a side yard or garage to park it while you're off the road.

It will be helpful if someone knows or quickly learns how to back up a van and trailer. Although you'll be moving forward most of the time, there will be the day when you need to back it up–to park, to avoid a parked car while turning, to back out of a one-way dead-end alley behind a club, or to back the trailer door snug against a wall to keep it from being broken into.

You'll have to supply your own lock. The round lock–also called the yo-yo, the circular, or the disc lock–is recommended by tour managers as being the hardest to break.

LOADING YOUR TRAILER

There's a method to loading your trailer. The band gear goes in first. Suitcases go in last. Trust me. It makes sense in the morning. It makes sense in the afternoon. You want your stuff and you don't want to unload a keyboard and an entire drum kit to get to it.

The heaviest items–the amps and drum hardware–should be placed over the wheels. Cases should fit snugly against each other in the trailer. Too much bouncing around may cause instruments to crack or tubes and wires to disengage (i.e. crackling or intermittent signal during the show). Once you've got a full, well-packed trailer, consider making a diagram of what goes where. That way everyone doesn't have to figure out the best approach to loading the trailer every single night after the show.

Then, please remember to check that the trailer door is actually closed and locked before you walk away or drive down the road.

> We stayed at Keith's parents' house. His mom served us a lunch of spinach lasagna and brownies while Keith offered us a breakfast of bagels. Later, we drove away with the trailer door wide open and things falling out as we made our way to the highway. Someone honked and eventually we stopped. Moments later, his parents showed up with a car full of items they had been retrieving off the road.

SEATING IN YOUR PASSENGER VAN

Since most bands travel in a fifteen-passenger van, we're going to use it as our model from here on out. It has two seats up front and four benches.

Riding Shotgun

Only if you have the van in sight may you declare "shotgun" and ride co-pilot. The seat is comfortable. You have a panoramic view. You can be more in charge of the CD player. It's hard to sleep there on an overnight drive, having to sit upright, but you should be helping the driver stay awake anyway. It will usually be your job to read the map or give the driver directions and help look for highway and street names.

Author Note: Often it seems like a great idea to buy a cooler and put it up front between the driver and co-pilot. You've got a place to keep drinks cold. And you've got a little table. In reality, don't bother. The ice melts quickly; the food gets soggy; the table is unsteady.

> The cooler is nothing but trouble. We never put anything in it because we put everything on it and then it all slides off as we make a sudden turn or stop.

First Bench

If you're sitting on the first bench, you're right behind the driver, the co-pilot, and CD player. You can see fairly well out the front windshield. If you're trying to sleep, it will be noisy with the talking and the music. However, you can be one of the first ones out of the van since the big side doors are to your right.

Second Bench

The second bench is the ideal bench. You'll have easy access out the side door and you can talk to those in the front of the van or turn and talk to those in the back of the van. You'll be able to be a part of either conversation. You'll be asked to be the intercom between the two, relaying halves of conversation that can't be heard. Musicians have a theory that as the van is moving forward, sound travels to the back of the van fairly well, but cannot make its way forward. We think this has to do with physics of sound. We wish we knew about this. We're musicians, after all.

Third and Fourth Bench

The musicians on the third and fourth bench are usually troublemakers, sort of like the younger brother who sat behind you in the family car tormenting you. They may have pot. The fourth bench, the back bench, is the longest, extending the entire width of the van. Sometimes it's taken out before you leave home to store extra luggage or gear. If you know you'll have long drives on your tour, keep all the benches in, if possible. That way, there are more places to lie down and try to sleep. The back bench bounces the most and can be a bit claustrophobic, although the nearest exit is right behind you.

Author Note: You can't really claim a bench or a particular spot on a bench for an entire tour. Then again, you might try.

SIMPLE VAN ETIQUETTE

Before we go too many miles, before you piss off your bandmates or get moody because everyone seems mad at you and you don't know why, here are some van rules for you to consider, or not:

- Be at the van at the scheduled time.
- If you're the last one in the van, shut the side door. Who do you think is coming to shut it after you?
- If you are going to smoke, sit shotgun and blow your American Spirit health food cigarette smoke out the window. Don't even imagine that this will not make it smoky in the van. It will.
- Limit the length of your cell phone calls unless you are way in the back bench talking under your blanket. A cell phone call in the van takes up all the room. It's really all anyone can do–listen to your half of the call.

   Long cell phone calls in the van are thankfully interrupted with, "You're cutting in and out, hon, you're cutting in and out." That's the end of the call.

- When in doubt, just shut up. You don't need to make everyone your captive audience about everything that wanders through your head about your past, your mother, other bands you've been in, and friends no one else knows.

   "If one of the van rules is 'shut the fuck up,' it's also true that some of the best conversations I've ever had, I've had in the van."–Jon Dee

- Farting, belching, personal hygiene . . . oh, come on.
- When you get out of the van, you could take your trash with you.

   "Do you know which water is mine? Which of these ten waters is mine?"–Alejandro. We've all been tripping over these half-empty ten-ounce bottles rolling around under the seats for days.

- If you're the last one out, please close and then lock the doors. More than once we'd all go into the convenience store only to come out and find our van unlocked and still running in the parking lot. But before you press all doors locked, make sure the keys are not still in the ignition or dropped on the floor by the driver's feet.

"Who would lock the keys in a running van?"–New York City

CHARTING YOUR COURSE

Where are we going? What road do we take? When do we leave? A tour manager told me that before every tour, the first thing he does is decide the leave time each day. He notes the distance to the next city and how long it will take to get there and then writes down the leave time every single day.

Maps and Routing

You'll be routing yourselves from one city to the next. Buy a current road atlas so you can see on a map where you're going. You can purchase one at a bookstore or truck stop. A Midsize Deluxe Rand McNally road atlas costs about $10. A Michelin road atlas with a wire binding is $18.95. Michelin knows tires, so I guess they know roads as well.

Get one with a laminated cover to help keep the pages from tearing out. Make sure the print is big enough for you to read the numbers on the highways. The day you get home the atlas will be all beat up, stepped on, torn, and muddy in the back of the van, and you'll have lost it before the start of the next tour. Just buy another.

Routing between cities can also be done by going on-line to Google Maps or Mapquest.com. You type in your beginning location and ending address and directions will be listed. Double-check the route the old-fashioned way with your deluxe road atlas. Sometimes the ten steps Mapquest gives you can be translated into two easy steps if you just look at the map. Mapquest is most useful to find your way within a city, as it will give you directions and a map of the town. Your atlas won't always have a city map of each of the towns you are visiting.

Three Routing Tips:

1. If you don't have a tour manager, routing should be agreed on by at least two band members.

   > Martin routed us west to avoid NYC, but an eight-hour drive became eleven, and we got to Erie, Pennsylvania, after 2 AM. We drove through the Berkshires and Tanglewood in pitch black. I did enjoy the shadings of black–mountains, trees, rivers, all in degrees of blackness.

2. Stay on the main roads. They will be faster, plowed, well lit, well marked, and more direct than little side roads. Even though the

map may have you believe that a shortcut via the Western Kentucky Parkway is quicker and more scenic, are you sure it's an interstate the whole way? Will it turn into a two-lane road? Will it become full of cars during some unfathomable, unforeseeable rural rush hour?

3. You can leave the main roads if three separate sources who live in this particular town tell you there's a shortcut from say, Columbia, Missouri, to Springfield, Illinois.

> "You know what I say: the longest distance between two points is a shortcut."–Heinz

Directions

You got directions from the main highway to the club when you advanced the gig. You also got directions to the hotel when you booked the hotel rooms. The driver and co-pilot should have these directions up front with them. Someone in the third bench should not be shouting them up to the driver who can't really hear "Turn north! Left! Here!"

> We missed the last turn to Lawrence and had to go all the way to Topeka and back.

Reversing Directions

There's a lot of reversing of directions on a tour: to return to the hotel, to return to the club, to return to the main highway in the morning. This sounds easier than it is.

> I navigate. But I can't read directions backwards in the dark at 75 miles per hour. I just can't sort it out. I admit this freely. It helps if I draw a map.

It's hard enough to reverse directions if you're navigating, but for the driver to turn on the overhead light, read and reverse directions, and drive is not so easy. The co-pilot must help him.

> "The road in is the same road that leads out."–Alejandro. We can't find the highway we came in on.

Estimated Time of Arrival, or, How Long Till We Get There?

Nothing happens quickly on a tour. The tour will unfold and settle in to its own pace. I used to add up the mileage between cities and look forward to arriving with enough time to go see the Liberty Bell in Philly, the Paul Revere House in Boston, or the Ford Theatre in D.C. I'd be frustrated when we'd leave late and have a long stop at a truck stop and then someone had to pee and there was another long stop and then we got lost, blah blah. Lesson #1 of tour: Everything just takes longer.

50 MPH FORMULA. Use the 50 mph formula to estimate your arrival. When judging time between cities, our tour manager always budgeted us at 50 mph. For example, if you divide 50 mph into 250 miles, it will take you five hours to get there. Even if you're traveling 75 mph, by the time you leave late, make a wrong turn, stop to pee, stop for gas, stop to eat, it'll average out to about 50 miles driven in an hour. Now, if you need to get some sleep after a very late night, remind yourself you'll actually be driving 65 mph, and if you don't stop and dawdle you could leave a little later and get a little more sleep.

Author Note for the future: The time it takes to drive with your bandmates in a van with nine people from Los Angeles to San Francisco is seven and a half hours. Don't listen to anyone else tell you "it's five or six hours" in their little red car.

RUSH HOUR. The thing you often completely forget about is that sound check is at 4 PM or 5 PM, the same time as rush hour. It may be impossible to avoid a traffic jam. You can leave a little earlier to avoid rush hour altogether, or you can figure your travel time will be two hours longer in heavy traffic.

We left Austin early, slammed into thick Houston morning rush hour and then early afternoon Mardi Gras traffic on our way into New Orleans.

Author Note: When you advance the date, you hope the production manager will alert you to any Mardi Gras parades, Caribbean festivals, or street fairs causing traffic jams and street closures in the city the day you arrive that would be nice to avoid.

CHANGING TIME ZONES. The four time zones in the United States (Eastern, Central, Mountain, and Pacific) will take you by surprise. Louisville's on Eastern time? Nashville's on Central time? You often figure it out the morning you arrive early or late. There's nothing to really alert you to the time change.

We're an hour out of Chicago. Bruce is driving like a madman.
"We're supposed to be there in fifteen minutes!"
"Bruce, relax. We'll gain an hour!"
"Oh, we're going to be late for a little while and then we'll be early."

Your road atlas has the time zone lines on it, but these lines look like small farm-to-market roads, and if you're not thinking about a time change you'll miss them. Your cell phone might adjust automatically to the new time zone, but by then you're already in the new time zone and it's too late to leave earlier or later.

> "If it's 11 PM here in Erie and 10 PM in Chicago, you lose an hour going to Chicago"–Matt Morrison, our sort of tour manager says.
>
> I try to explain to a slightly drunken room of travelers that "Actually, you subtract an hour on the clock, but by doing that you'll gain an hour of time."
>
> As everyone considers this, Frank asks, "If you have twelve band members in two vans leaving Erie, Pennsylvania, with a case and a half of beer and a pack of cigarettes between them, how long will it take them to get to Chicago?"

DAYLIGHT SAVING TIME. Daylight saving time begins the second Sunday in March and ends the first Sunday in November. Arizona and Hawaii are the only two states that don't change to daylight saving time, although the Navajo reservation in Arizona does observe it. And incidentally, why is there daylight saving time anyway? Benjamin Franklin tinkered with the idea, but why? Everyone in the van will have a theory how it began, none of which will be entirely accurate. It did not start with the farmers. They actually don't like it. (*Short history:* It was first used in the United States in 1918 during WWI to conserve resources. President Roosevelt implemented it again during WWII, calling it "War Time." After that, the use of it was sort of hodgepodge. Some counties kept to it. Some didn't. Some places started and ended it at different times than others, making it hard for buses and trains to keep a schedule. The Uniform Time Act of 1966, signed by President Johnson, didn't require anyone to observe daylight saving time, but if you were going to, you had to agree to begin and end at a specified date.)

ENTERTAINING YOURSELF

There is tremendous liberation in finally driving out of town. Your heart soars. You are so ready to go somewhere, to see what's out there down the road. What do you do on the twelve-hour drive to your first show when conversation winds down?

Look out the Window

Watching the world out the van window is a lot of your entertainment. Really. It's not thrilling, but it is time consuming. The light, the landscape, the signs, the little towns—it's a collage of hours unfolding.

"I like all the brick houses."

"Well, that's just in case Sherman comes through again."—Club owner in Georgia

"Hey, this lake has been on fire three times."—Josh, looking out over Lake Erie.

Driving into Detroit, I see people sitting on their front porches, thinking and looking at us as we go by. And we roll along in the van, watching them as they go by.

"Isn't it interesting that any time you go past a huge cluster of buildings with smoke billowing out, they never have a sign telling you the company name?"

As you drive through and pass all these cities you'll see some poetic graffiti:

"Love's fumbling futility."—On a bridge overpass in Philadelphia

"This life ... is not life."—On a wall by the Thames River in London

"You just have to try ..."—On a garage door in Chicago

You'll find signs that may amuse and intrigue:

Ghetto Burgers

Fag Bearings

Bong Recreation Center

Espresso & Oil Change

Just Say No to Bugs

Panther Crossing

You'll read signs with words that don't go together:

Liquor, Guns & Ammo

Nutmeg Power Equipment

Old Newgate Prison

You'll come upon signs of places you would like to visit if your tour manager said yes:

Biscuitville, North Carolina

Liquor, Guns & Ammo

We tattooed your father here.

"Did you notice C&B Darts is right next to B&C Antiques?"—Howe

Listen to Music

The music we listen to on tour is bound to affect our performance. (This is also a reason you may not want to watch the opening band right before your show.)

> We're listening to *20 Explosive Hits of the '70s*, and we've got a long, long way to go.

> "Hey, that music doesn't go with the landscape."–Luke

If you're co-pilot or driver and in control of the radio or CD player, don't just assume the whole van wants to hear what you want to hear at the volume you want to hear it.

> "I can't stand rap music. It sounds like I'm listening in on someone's argument next door."–Luke

Some vans don't have CD players. Some vans think they don't have a CD player.

> "For those traveling in the maroon van all this tour, I just want to inform you that yes, you do have a CD player with a flip-down face."–Josh. We traveled all these miles thinking we had no CD player. We listened to country radio and Christian radio and nothing at all. And now we feel like idiots that the radio we have been looking at all these hours of traveling is actually a CD player. The crew will never let up on this. They already think the musicians aren't very bright.

Read the Local Paper

Read what's happening locally. The writing styles change with each city. What seems to be important is unique to each area.

> "Shark Sighting at Sunset Point"–*Honolulu Star Bulletin* headline

> "A forty-year-old woman called police to report that her husband doesn't do enough work around the house and she is fed up with him."–Police report, *Honolulu Star Bulletin*

> They canceled the Christmas parade because the permit was going to include a Klan march with it.

> The *Tucson Weekly* says that because of the dry and mild winter, be on the lookout for bears, and there won't be as many wildflowers. And this spring has an active population of diamondback rattlers and Africanized bees. When I tell this to my Tucson friends, they say it was written for tourists.

> From the *Bangor Daily News*: "Horace Rudy Peabody, a well-known lobsterman/fisherman, has died. He grew up on the *Lizzie J. Clark*, which his father owned and operated up and down the coast of Maine. He enjoyed playing with his dog Juju, who could be seen riding alongside Rudy, sitting

high upon his toolbox with his head out the window."

"A pair of air conditioners were stolen from a Bolingbrook subdivision and police said they had no leads–everyone had a motive."–*Chicago Tribune*, during ten-day heat wave.

Read Your Books

You brought them, so read them. The sun goes down at different times depending on your latitude, so I hope you brought a little book light. If you turn on the overhead van light for hours, it may interfere with the driver's ability to see and your bandmates' ability to sleep.

> We drove out of Oklahoma City, and it was tornado flat with a fuzzy moon and no stars except a few braves ones. Frank read an Allen Ginsberg poem out loud about his mother's death and then asked if he should read more, but we were still hearing the old words rolling in our heads.

Write in Your Journal

Write your tour stories down. Years later, write a book. Also, if you write, you won't have to talk all the time to sort out your conflicting emotions with your bandmates.

Play Games

I'm too bored to play games in the van, but if someone brings out a travel scrabble, I'll play. Playing a game is another kind of band rehearsal. Whatever you do during the day will often find its way to the stage that night. If you play a game, or share dinner, have a cocktail and a conversation, or watch a DVD this afternoon, you'll feel it onstage tonight.

Conversation

The first hour of driving, everyone is talkative. Slowly everyone runs out of energy or thoughts. It's like you've burned off the first layers of thought and conversation. Tour conversation today: movies, sex, other bands, sex, actors forming bands....As we drive and rock back and forth in the van and watch the landscape and light change, our thoughts have time to stretch out. Conversation on the long drive becomes confessional and reverential. Much like drinking conversations, topics often come back to our own vague understanding of religion, other bands, actors forming bands, families, love, and sex.

> "If you were going to sleep with anyone in the band who would it be?"– Adam. We're sipping little Maker's Mark bottles we bought at a 7-Eleven near the distillery and continue our overnight drive.

We plan the first sentence of our Great American Novels simply by what the morning brings. "All she wanted was a good cup of tea with milk," is mine. "Consider me a dead man." Alejandro thinks this is great, although he admits he doesn't know where it came from or where it goes.

"Why must mankind's blunders be repeated in my life? Why hasn't someone figured it out?"–Luke

STOPPING FOR FUEL

Pretty much the only reason we stop between cities is to get gas. Every other reason to stop is organized around the fuel stop–to eat, to pee, to stretch our legs, to make a phone call home. There is an odd push to keep driving and not stop at the very service station we're looking at. We need gas, yet we keep driving.

"You can't stop here. It's the gang capital of the world." There is no gang capital of the world. Is there?

Tip #1: Buy gasoline now, not at the next gas station that may or may not appear in time.

Tip #2: Buy gasoline at a service station you can see from the highway with easy-off, easy-on access. You don't want to drive three miles into town looking for gas. You don't want to exit to another freeway and drive a long way before you find a gas station. Then you've got to pull out a map to find your way to back to the original and correct freeway.

Tip #3: Pee when you can, not when you have to. When the van stops for gas, take this opportunity to pee. Why would you wait until you're twenty minutes down the road and ask to stop again?

Half-moon sunset. We stop to pee in a canyon. They all pee like their dads must have taught them. Legs apart. One hand on hip, looking off, like there is a vista over there to the left. I try to avoid peeing on my shoe.

FOOD STOP

You're not in town near the square, the coffee shop, or the Thai place. You're at some exit off the highway on your way to the next gig. Your choices are usually slim: Cracker Barrel, maybe a Chinese place in a strip mall, a Subway, or the restaurant at the truck plaza where you will find a good diner breakfast, breaded everything, white-lettuce salad, and creamy additive-filled dressing.

Why does Middle America, the nation's bread basket, serve up such tasteless food?

With a place in sight, everyone sort of agrees on the stop. Band members will "negotiate" with each other as to how low on the food chain the band is willing to dine. Sometimes when the van or bus stops, the band will split up as several go looking for a better choice. Before everyone leaves the vehicle, declare a return time. If there is no plan, these stops get ridiculously long and the tour manager has to go find the keyboard player who is innocently shopping for socks at the Wal-Mart after his Chinese buffet.

Author Note: After you travel together awhile you'll start to sync to each other's timing and all come out of the convenience store or diner at the same time.

THE FIRST PHONE CALL HOME

It's time to call home. Have one anecdote ready even if you've only seen a highway and several gas stations and there are seven more hours to drive. The first few conversations home can be weird. The one on tour is either dulled from the monotony of driving or stimulated by the new people, new conversations, and new landscape. The one at home will feel the emptiness of a best friend gone.

> "Do you think it's harder for the one going on tour or the one staying at home?"

You'll find your own way to stay in touch on the phone. Have the kind of conversation you have at the kitchen table. Consciously include details–the okra you had with dinner or the Southern accents you heard in the restaurant. If you leave these out, you'll slowly lose touch with each other. Talk about something in addition to the day's events. Let a conversation unfold.

Be sure to ask how your loved one is. Make an effort to listen to the answer. You may need to refer back to that answer when told, "You don't ever listen to me anymore."

It takes a while for the rhythm of the one at home to roll smoothly again. You've just left their life. Left a big hole in it. She thinks you've got a lot of fun and entertainment going on out on the road. She feels a little left out. Although when you call home you may find she's filled up that big hole quickly with a raging dinner party with all your friends. You feel a little left out of your own life. What can you do? You're miles away and weeks away from getting home. You shake it off and get back in the van.

DRIVING TIPS AND TROUBLES

Everyone shares in the driving, but you'll have a few people who drive more than anybody. Thankfully they're usually the better drivers. Each of your bandmates has their own driving method and style.

> Ted drives in S patterns. His distance between shows is significantly far-
> ther than any other driver. John drives so that the trailer wags like a dog.
> We surmise John is driving "Isabella" (the other van, the smoking van) right
> now. Howe drives like he plays guitar. Luke is dodging butterflies to no
> avail. They still smash the windshield or fly into the tires like Bambi meets
> Godzilla; butterflies meet iron machine.

Airplane pilots have a saying: aviate, navigate, communicate. This means
fly the airplane safely first, then navigate where you're going, then communicate to the control tower. So pay attention to driving the van first. It's
the most important thing. Then look for the highway signs to get you to
the next city, then communicate on your cell phone to your friends you've
invited to the show tonight. It also means if there's any problem, return
immediately to the most important thing: driving the van.

Author Note: In many cities (Chicago and New York City, to name two),
it's illegal to drive while talking on your cell phone unless you have a
hands-free device.

Author's picky and obvious driving editorial:

1. Use your turn signal. It's really an indicator light. You are indicat-
   ing that you are going to turn right. Signaling that you are turning
   while you are turning is really rather pointless.
2. The left lane is for passing. When I asked a cellist why he always
   drove in the far left lane, his response was, "Why Susan, I like it in
   the left lane. There's never anyone in front of me I have to pass."

Getting Lost

Getting lost could be a matter of bad directions. It could be that your bass
player driver is not paying attention at all and the co-pilot is asleep. It
might be too dark or foggy to see the street signs. Maybe the signs have
fallen down. Anyway, what the directions say and what you see out the
window do not match and you're lost.

> "We want to go northeast so we take the highway that says west?"–David,
> 75 mph, driving into Chicago

It makes you crazy driving an extra forty-five minutes circling close to your
destination. It just happens some days. You'll find your way again.
Unfortunately, you now won't have time to stop at the hotel and rest, or
get a little food or shop before sound check. Maybe you'll get up early and
have some time in the morning to see this city, you think, but you know
it's not true.

"We weren't exactly lost. Let's just say we could have gone more straight."
–Heinz

If you are driving late at night and see a WELCOME TO DELAWARE sign but it is not the welcoming state you expected, just turn around and arrive late. No need to account for the missing hours to the musicians asleep during the turnaround.

Speeding

There may be long, long drives between cities. This may cause speeding and speeding tickets and encounters with police.

"In the U.S., they'll never have gun control. In Germany, they'll never have a speed limit."–Heinz, speeding to Portland

If you have plenty of time to get to your gig, then the person speeding because he or she felt like it should pay the damn ticket. They never do. We hear there will be a warrant out for their arrest, which will give them trouble should they return to this state and be driving and get pulled over again. It seems so far-fetched and so far away. The tickets rarely get paid.

"What's our speed limit?"
"As fast as she can go until she starts shaking."

If the officer asks if you've been drinking, it's not helpful to answer, "Not since I left the bar." When the officer asks what kind of music you play, country and western is a good answer. Tell them you have an acoustic guitarist and a violin player (if you do). Tell them anything about your band that seems quiet and lawful.

"Pull-over country." It's what Alejandro's band is calling Lafayette County, Texas. Everyone gets a ticket driving through there.

Traveling with Cannabis

In the music world we often forget that marijuana is not legal. Whatever the unwritten tolerance to pot is where you live, it will be different and probably more serious once you start traveling the U.S. highways. If you say you have no pot and the police find a joint in someone's pocket, they have been known to haul everybody off to jail, threatening to confiscate instruments. Your bandmates may bring other drugs with them, but the most common and "acceptable" is pot. They call it a soft drug in Amsterdam.

Vans with Texas and Florida plates look suspiciously like they are transporting drugs or dynamite, which is another reason not to speed radically and to make sure your lights are all working properly. No need to get pulled over. Nothing of interest in here; just some hippies having breakfast from their cooler.

Driving in Bad Weather

Mother Nature has a greater affect on you traveling in a van than in a bus. A bus is heavier and is driven by a professional driver. A van pulling a trailer is lighter and slides easily and is being driven by a sleep-deprived musician. You might want to become familiar with how the defrost works, how to turn on the windshield wipers and the headlights, as well as how to turn on the overhead light *before* getting on the highway and encountering weather.

> "That's not snow. I've seen pictures of snow."–Adam, Chicago in November

Author's Driving-in-Fog Tip: If you find yourselves in thick fog, don't use your bright headlights. The more intense light will only reflect off the fog, making it even harder to see anything but fog. Proceed with caution but do keep moving forward. Wrecks are often caused when someone stops and no one can see them for the fog and they get hit from behind.

> We're driving twelve hours back to San Francisco. I stay up with the driver through bad fog. As he gets sleepy so do I. But now it's my turn to drive. I make it through a tape and a half, invoking Jesus, the Buddha, and all the dead I know to guide this van and keep us safe.

Author's Driving-in-Snow Tip: Have the person with the most experience driving in ice and snow behind the wheel; someone who can react instinctually. Most importantly on slippery roads, you don't want to make sudden moves. Give other cars a wide berth, a wide margin of safety. If the van starts to slide, turn into the slide–sliding right, turn to the right; sliding left, turn to the left.

> Kansas is socked by an ice storm and four inches of snow. We drove through the most beautiful ice-covered landscape. Trees, fields, barbed wire. At sunset the land is blue. End the joy on thirty yards of sheer ice. Eric is driving the trailer van. I am driving the red van. Police are waving us to continue on as if we had a choice to stop. I am so scared my teeth are chattering. We continue at 25 mph for three hours on packed snow and ice in the night. We stop for a "nerve stop," and Eric gets out and we hug as drivers. We've got 322 miles to go at 30–35 mph. Spinout ahead. "Is there a pillow?" Frank is going to take a nap.
>
> "I grew up on this stuff. I know what I'm doing," says Daren, the next driver (who five years from now will be unable to stop a rollover crash and a band member dies).

The next morning we see hay bales covered in snow like giant marsh-mallow crops in the fields, now that "hot chocolate is in season." Dead cars are strewn about from the night before. Everyone wants to cuddle up, curl up, and make love with the freezing outside pulling the loving inside.

"Though love be a day, and life be nothing, it shall not stop kissing."
—e.e. cummings

I've driven on glare ice in Kansas, a blizzard in God-knows-where moun-tain state, fog outside of Houston, and an ice storm outside Nashville, only to have our booking agent tell me later, "If you can't make it safely, just stop." Really? Really. To avoid problems, don't drive if there's a blizzard, even if you'll miss a gig.

Snow definitions—
  Blowing and drifting snow: snow from adjoining counties
  Lake effect: snow without a proper purpose; aimless yet cumulative

Breakdowns

The oil light comes on. There is no power in the gas pedal. A "that's not good" clanking noise is coming from somewhere. You glide the van over to the side of the interstate. Yours is not the first rock band to be stranded fifty miles between cities.

We drove and drove. We drove until one van broke down and we climbed aboard the other one and moved the trailer over and kept driving.

If you're driving a commercially rented van, give the company a call and ask them what you should do. There will be a phone number in your contract to call. They will find a repair place and call a tow truck to come get you. The rental company is responsible for the repair costs. If the repair is going to take too long to get you to the next gig, they will help find you another van.

If you're driving your own or a friend's van, call AAA if you're a mem-ber. If not, find and call a tow truck to tow you to the nearest garage.

Once the mechanic has diagnosed the problem, call the club and let them know you'll be a little late. Hopefully the van will be repaired in time for you to make the show. What do you do if it won't be repaired until morning? Pull out the yellow pages and search for a rental van with a trailer hitch in whatever town you're in. If you find a van but it isn't able to pull the trailer, load as many instruments, amps, and musicians into it as you can. Call the club to see if you can borrow backline (amps and a drum kit) from another band on the bill.

If all you can find to rent is a Winnebago, fill it up with your stuff and hope you don't sideswipe any cars while driving a narrow road to park behind the club. If you can't find a rental vehicle and you're only an hour away from the club, maybe someone from the club can come pick up the band members and instruments and you can borrow backline for the show. (How about the sound guy? He's got nothing to do until you get there anyway.) The club doesn't want the show to cancel either, so they may be willing to help you out.

Tomorrow, you'll be getting up early to return the rental vehicle and pick up your newly repaired van. Cross your fingers that the problem is fixed as you continue on to the next gig.

Close Calls

There are so many close calls–barely missed accidents, the wrecks you almost have–when you drive day after day and tour after tour. It could be losing control of the van on ice, or trying to avoid running over an animal crossing the road in front of you, or being cut off by another car.

Most of these are unexpected, heart-stopping, and memorable. You'll still be talking about your close calls years after they happen. You shake your head at what might have happened and in disbelief that you are all safe.

> We made it to Muskogee, Oklahoma. At 4:30 AM the van went hydroplaning on the ice. Ted was driving. At first it felt just a little out of control. Then suddenly the jerkiness got bad. The trailer–back and forth like windshield wipers. I was thinking, "Ted from Hawaii doesn't know about ice and snow." But he got us through and we stopped at the next hotel with three double beds in one room.

> Earlier today a highway truck did a U-turn right in our path. Are we invisible?

Minor Wrecks

By definition, a minor wreck is not a major bad accident. It can be expensive and inconvenient, but usually no one is hurt, just jostled around a bit.

> "If your record's spotless and you've never had an accident, chances are you're about to have one."–Howe

If you've been driving a Honda Civic at home, you'll have to adjust your driving significantly once you get behind the wheel of a van or trailer. The most common minor wrecks are caused by not knowing your rented vehicle. The van is wider and longer and responds differently than a little car. You can't stop as fast or turn as quickly. And if you've got a trailer attached, you lose the ability to look out the rearview mirror. Use the side mirrors and ask your bandmates for help when changing lanes or passing.

A van is taller than you think. The driver should know the height of the vehicle. You don't want to dent or scrape the roof going into a parking structure you won't fit in. One time we made it up into a parking garage but for some reason were hitting the ceiling on the way out. The solution was to lower the antennae and take some air out of each tire.

Most minor accidents occur on tour while backing up the van. There's a sign etched onto side-view mirrors: OBJECTS IN MIRROR ARE *CLOSER* THAN THEY APPEAR. This means the front bumper of the car behind you is CLOSER than you think it is. It will meet your bumper sooner than expected.

> We backed into a mother and daughter at the gas station restaurant by the hotel. Their car was overheating. "Oh honey, it ain't nothin'. It's already a bad day," the mom said. We drove on.

You could take a picture or video with your cell phone of the car your van barely dented while backing out of a parking space during an Atlanta rainstorm. A picture gives you some proof and half a chance of not being taken advantage of by an attorney in a faraway state.

Bad Accidents

The bad accidents are bad stories that musicians don't bring up. They chill us. There are so many hours of driving. You do what you can to be safe. You hope the driver will admit he's tired even if he's only driven an hour. You hope no driver around you does anything stupid. You hope the universe is with you. There are many close calls. And then there's a wreck.

> Alejandro tells me about the Silos' rollover wreck as we are leaving on our West Coast tour. Manny flew out the window. He was probably waiting for the wreck to end. Daren was driving, and Daren's a good driver. He was my co-driver on the Kansas ice. They were out west heading to Portland, Maine, Manny's hometown. The bottles of wine they were taking to his mom were not broken, but Manny slowly died because it took the ambulance so long to arrive. We feel especially bad because we had made fun of his demo tape on an earlier tour. We drive and don't say much.

When Friends or Fans Want a Ride

When friends or fans want to ride with you from this city to the next, consider this very carefully. Yes, they're your friends. Yes, they're your fans. Yes, we had a lovely after-party last night. But you're asking for a heap of potential trouble.

> In the morning I walk by David and the drunken radio guy who obviously
> hasn't been to bed since the show and who announces he's coming with
> us today on our six-hour drive to Memphis. We drive him home instead.

Every band handles this request differently. Somebody sometime has to
remind the band that this is a business. You're out on the road supporting
your independently made record. You're gaining fans in each city you play.
You start to get some press. A record label takes note of this activity and
flies in to see you play somewhere. Piling more people in the van only
takes space that is really for the band and crew to travel comfortably to the
next show.

> "These are the people the tour manager hates but the band loves to have
> around. The freeloaders who want rides and to crash in hotel rooms."
> –Mark

Conversely, if you give a fan a ride, they'll appreciate it and feel a part of
the band and tell their friends about you. I know you want to be generous,
but what's going on here may not be simple generosity. One of these three
girls is probably the bass player's new "girlfriend."

THE OVERNIGHT DRIVES

> We drove until the night broke into dawn. "Coffin call," Charlie used to
> call it.

Overnight drives occur when your booking agent books your next gig in a
city too far away to drive to the next day. It could be your own tour or
you're the opener for a band more famous than you traveling in a tour bus.
You've got to keep up with their schedule. On a tour bus the overnight is
expected and easier, provided you can sleep. You've got a professional
driver and bunks to sleep in. An overnight in a van is just hard. One of you
drives; the rest bounce around curled up on the benches.

> Dave, Frank, and I watch *The Spirit of St. Louis* with Jimmy Stewart tonight.
> Poor Lindberg stayed up for three days flying. It's like us trying to stay
> awake yet drifting off to sleep while driving the van.

There are three options to reaching the faraway gig on time.

> 1. Leave directly after the show, full of adrenaline, and drive through
>   the night until you arrive in the next city. You might follow the warm
>   glow of the headliner's tour bus. At 4 AM you might imagine the front
>   lounge of the bus full of trip-hop music, shoulder rubs, wine from
>   Argentina, and then sleepy good nights and bunk curtains closing.

And you drive until dawn. Then you stop and have breakfast with their tour bus driver. And then you drive until early afternoon.

> "You know my new rule: The last one to pack up their stuff is the first to drive the van after the show."–Tour manager

2. You can break up the long drive by driving two or three hours, stopping to rest a few hours in a cheaper hotel out of town, and continuing on in the morning. That way you make a dent in the drive time but also get some sleep. However, once you start driving overnight, it's hard to decide exactly when to stop.

> "There was a whole range of road pride on that tour. They got all road-doggy. 'No, we can't stop. We've got to burn thru the night.'"

Author Note: If you've decided to drive out after the show, you probably won't book a hotel in the city of the gig. You arrive in town and have your sound check. Then you find some dinner. And then there's four or five hours with no place to go until the 11 PM show. These are the oddly homeless, aimless, and lonely hours. Your show can feel a little pale after waiting around so long.

3. As a third option, you can sleep a few hours after the show, then get up really early and drive eight hours straight to make your sound check at 4 PM. You might feel dizzy, mindless, and somewhat nauseous for awhile.

> I told Jackson I think I'm getting that sickness. "No. You just have van." I've been in the van way too long.

Who Drives When?

In theory, everyone shares the driving, although two or three people tend to always drive. When there's an overnight coming up, you'll notice the frequent drivers jockeying for early driving position. "I just want to make it to Los Cruces," the drummer says during a long day of driving. Yes, it sounds generous. But it may just be his strategy to drive all day so it's not his turn late that night. It's usually the ones who don't drive as often, the junior varsity drivers, that are brought in off their bench to drive the overnight. They aren't your best drivers, but late at night you don't need a lot of finesse or speed. You want someone who has good night vision and can not only stay awake but be alert enough to respond to sloppy driving by other drivers around you, a deer suddenly crossing the road, detours, and road construction and keep on the right highway. All in the dark. All while a little tired.

Staying Awake While Driving Overnight

Coffee and plain water are amazingly helpful to stay awake, but you can still fall asleep. If you've had too many drinks, don't risk your bandmates' lives by driving. Even a beer or two will make it harder to stay awake once the stimulation of the show, the club, the night, and your bandmates' banter winds down.

The weird thing about falling asleep at the wheel is that you won't know it until you wake up. Your eyes involuntarily close and by then you're way past the point of safety. You learn to recognize when your body is too tired to continue and it's time to stop driving. For me, my body is too tired when I start seeing bridges that aren't there, like a mirage in the night. They always appear at the horizon, linking the tops of the trees from either side of the road. But they never get closer. We never drive under them.

The Handoff

After two or three hours of night driving, you switch drivers and probably get gasoline. There's an unwritten rule that, if possible, the one who just drove gets a bench to himself to rest. Before collapsing on the back bench, he should point the new driver, holding weak yet hopeful coffee in hand, in the right direction on the right highway to continue your journey.

> "This coffee has already stuck its tongue down my throat."–Steve Goulding

It has happened that the new driver has accidentally driven the van back toward where it came from before someone noticed we were returning to Los Angeles and were intending to be in Las Vegas.

Make sure the driver knows to wake up the next driver when he needs to stop. "If you get tired, just pull over and rest," was the last thing my bandmates told me before they fell asleep. At about 3:45 AM, I was tired and pulled into a rest area, reclined the driver's seat, and promptly fell asleep myself. When the sun woke us all up about two hours later, Alejandro asked me, "What are you doing?" I thought we'd all get some rest, okay?

Sleeping on the Overnight

How do you sleep in a van on an overnight drive? If you didn't bring your pillow, roll up your jacket for a pillow and lean onto the side window or your bandmate's shoulder. Or you can press your head forward into the bench in front of you. You can also squeeze to the floor and sleep a little claustrophobically, hoping there's no wreck while you're wedged in.

The Drive Home

Driving home after the last show or an out-of-town gig can be a dangerous trip. It seems you are too close to rent a hotel room. If you begin your three-hour drive at 3 AM, there are no sure ways to stay awake. You just have to know that fatigue can't always be overcome. Your co-driver becomes really important. Be careful. I remember hearing of World War II pilots who stayed awake for twenty-four hours on difficult missions. Once the battle was over and the adrenaline and concentration could ease, they fell asleep and crashed flying back home.

FINDING INEXPENSIVE LODGING

Your first van tours are low-budget tours. There may not be enough money to stay in a hotel room each night. You might be offered the floor at a friend's house, a parent's basement or attic, or a small apartment connected to the club. These accommodations are welcome and free (although your hostess may ask to ride with you in the van to the next city) and vary widely in their comfort level.

> We stayed at a friend's apartment, about the size of a table, two blocks from the beach.

> We stay at someone's house. "There's a bedroom for each of you and a towel on each bed." I could cry. I think I do.

The apartment offered by the club is going to be messy and funky, probably full of cat hair and none of those sheets have been washed in years. Bring your own pillow and blanket in from the van. I don't care what the shower looks like. If there's hot water, take a shower now. Remember, shower when you can, not when you have to. It may be days before you have another.

> *The owners let us stay in the apartment above the club but they had to lock us in. We had free access to the bar but if there had been a fire we'd have been in trouble.*

GETTING BROKEN INTO

Always take with you what is valuable when you leave the van. It *will* be broken into. For this reason it's a good idea to insure your gear before you leave home. (See "Purchasing Insurance for Your Instruments and Gear," page 35.) Some cities are notoriously dangerous–Vancouver, D.C., Detroit, Atlanta, Oklahoma City. It may not be the city but the part of town you're in or just your luck on that particular day. When you arrive at the club, arrange parking in front for your van and trailer. The doorman will probably be able to keep an eye on it while you're onstage. If he says you can park there but you might get a $20 ticket, risk the ticket. If you park down the street and someone breaks the window and ransacks the van, the loss will be a lot more than $20.

And at this point you've got a broken window in D.C. at 2:30 AM. It will most likely be raining or snowing. Someone is going to have to sleep in the van tonight to make sure it isn't hotwired or vandalized further.

The next morning, someone will get up early to find an auto-glass repair shop. Does your van insurance cover a broken window? Is there a deductible? How much money will the tour have to come up with to repair the window? You might have to use your merchandise money. Have you sold enough T-shirts to pay $200 or more for the window replacement?

FIVE DAYS INTO YOUR VAN TOUR

Five days in your van. There is no privacy. You look at your bandmates. You listen to them. You may be lucky and the cellist studied the theory of comedy in college and the guitarist studied comparative religion and the songwriter studied Buddhism and one of you is genuinely crazy. This is high entertainment during the long hours of travel.

You've probably played five shows and already traveled 1,500 miles, met club owners and bartenders and a few fans, had diner breakfasts, listened to hours of music, and bantered witlessly with sleepless musicians. You're a little stressed, with too much stimulation and not enough privacy to absorb it or a dream to make peace with it.

If there are problems to solve with your bandmates, remember that you want a positive outcome. You've probably got weeks and miles left to travel. You want to keep the peace. Part of the stress is that you are so close to each other all the time—in your van, in the small dressing room, sharing hotel rooms. Add to this alcohol, egos, no sleep, and that you're not around your lover who adores you and your home things that comfort you.

"Tour can separate you from the things in your life that fix you."–Frank

You can almost see trouble coming. There are two predictable problems on most van tours. The first is being consistently late. When you arrive late, with your double latte and Egg McMuffin, everyone wishes they too had gone to get a double espresso drink and a bite to eat. But no, they came to the van on time and have had no coffee and no Egg McMuffin. You have made them wait. And they are empty-handed and hungry. They don't like you as much as they did last night. You have been inconsiderate this morning. You have been selfish. Suddenly they think you don't play as well as you did yesterday.

You've also started a bad precedent as time begins to unravel and everyone loses faith in the stated leave times. Now 4:30 PM will mean sometime before 5 PM. No one will know exactly when they are to meet at the van. The band will never recover its sense of time until a bus is leased and your bus driver scares everyone into arriving at the actual stated time of departure.

The second predictable infraction is not doing your job so others have to do more. In addition to playing for all your worth, your job is also to help load gear into the club and at the end of the night to pack up your gear and help load out. If you're the one always missing load-in or load-out, you're forcing someone to take care of your stuff and you're never around to carry theirs. The band will think you're on a star trip. The band may think you are getting too full of yourself and are a drag to be around. Morale suffers. The show onstage suffers.

TAKING SIDE TRIPS

It's time to take a side trip. One way to improve morale is to see something besides a highway, a truck stop, a hotel, and a rock club. Traveling by van, you can actually see more of the country you are crisscrossing than if you were in a tour bus—and not only because you'll be awake all the time. A van is more nimble than the bus, easier to park, and doesn't eat as much gas driving a little out of your way.

> Howe, John Convertino, and I go to the Saguaro National Park. It's a forest of cactus trees but no shade. We climb up and up. Desert and sky go on forever. The wind is bathing. We watch a "devil spout." The rocks smell like a sauna—deep, musty, rich.

> We arrive at the Redwoods after dark. We stop, get out, and touch the trees. They grow in clumps—in families. At 7 AM the next day we see elk standing so still in a trailer park that we think they are lawn ornaments. We drive through the redwood tree and buy redwood souvenirs. Before we reach LA, one of them tells me he slept with a lesbian in San Francisco.

> We stop and buy baskets by the Conoco Gas Station outside Amish country. We wonder about the Amish and then the Shakers. "I want to go back to school on the 'I want to learn this today' program," Frank says. We want to know about the Amish and the Shakers today and he wonders about the evolution of civilization and language, like why does Russian look like Greek.

TRAVELING IN TWO VANS

When you can afford it, you'll want to bring a sound engineer or tour manager out with you on tour. You might want to rent another van so everyone can have a little more room. One van will be towing the trailer. I'm not sure why, but usually the van with the trailer will become the smoking, drinking, nastier van.

"I am in the van with endless flatulence."–Luke

The other van will be the nonsmoking, reading, massage-giving van. Each van will make fun of the other, but when it's time to stop and have dinner, you will have missed your bandmates in the other van.

"Smoking kind of defines where people hang out. One van becomes the smoking van, just like one lounge is declared a smoking lounge on a bus. Do you talk in the book about how one is cooler?"–El John

MAYBE WE SHOULD RENT A WINNEBAGO

Someone will suggest that renting a Winnebago or an RV is a great idea. It costs about as much two vans and a trailer. You'll be driving it yourselves, so you won't have to pay for a driver like on a tour bus. You can stand up and walk around. There appears to be places for six musicians to sleep: above the driver, the front couches, and the back bedroom. You can store the gear in the shower and bathroom.

"Old people drive them. How hard can it be?"–Jackson

But old people drive at 50 mph and aren't drinking and aren't in a hurry to get to the next gig.

"An RV doesn't go fast well. It feels like it's going to blow apart. You can't sleep in the back while moving, so everyone piles up front. On the plus side, it has the feel of a bus. You can talk while looking at each other instead of looking forward like a van. You can get up and walk to the fridge."–Frank

There's a reason bands wind up in vans or a tour bus. Most likely nobody in your band is familiar with driving a Winnebago. The chance of sideswiping a car or a car rearview mirror is very likely. It sways a lot in the wind and rain and snow. The interior is not as sturdy as a bus. The little things break easily. Parking is difficult. You're not going to an RV park but a densely populated part of town where streets are narrow.

"Well, the Winnebago was towed this morning. We thought it had been stolen."–Day one, Vancouver

If you're thinking of renting a Winnebago, it's probably time for you to look into renting a tour bus. Raise your ticket prices if you have to. You'll be far more rested, your shows will be more fun, your band will stay together longer. I know you are excited to be in your van on the big rock tour and a bus is very expensive, but after a while you will have used up all your safety juju. (See "Minor Wrecks," page 62, and "Getting Broken Into," page 67, or perhaps it's time to see "The Kitchenette," page 76.) A bus is what you want.

"I just don't want to see another 7-Eleven at four in the morning."–The end of van touring

3. Touring by Bus

Musicians love a tour bus. It feels like you're traveling down the interstate in a long living room, and you are. You can sit across from each other and have a conversation (rather than always facing forward or twisting around as you have to do in your van). You are able to stand up and walk around to see what's happening in other parts of the bus. You can play a board game around the front table, watch a movie, use the bathroom (liquids only), then climb into your bunk and close the curtain for a nap or some privacy. A professional driver is provided, whose only job is to get you to the next gig safely. Arriving at your show in a tour bus is arriving in style. And being able to use the bus as your own personal and comfortable dressing room before and after sound check and show each night is fabulous.

GETTING YOUR TOUR BUS

To find an affordable, reliable tour bus, search on-line or get a recommendation from bus-touring musician friends. Bus companies offer crew buses, band buses, and star buses. Your first tour bus will most likely be the one that fits within your budget and that's available for the dates of your tour. Some companies offer different models of buses to choose from with limo-sounding names–Eagle, Van Hool, PreVost. There are also newer and older, shorter and longer buses to consider. (*Author Note:* A forty-five-foot-long tour bus is significantly roomier than a forty-foot bus.) I'm happy to be on any bus where the air-conditioning works, the bathroom doesn't smell funny, and the front door lock is easy to open.

What Does It Cost to Lease a Tour Bus?

The average cost to lease a tour bus (or "coach" as the bus companies call them) is somewhere between $7,000 and $8,000 per week. You might be able to find a less expensive one, but don't forsake reliability. You don't want a bus that overheats, breaks down, or loses its air-conditioning. The lease information below is an average cost per week. (Source: Snowden Custom Coach, Austin, Texas; Staley Coach, Nashville, Tennessee: staleycoach.com.)

Coach lease rate per day, based on type and year model	$300–$750 × 7 days
Trailer per day	$25 × 7
Driver wages per day	$185 × 7 days
One overdrive	$185
Driver hotel per day	$100 × 7 days
Daily In-Motion satellite service	$10 × 7 days
Exterior wash once a week or end of short tour	$50
Linens cleaned once a week or end of short tour	$45
Comforters cleaned end of tour	$10 each × 12
Carpet cleaned end of tour	$65
Generator service every 100 hours or end of tour	$50
Engine/transmission serviced	$175
End of tour coach cleaned	$250
Plus fuel,* oil, tolls, permits, parking fees, bus supplies, taxis, and parking	$2,000 estimate

"Gas costs . . . you never know. It's always way more than you want it to be."–Heinz

Key Elements of a Vehicle Lease Agreement

A tour bus lease agreement puts in writing the details of the lease so that the parameters of the deal are clearly understood. Below are some of the

*Most tour buses use diesel fuel and have a 150-gallon tank. You'll get between six and ten miles to the gallon, depending on how much gear the band is traveling with. To fuel up today costs over $400.

main points you'll want to be sure your agreement covers:

1. *Bus and dates reserved.* The model of bus to be leased, the number of days it will be leased, and the dates the bus will be in use are specified.
2. *Charges.* The cost of the vehicle, the driver, and other expenses are specifically laid out. A bus budget for the entire tour may be attached to the lease.
3. *Insurance.* The insurance paragraph will detail what insurance the bus company is carrying on the vehicle and whether it has "contents insurance" for the band gear (usually not).
4. *Breakdowns.* If the bus breaks down, the leaser (bus company) will furnish an equivalent replacement vehicle for the remainder of the lease or pay the cost for alternative transportation up to the amount due per day stipulated in the lease until the vehicle is repaired. If the bus can't be repaired, the band may cancel this lease.
5. *Missed engagements.* If the bus breaks down, the leaser will not be held liable for the missed engagement.
6. *Road conditions.* If weather gets bad with snow and road conditions call for chains, the coach will park until the conditions improve and it can proceed in a safe manner.
7. *Illegal substances.* Bus cannot be used for illegal purposes. If it is seized for any type of illegal substance or action, the band will have forty-five days to return the coach or pay fair market value for it. The band has to continue the terms of the lease regarding payment and damage during the time it is seized and pay any and all fines. (Bus drivers are aware that some band members are smoking pot. Usually they ask that pot be smoked in the back lounge. That way paraphernalia and skunk odor are not immediately discovered if the bus is boarded by the state highway patrol. The police are aware that tour buses are carrying musicians who may be smoking pot. There's some unwritten agreement that everyone leaves everyone else alone. The bus drives the speed limit. The band smokes pot in the back lounge. The police have no suspicion to board.)
8. *Bus driver log.* Bus drivers are under federal regulations to drive no more than ten hours straight and then rest for eight. This is to keep everyone safe. (In reality, your driver may drive longer than ten hours in order to get the band to its destination or he may simply prefer to get the drive over with in one long drive. I have heard

of drivers who keep several different log books that falsify the actual drive time. If the bus is pulled over by the police, the false log book will corroborate that he is not overdriving. If the police ask band members how long they've been driving or what city they left, everyone should be in agreement. If not, the police are not happy being lied to and the bus driver could be fined $250.)

9. *Local transportation.* The tour bus is to be used between cities. The band will be responsible for its own local transportation. Normally the coach will proceed directly to the venue and remain there until after the show or, time permitting, a brief stop at the hotel for check-in, then to the venue.

10. *Float.* It is customary to give the driver $700 fuel float to keep up front with him so that each time he fuels up he doesn't have to go looking for the tour manager.

11. *Damage to vehicle.* Any interior or exterior damage to vehicle will be repaired or replaced by the band.

12. *Things left on the bus.* If anything is left on the bus, the bus company will not be responsible for it. All postage, freight, time, and telephone charges will be paid for by the band to recover the items.

Two Tips Regarding Your Bus Tour Budget:

1. Cab expenses will go up. To get to the hotel (or go anywhere) you'll walk or cab. Your bus driver will park the bus at the venue. His day is done until the trailer is loaded up after the show. So when possible, book hotel rooms within walking distance to the club. You may find a cheaper hotel out of town, but the cab rides will add up.

2. Hotel costs change. If you sleep on the bus most nights, your hotel costs will decrease, but not entirely. Each day, you'll need to buy one hotel room for the bus driver to sleep and one for the band to take showers. Realistically, at least once a week you'll want to pay for hotel rooms for everyone so the band can get some deep sleep in a stationary bed. As the income of your tours increases, you'll drive overnight on the bus only when it's necessary to make it to the next gig on time.

GETTING ACQUAINTED WITH YOUR TOUR BUS

This morning you heard that your tour bus is somewhere near Lexington, Kentucky, and should arrive around 4 PM. It was just out with some other almost famous band you think you might have heard of but then again are pretty sure you haven't. You finish your last errands and your girlfriend or boyfriend drives you and all your stuff to the meeting point. And there before you—your first tour bus. It's so tall—tall as the tree branches—and as long as a semi. It's a weird aqua blue color, and there's a strange painting of a tropical island on the side, but it's your tour bus, taking you on your first bus tour.

"How do you get on this thing?"—Bass player, looking for the door

The only door is on the passenger side, like a city bus.

The Driver's Area

Up front is the driver's area. It consists of his tricked-out driver's seat surrounded by knobs and levers that you rarely touch unless he has shown you how something works and a co-pilot chair. Very often a bandmate will announce, "I'm going to go sit up front with the driver," and will sit co-pilot where he can smoke, look out the front of the bus, or share stories with the driver.

There is a sound and privacy curtain or door between the driver and the front lounge so he doesn't have to hear our bad movie and we don't have to hear his bad choice in radio. The rest of the bus is divided into thirds—the front lounge, the bunks in the middle, and the back lounge.

The Front Lounge

The front lounge is your main living area. It's the most sociable place on the bus. People hang here in the morning, for movies, after sound check, and for after-show parties.

There's a long row of windows on each side of the front lounge. Although floor plans vary a bit from bus to bus, there is usually a long couch, a smaller couch across from it, and a kitchen table with loveseats on either side of it. Although there are a few recessed cup holders for drinks, it won't take long for you to realize that every time the bus stops quickly or makes a turn, things on the table will slide to the floor. You could tape everything down or move items to the kitchen counter, where you'll quickly discover they fall off here as well. It's helpful to put these small random items in a big bowl or basket to keep them stationary.

There's a TV, DVD, VCR, and stereo system in the front lounge (as well as the back lounge). Ask the bus driver to show you how it all works. There will always be a trick. If you don't know this little trick, you'll have picture but no sound, and now the bus driver is driving and can't help you. As you travel from town to town, you'll lose whatever satellite TV movie you were watching. It's incredibly frustrating to be engaged in a movie and then it digitizes. The blank blue screen tells you THE SATELLITE IS LOOKING FOR THE SIGNAL, and then it's gone.

The Kitchenette

Toward the middle of the bus, at the back of the front lounge, is your small kitchen, called a galley on the tour bus Web site. It usually includes a microwave, a coffee maker, a dorm-size refrigerator, and a built-in cooler. If you have a choice when leasing your bus, choose one with a full-size refrigerator. It will hold a lot more leftover dinners and beer than the dorm-size fridge often found in the kitchenette.

Author Tip: If you don't want your boxed-up dinner to get thrown out in a random frustrated sweep of the refrigerator, put your name on it and the date. Even then, after a day or two, it will be thrown out to make room for the next wave of leftover dinners and deli items.

If it's not yours, don't eat it. The tortilla chips and Diet Coke cans you've seen backstage for weeks on each deli tray are for everybody. Chances are the chicken Caesar salad and Hawaiian Punch is someone's private food. I have witnessed great emotional upheaval when a missing chicken Caesar salad sent a singer to her bunk for days. And it was another singer who wouldn't be consoled for her missing Hawaiian Punch at 9 AM.

There may be a sink in the kitchenette. Don't use the water from the tap except to wash dishes. (I use bottled water to wash my cup and silverware.) In drawers or cabinets, there may be plasticware, plates, and cups supplied by the driver or left over from the previous band out on tour in the bus.

There's a trash door (like a kitty door) to send garbage to a bin under the bus in the bay. The trash chute will get jammed easily with pizza boxes unless they are somehow folded flat. On some buses, the trash bin is in a pull-out drawer. (As part of bus maintenance, the bus driver will empty the trash.)

Windows

There are sliding windows that open in both the front and back lounges and accordion shades over all the windows. To raise or lower, use both hands and raise or lower both sides evenly. Bus drivers will charge you a lot for broken shades, and they break easily unless you follow this little direction. The last one off the bus should close and lock the windows. It's an easy point of entry for thieves. Also, a rainstorm could soak the lounge cushions if a window is left open. Everyone agrees to close the windows, but often you just don't notice the open window behind a shade, and everyone leaves the bus for sound check and a window is open.

Thermostat

There's a thermostat somewhere on your bus: up front by the driver, in the kitchenette, or maybe in the bunk area. One of you will always be changing it. Buses get hot. Buses get cold. It's hard to keep a bus temperate. It's the bus from hell when the air-conditioning is out. This may sound like so much whining to those still traveling in a van, but the bus windows and the small portal window on the ceiling of the bunk hallway don't bring in much breeze.

We traveled across the Southwest without air-conditioning and had to wait hours in a truck stop for the sun to go down and the temperature to cool off. Back on the bus, with the windows open, the bunk curtains flung back, and all of us essentially in swim attire, it still wasn't cool and the air was too thick to breath.

> The generator is overriding the A/C. The farther back on the bus, the hotter it gets. Hell I to Hell II.

This was the same bus that couldn't make it up steep mountains and only occasionally had reverse. We arrived at the Telluride Festival only to have to push our bus to make the turn onto the grounds. This is not making an entrance. Go over your budget thoroughly to make sure you can afford a nice, reliable bus.

I have heard stories of bus drivers who say the air-conditioning is out when it's actually just fine. They are making the band suffer for some infraction committed by management or an annoying band member.

> "We never could convince the last bus driver we were cold. It was always freezing on that bus."
> "You know why they do that, don't you? To keep you all in your bunks."
> "Really? Why would they do that?" Evidently, to get us to turn off the movie or music he didn't like and make us go far away from him.

The Bus Bathroom

Yes, there's a bathroom on the tour bus with a toilet and a sink and sometimes a shower. I've never seen a bus shower used as a shower. It's always used for storage or hanging clothes. When choosing a tour bus, consider that a bigger bathroom feels like a cleaner bathroom. In a small one where you're trying to avoid touching anything, it feels even smaller than it is.

Bathroom Rules:
1. Liquids only. No poop, puke, or paper. Pee only.
2. Never drink the water from the sink. Use bottled water to brush your teeth.
3. Don't sit down. I know it's hard to balance standing up, but hold onto something and aim. If you miss, clean up.
4. You don't want to be barefoot in the bathroom. See Rule #3.
5. Always keep the door closed.

There are regulations as to where the bus driver can dump all the liquid collected. If you see a stream of green liquid coming from under your bus, walk away. It may be a scheduled dumping or it may be a small revenge for a convenience clerk not willing to wait on a black band member or a hotel that is extremely unhelpful.

A Closet or Two

Some of your performing clothes can be hung in one or two small closets on the bus if there's any room left in them the morning you arrive. Clothes will be less wrinkled, but one day they'll wind up on the bottom of the closet under a guitar case or some cowboy boots and there will be no one you can blame. Perhaps someone has an iron. Perhaps someone has a little spray bottle of water. Hang the clothes up in the unused shower, lightly spray with water, and wait to dry.

The Door to the Bunks

There's a sliding door or a hinged door dividing the front lounge and the bunk area. Sometimes the door just will not stay shut as you round the bend in a mountainous state or stop quickly during a rush hour you couldn't avoid. You can apply some Velcro to the frame and to the door. This may be a better method than shoving a gym shoe under it again and again.

Keep the door to the bunks shut. Musicians' nights are short. Bus call may have been three hours after going to bed. Those sweet, sleeping faces shouldn't have to breathe the cigarette smoke that floats in from the front lounge. Also, musicians are sensitive to sound and can't help but listen to the movie explosions, dance music, and peels of laughter coming from the front lounge instead of taking a short nap.

Author's picky and obsessive comment: Door slams open. Door slams shut. Didn't you learn as a kid not to slam the door? It scares the person in the middle bunk who almost gets a doorknob in the face. It startles those who are trying to sleep. Pay attention to the sounds you make, just like you're supposed to be doing onstage.

The Bunks

In the middle of the bus are twelve bunks, six on each side, stacked three high with a hallway down the middle. (Some buses have fifteen bunks, but the additional three are smaller and across from the bathroom, which may smell weird. Some have nine, taking two out for hanging clothes.) There are four top bunks, four middle bunks, and four lower bunks. Unless you are over-filling your bus, everyone gets their own bunk. It's your little "apartment" that looks a lot like a coffin. You'll use your bunk to sleep on an overnight drive, to read, have some privacy, and rest before your show.

Each bunk has a curtain you can close for privacy, a light, a mattress, and bedding of some sort. (Some musicians bring their own sheet, blanket, pillow, or pillowcase from home to be more comfortable.) Usually there's no window, which can add to some mild claustrophobia you might already be experiencing lying in a low-ceilinged rectangular box. Some buses do have small portal windows in each bunk. There's a leather curtain you can snap around the portal, but light leaks through and you don't get that deep restfulness of a windowless bunk where you have no idea of the time of day.

On some tour buses there will be a TV monitor hanging by your feet in your bunk. It means you have less room by your feet, but you can plug in headphones and watch a movie, all cozy in your bunk.

There are electrical outlets in the bunk area for laptops and iPods and cell phones. Check if the bus you are considering leasing has outlets in each bunk, otherwise power cords wind up dangling from various bunks to the two floor outlets.

CHOOSING YOUR BUNK. Inspect the bunk before choosing. The drivers care for and clean their bus. Still, you want to be sure there's no weird crust on the inside of your curtain and that the light works and has a cover.

Lie down in the bunk to try it out. If you don't like it, quickly choose another. Bunks will likely be first come, first served. You can't declare a bunk yours the night before the bus arrives. You have to climb on the bus when it arrives and put something on your chosen bunk. You can ask a band member to claim a bunk for you if you know you'll be late. After several tours you start to know who's usually in what bunk and you may respect that or not.

Top bunk. The top bunk "high-rise" is the highest. If you wanted to be on top as a kid, you might still. Sometimes this bunk has a slight bend in the ceiling so it feels less roomy. It also rocks the most. To enter, balance on the two opposing middle bunks and leap. As you look out from your bunk you'll see the top of your friends' heads.

> I chose my bunk badly. The three available were up front, short, and across from the bathroom door. So I found an open high-rise that rolled me around all night, even after taking a half a Benadryl.

Middle bunk. This is the choice bunk and the first to be claimed. I think it's the tallest. It doesn't sway as much as the top bunk and it's not as loud with engine or generator noise as the bottom bunk. If the door to the lounge is banged open you may almost get a doorknob in the face, though. This is the easiest bunk to enter, and when you look out, you will be at belt level.

Bottom bunk. Garden apartment. Those who love it sleep best down here. It rocks the least. The bottom bunks are closest to the generator, so you'll hear a loud deep hum. You might want to wear your squishy earplugs so your hearing isn't all muffled in the morning. To enter, aim and roll on in. You'll have a view of shoes.

Bunk Rules #1–5. Now that you've chosen your bunk here are a few safety and privacy tips for you:

1. SLEEP WITH FEET TOWARD THE FRONT OF THE BUS. "In the unlikely event of a crash or sudden stop, it is better to break your ankles than your neck." One-time tour manager Ken Wagner's advice in an early tour itinerary.

2. If someone is in their bunk with the curtain closed, never open it. Usually, don't even knock unless it is a tour manager emergency or a really good movie is starting up front.

3. You can leave your shoes outside your bunk. Keep them as clear of the aisle as you can or musicians will trip over them in the dark. In the morning, you will never find them together.

   > "But what I want to know is, how did her shoes wind up in my bunk?"–Adam, the morning after a bus party.

4. When you crawl out of your bunk to have a diner breakfast or to find the hotel and start looking for your shoes, please be quiet. You may not see your bandmates, but we are all getting barely enough sleep behind our curtains, which are not soundproofed.

   > "You're like the stupid-question guy in the morning."

5. You might want to bring a day bag to store things in your bunk. Otherwise, your pajamas, toothbrush holder, journal, cell phone charger, books, or water bottle will fall about. Some things may

slide between bunks. Rather than beginning your search with "Who stole my itinerary?" you might want to check downstairs.

The Back Lounge

The back lounge is about half the size of the front lounge. It's got a horse-shoe-shaped couch that fills up most of the space. There's a TV, DVD and CD players, and cabinets on the back wall. Sometimes the lead singer and his wife take this as their apartment if his name is on the marquee. Other tours, it's the smoking lounge or the game room. Sometimes it becomes the temporary office of the tour manager. Other times it becomes the girls' dressing room. Late at night, it may become a down-tempo lounge. As Bohb Blair, sound engineer, told me, "It's common knowledge that the front lounge is for pleasant discussion and decent behavior and that the back lounge is for debauchery, drug use, and immature fart jokes."

Our first bus had been Reba McEntire's tour bus. I couldn't believe that no subsequent bus had a movie-star makeup mirror and dresser in the back lounge. On one overnight drive, we were pulled over for speeding. Now, truckers and store clerks often ask who's on the bus. Usually it's a young band they've never heard of, but I think they keep hoping for Willie or Loretta Lynn. When the police officer asked our bus driver whose bus it was, the driver was able to say it used to be Reba's bus, and we didn't get ticketed.

Loading Gear in the Bus Bays

The band gear and suitcases are stored in the bus bays. The bays are the empty compartments under the bus. Your driver will show you the very specific way to open, close, and lock each bay without jamming the metal folding door, pinching your fingers, or banging your head on it. If you've got a big band with lots of gear, you may not have enough room in the bays, so you'll rent a trailer for the gear and pull it behind the bus.

The bay key hangs on the inside door of the bus and is always returned there–not to your bunk under your pretty little head. The bus will not move until the key is found. Newer buses have bays that air lock. The driver will show you how to unlock the bays with the black knob to the left of the steering wheel. Older buses may have line-up-the-number locks that are incredibly hard to read after a beer, in the dark, after the show.

Author Note: If there is an extra, unclaimed bunk or two, sometimes guitars are stored inside the bus to keep them warm and keep them from sliding around in the bay. This bunk–the junk bunk–winds up with not only guitars but T-shirts, boots, books, and road purchases.

YOUR TOUR BUS DRIVER

As you're getting acquainted with your tour bus the day it arrives, there will be a guy walking around on it you don't know. "Who's this guy on our bus?" you'll wonder. He's your tour bus driver and he's thinking, "Who's this band I've got on my bus this time?"

Ken Wagner's tour manager advice: "Be respectful of the driver. Treat him as one of us, not 'the driver.' Ask him his name and what tours he's been on. He's probably quite experienced and can help in a lot of areas you may never realize. The driver only takes instruction from the tour manager, or whoever is 'in charge' at the time. If you need the bus to stop, move, etc., find the tour manager."

Offer your bus driver a copy of your CD.

"Thanks for the CD. I get tired of talking on the radio. They always ask me the same thing: 'Who you got?,' 'Where you going?,' and 'Can you get me a job?'"—Our new bus driver

These drivers are usually amazing drivers, maneuvering calmly through heavy traffic and city streets and dead-end alleys with a forty-five-foot bus and a trailer. Ask if he needs any help making tight turns or backing the bus up. Sometimes it's helpful if one of us gets off the bus and stops traffic so he can back out of the alley.

You always hope for an easygoing, friendly driver. A mean, cranky one will influence your tour. You could have the Bible and gun-carrying driver or the one who just got out of prison and still seems like a volatile outlaw. Or "Crystal Mark," who appeared to never sleep and laughed at smaller vehicles, telling us, "The law of tonnage is on our side." Or the bitter guy who had to fly back to Lexington for a court date, leaving the tour manager to drive the bus from the hotel to the venue that afternoon. Or the one whose wife took a taxi from Lexington, Kentucky, to Birmingham to find him. We don't know why. Or the one who tells you he was wearing cotton briefs during the fire so he's okay "down there."

Or Bob, the best driver we ever had and the owner of the company. He scared himself when he took the wrong route into Telluride, Colorado, and he knew a forty-five-foot tour bus can't maneuver the hairpin mountain turns. Our bass player had brought his young daughter on that tour and he was white with fear as we slowly made turns. In the back lounge, a singer, his almost ex-wife, and his road romance were talking things over, a plummeting cliff inches from the back wheels.

Most bus drivers use GPS (global positioning system) to route from city to city. The tour manager will still have physical directions (and phone numbers) to the hotel and the club because GPS can fail if the bus is surrounded by concrete or if the address punched in is slightly inaccurate.

Once you've made it to the club in the next city, give your bus driver the key to his hotel room first before the band. His job is done. Now leave him alone. Do not call him on the phone. This is not only etiquette, it's a safety issue. He needs to be well rested to be alert for the next drive. Bus drivers are required to sleep at odd intervals—sometimes at night, sometimes in the late afternoon. Do you think it's okay to wake him while he's sleeping to complain that he threw out your salad while he was cleaning out the bus refrigerator this morning? He may be called, however, if the monitor man is stuck in the back lounge because the air locks have locked him in.

> "If the bus catches on fire, you make sure everyone is off the bus, call 911, put out the fire, and then you can call and wake me up."–Our bus driver

YOUR CREW

Once you have a bus, you probably have a crew. At the very least, you'll hire a tour manager who might double as your front-of-house sound engineer. Soon he'll get tired of working all the time and convince you to hire more crew.

You'll probably start by hiring friends, who will learn by trial and error and from watching other band's crew. If the crew does a good job, the band never knows all the problems they fixed during the day. The band just walks onto a stage that is ready for them to sound check or have a great show.

Your Tour Manager

On a bus tour you need a tour manager. He's the boss man, trail boss, cat daddy out on the road. He filters all the information between the band, management, bus driver, venue, and hotels. He's in charge so the lead singer doesn't have to be. (Imagine that tour!) He's not your babysitter or bodyguard (do you think you're Whitney Houston?). He's not your own personal assistant, unless of course that is how you set it all up before you left home.

Author Note: You'll be able to find the chink in your tour manager in a few days. What drives him crazy. What you can get away with.

Before you leave town, your tour manager does tour preparation, like advancing the show with the club (See "Advancing Your Show," page 29) and deciding on reasonable leave times to arrive at the next load-in on time. He compiles all this information, creating your itinerary. (See "Your Tour Itinerary," page 89.)

Each day he'll print and post at the front of the bus a day sheet (Figure 6) of that day's schedule. It will support or update your itinerary. The day sheet lists the day, date, and city, bus call to go to the club, load-in time, sound check time, showtime, and any interviews. It will also let you know what time the bus is departing for the next city.

```
DAY SHEET          SAT/NOV 4
MADISON, WI
BUS CALL           10AM
LOAD IN            4PM
SOUNDCHECK         5PM
DINNER             BUYOUT $10
DOORS              8:30PM
SUPPORT            9:30PM (60MIN)
ALEJANDRO          10:45PM
BUS CALL           2AM
MADISON-AUSTIN
1245M              TBA
ETA AUSTIN/ MONDAY EARLY PM


                INN ON THE PARK
                22 S CARROLL ST
                 MADISON, WI
                    53703
                 608-257-8811
```

FIGURE 6

Your tour manager is the one who keeps things rolling. He will do his best to gather everyone in the morning to travel to the next city, and at the end of the night he gets everyone out of the club after the show. He'll accompany the band to in-store performances and radio shows to make sure they're well run and the band is well treated. (See "Performing at an In-Store," page 111.) He oversees the stage if there's no stage manager, getting tough if the crew is slacking off or if the lighting guys are slowing down the sound techs. He'll let the band know when it's ten minutes until showtime and walk you from the dressing room to the side of the stage so you don't get lost on the way and can start on time.

A tour manager, guitar tech, and monitor guy are under the stage looking for some wood to prop up the monitors, and the guitar tech finds a lantern and brushes it off. Poof, out comes a genie and offers them each three wishes.

The guitar tech says, "Wow, really? I'd like to be on my own tropical island with a beautiful big-breasted blonde woman and an unending supply of beer." Poof; he's gone.

The monitor guy says, "I'd like to be on my own tropical island with a beautiful big-breasted blonde *and* a brunette, and an unending supply of champagne." Poof, he's gone.

The genie turns to the tour manager and asks what his wish is. The tour manager says, "I want both those fuckers back here in five minutes!"

Your tour manager is the problem solver for all the things that will fall apart. He prearranges parking for the bus at the venue and at the hotel. Then he makes another plan if the hotel has forgotten to save that parking space. He finds lodging for the bus driver first and the band second if the hotel has "lost" the reservation. He's firm if the club is not fulfilling the rider as agreed to in the contract.

He's the one who settles with the club at the end of the night and does the tour accounting. He'll let you know when he's setting up office hours, when he'll exchange your cab or guitar string receipts for cash, or give you your per diems for the week. (See "Your Per Diem," page 91.)

It is usually the tour manager who also makes departure arrangements for individuals leaving the tour due to health or firing. (Be wary if the tour manager asks to take you to breakfast.)

Your tour manager could be on call twenty-four hours a day until he learns to turn a cold shoulder to your little problem like the phone won't dial out in your room. (You dial "0" to reach the front desk and sort it out with them yourself.)

"No es mi perro."–Tour manager. ("Ain't my dog.")
"Es tu gato."–Any band member. ("It's your cat.")

The tour manager and the band manager should be on speaking terms throughout the tour. I think these two have the potential to become suspicious or jealous of each other. The tour manager is in charge of the band out on tour but is aware that the manager holds the purse and power strings. The manager usually doesn't tour well and feels a little left out of the adventure of a tour. If he comes out on tour to NYC, he should respect the tour has been up and running well so far. He shouldn't try to be the one in charge. The tour manager is in charge. In other words, the visiting manager is advised to leave well enough alone.

Your Sound Engineers

Your soundman is God. Your monitor person is also God. This is what they have told me themselves. I pass it on to you. You don't want to piss them off. They have the power of the fader. A fader is a volume knob and volume is your spotlight. Your sound guys have the ability to make you disappear or make a crowd cheer for you. You want to be on great terms with them. They both work hard and long days. They load in, set up, mix the show, tear down, and load out. Thank them. Buy them a double latte or a shot of Petron.

YOUR FRONT-OF-HOUSE SOUND ENGINEER. Your front-of-house sound engineer mixes the band in the house for the audience each night. All instrument and vocal inputs from the stage are sent to the front-of-house mixing board or console. Your front-of-house engineer can add effects to each, pan the sound left, right, or center, as well as bring each volume up or down. He or she also adjusts the high and low frequencies, making sure the bass doesn't rumble around like a thunder cloud or high-pitch feedback doesn't split eardrums.

Some engineers have a hands-on approach during the show, adjusting faders and massaging the sound throughout each song. Other engineers let the band do most of their own mixing from the stage with effects pedals and volume pedals.

YOUR MONITOR ENGINEER. All the instrument and vocal inputs also route to the monitor board, usually located just offstage either right or left. Your monitor engineer will create the mix you want to hear in your monitor (speaker facing toward you) each night—a general mix of the band or simply more you. This mix helps the band play together. A good monitor engineer is especially important on big stages when you're far apart and can't hear each other or on very small stages where you're so close to each other all you really hear is the amp nearest you. (See "Sound Check," page 125.)

Author Note: The club will provide a front-of-house sound engineer and a monitor engineer if you don't bring your own. Even if you do bring your own, it's helpful to have house engineers nearby if your engineers are having any trouble or the house soundboard is quirky.

Your Instrument Tech

Don't start hiring all your friends as guitar tech or drum tech because they're available and would love a ride to New York or Chicago. Hire them if they can do the job. The job of a tech is to load in, set up the gear the way the band member wants it, tear down, and load out. It's also up to him to keep the instrument show ready–change strings, change drum heads, polish things as needed. The tech should be able to play the instrument. He'll be asked to play a bit before sound check begins to give the front-of-house and monitor guys a basic tone and volume level.

During sound check, if there's a gear problem onstage, your tech will track it down and fix it. Forty-five minutes before the show, your tech will rearrange/adjust anything onstage that has been moved for the opening act, tune the instruments, and place them on stands.

Your techs need to be very, very alert during the show. They'll stand just offstage watching the entire stage through the entire set. They're the trouble-shooters once all hell breaks loose. Techs need to have spare short and long cables, a flashlight, a Leatherman all-purpose tool, and be armed with the belief that they can fix that terrible noise coming from the guitar amp or figure out why the bass has suddenly gone out completely. All in front of a curious audience.

> "Dumb luck; you can't have enough."–One of the crew twins surprised himself by fixing the broken pedal. We really can't tell them apart, so we just pretend to know or pretend it doesn't matter or don't talk to them.

Techs may also need to be security if a frolicking fan over-serves herself and joyously becomes an exotic dancer onstage with the band. They may need to help a crowd-surfing lead singer back up on the stage or mop up water or beer that has spilled thankfully right next to but not on a pedal board.

Once you've hired good people, make sure everybody knows what is expected of them. For example, are they helping load in and load out? Are they expected to wear shoes when they do this? Are they supposed to be at sound check until it's finished, which might include the band rehearsing for forty-five minutes? Or, would it be okay for them to go get their nipples pierced after placing the guitar amps? Some of this seemed obvious to me but not to the nipple-aching guitar tech.

> "He went out for juice at 8 AM and that's the last we saw of him."–Guitar tech Jimmy G. We waited on the bus, wondering why the drum tech had not arrived and never did arrive

> "Tell Luke if you see him that it's Sunday, June 28th, and he's on tour with Poi dog Pondering."–Tour manager

Your Merchandise Person

Your merchandise or merch person should be the best-looking, most flirtatious member of your party. Each night, he or she will set up a display of your CDs and T-shirts and get some singles from the bar to make change. It's helpful if this individual can do simple math and has actually listened to your band's records, as your merch person will be making friends with your fans, explaining how each CD shows the band's evolution, and that the newest CD is the one most like the show the fans just saw. At the end of the night he or she will dismantle the display, pack up the leftover merch, count up what has been sold, and determine if more should be shipped out from the manager. In addition to selling merchandise, the merch person often helps the crew load in, set up the stage, and pack gear up at the end of the night.

Author Note: If you're not traveling with a merch person, designate one band member to be in charge of merch. It's easy to leave boxes of CDs behind. The next day you look at one half-empty box of CDs and complain that the manager sent a ridiculously small amount of merch with you on tour when in fact there are four boxes still under the merch table back at the venue you played last night.

YOUR TOUR PACKET

It may not actually come in a packet, but as you gather for your first bus meeting, you'll be handed a bunch of items—a tour pass called a laminate, a bus key, and an itinerary. These will make your life infinitely easier for the next few weeks. At this meeting, your tour manager will also hand you your first week's per diem.

Your Tour Laminate

Your lead singer or tour manager will design and make a tour laminate for everyone. It looks like a ski-lift ticket covered in plastic. It's about the size of a playing card, with a picture of your record or maybe a foxy fashion model or a Leonardo da Vinci drawing on it. On the reverse side may be your tour dates.

Your laminate will give you all access in and around the clubs you will be playing. You'll need it all the time, so you wind up wearing it all the time attached to a lanyard around your neck.

Be sure to remove your laminate while you're playing the show. It just looks dumb wearing it while you rock. Give it to your tech or put it in your guitar case. You don't want to lose your laminate, and it's not a good idea to loan it to anyone. (I know you will anyway.) You can save them after each tour and make a big laminate collage as a souvenir.

At special events, the special-event people may make a special laminate for the band that is the size of a shoe. It doesn't fit in your pocket. It certainly doesn't look right around your neck, but you'll have to wear it to have backstage access. Whomever they are, they'll be happy about their big laminate.

Some tours have names that are printed on your laminate, itinerary, posters, and in print ads in the paper. Sometimes it's the title of the record. Sometimes it's an obscure phrase: "End your busy day on a high." Sometimes a tour will name itself mid-tour as it starts to reveal its nature.

> It's the "How many cities can you be in in a week?" tour. Howe believes he wins the prize for Madrid, Tucson, Hoboken, and Prague.

> It's the "Don't feel, don't speak" tour. Their father died while they were on the way to their Midwest dates.

Your Bus Key

At the start of your tour you'll be given a key to your bus. (Some buses have a code lock on the door to memorize instead of a key lock.) If you are the last person off the bus, you must lock the door. If you are the last person off the bus or if the only people on the bus are sleeping, you must lock the bus door.

You can clip the key onto the lanyard that holds your laminate. This is another benefit to always wearing your laminate–immediate access to your bus key all the time. You'll also be able to identify your band and crew coming down the hall of the hotel or down the street of some town because you hear their laminate (or several tour laminates) and the bus key clinking against their chest as they walk.

Author's Key Tip: If your bus key was working but now it won't turn in the lock, pour some olive oil on it. Insert the key into the lock, pull it out, push it back in several times. You've now lubricated the lock and your key should work. If not, throw it away and ask the driver for another one.

Your Tour Itinerary

The night before your tour leaves town, your tour manager will be at Kinko's putting together a tour itinerary–a bound tour book. It's your tour schedule, one day at a time, one page for each day. It should be the size of a folded piece of paper so musicians can easily put it in a backpack, purse, or day bag, or fold it and put it in a back pocket. If it's any bigger it'll just get left in a bunk or a suitcase and everyone will ask a lot of questions on the tour.

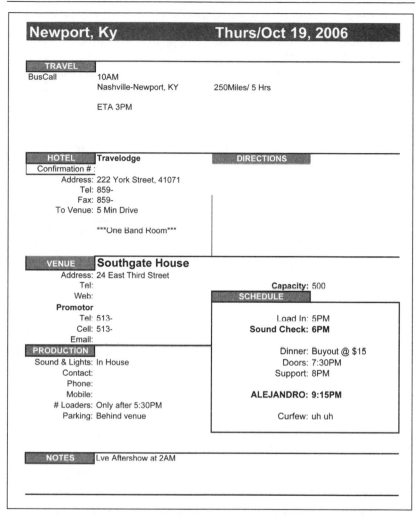

Newport, Ky — Thurs/Oct 19, 2006

TRAVEL

BusCall	10AM
	Nashville-Newport, KY	250Miles/ 5 Hrs
	ETA 3PM

HOTEL Travelodge

Confirmation # :
Address: 222 York Street, 41071
Tel: 859-
Fax: 859-
To Venue: 5 Min Drive

One Band Room

DIRECTIONS

VENUE Southgate House

Address: 24 East Third Street
Tel:
Web:
Promotor
Tel: 513-
Cell: 513-
Email:

Capacity: 500

SCHEDULE

Load In: 5PM
Sound Check: 6PM

Dinner: Buyout @ $15
Doors: 7:30PM
Support: 8PM

ALEJANDRO: 9:15PM

Curfew: uh uh

PRODUCTION

Sound & Lights: In House
Contact:
Phone:
Mobile:
Loaders: Only after 5:30PM
Parking: Behind venue

NOTES Lve Aftershow at 2AM

FIGURE 7

Figure 7 is a page from an itinerary. There are various styles, but basically each day will inform you of the date and city you are in, leave time for the next city, travel time, hotel info, venue info, load-in time, sound check time, and showtime. It's helpful if the itinerary informs you which nights you're driving out after a show and which days you have hotels and which days you have off. If you know what's coming up you can pace yourself. The itinerary will also list names and phone numbers of people you'll probably never call, like the promoter. (But then again, if you leave your computer bag somewhere in the club after sound check, you'll have the name and number of a person you can call to go look for it for you). It will inform you of the dinner situation each night as well. Is dinner going to be provided after sound check or is there a buy-out–$10 or $15 cash given to you by the club instead of dinner.

The itinerary doesn't need to include the weather, a map of Pittsburgh, or nearby parks. This information is easily gotten in the "Guide to Pittsburgh" in your hotel room or from the front desk, and it just makes the itinerary too busy. On a short tour, instead of an itinerary, management might e-mail you a two-page list of dates and cities and clubs. The tour manager will be asked a lot of questions on this tour, as the list is essentially a gig listing but not a schedule. You'll know where you are going but not when to be ready to go.

Always keep your itinerary with you. You may be off the bus wandering around a Canadian town and the bus may move or leave. Where will you be then? You won't know. And please, refer to it. Do not ask your tour manager, "What city are we going to tomorrow?" If it's written down, don't ask.

Your Per Diem

Once a week, your tour manager will have you sign a receipt to get your per diem (Latin for "per day"). This will be between $20 and $30 to buy food and drink. Some tours don't provide a per diem. You get your pay and you hope for a buy-out and a good deli tray. That's it.

"Hold onto your per diems, we're going to dinner with Frank."–Max

Quick Tax Note: You're allowed to deduct about $30 a day while you're away from home on business to cover your food and drink expenses. (The amount is based on what part of the country you are in.) A $30 per diem doesn't need to be included as income since you're going to deduct it as an expense. For this reason, you don't need to keep all your food receipts, because you can just deduct the $30 a day without the receipt. (See your accountant.)

ENTERTAINING YOURSELF

You'll entertain yourself on the bus much as you did in your van: listening to music, reading, writing, playing games, conversation. You won't spend as much time absorbing the landscape and signs and graffiti and bumper stickers out the windows. This is partly because you've got other things to occupy yourself inside the bus and partly because of the bus layout. There's often paneling dividing the front lounge from the driver's area, so you can't easily see what's up ahead. The side windows are big but sitting on a couch facing sideways, you see the world as it passes quickly by the side of the bus. I have seen a grizzly bear and caribou this way, but the perspective gets a little dizzying. After several tours, you may even long for a van tour to see more of the country. But trust me, take a road trip on your own. Don't go back to a van tour.

To entertain yourself on the bus, you can pull out guitars and play. You can bring a small recording rig. You can also sit up front with your bus driver and talk about all the weird tours he's been on, or walk to the kitchenette and make tea or coffee. You can listen to a really good stereo. You can write in your journal or read your book without getting nauseous, or play scrabble at the front lounge table. You can have conversations while looking at your bandmates. You can leave the room if someone is talking on and on, or talking on their damn cell phone. You can sleep in your bunk, legs stretched out and a pillow under your head. Or you can watch a movie.

Movies on the bus are lovely. On a long drive, you can watch two or three movies in a row. You can roll off the bus inspired by big-wave surfers in Hawaii or the Ramones or Jimi Hendrix. The band members who have learned how to use the DVD system from the bus driver will be the ones putting in their choice of movies, which you may or may not enjoy. You might pay attention on the first day of your tour when the bus driver shows everyone how the entertainment system works on this bus.

We watch a movie so dumb it offends Robert, who will not watch. I feel guilty every time it makes me laugh.

KEEPING COUNT OF EVERYONE

"Have you gathered everyone up?" Heinz asked Jon Dee this morning.
"Well, it's sort of like herding cats . . ."

Keeping track of everyone on a tour bus is more difficult than doing so in a van. Instead of one open space, you've got a forty-five-foot-long bus with a back lounge, a bathroom, and twelve bunks with half-closed curtains where musicians could be. Before the bus leaves the hotel or the venue, the tour manager usually finds and counts everyone, declares "We're a bus," and off you go.

You're more apt to get left behind during a fuel stop when you saunter off the bus into the diner or convenience store. Once the driver has paid for the fuel and you're ready to go, the tour manager should count everyone again. But often it's a general, "Is everyone here?" and the bus drives on. Many musicians and lead singers have been scooped up at the last minute as the bus is driving away and they are noticed calmly walking back to the bus in the wrong direction. And all the time it was thought they were still onboard.

Make sure that whoever is in charge knows if you leave the bus, especially if it's night and you get out of your bunk undetected. You risk being left somewhere in Pennsylvania with a very sleepy realization that you are now in a pickle. What we often do is tell one of our bandmates lying in his bunk that we're getting off the bus to buy a snack. Nonetheless, ten minutes later, as the bus starts to roll, he doesn't bother to get up to check if you're actually back on the bus or not. It's not that he wants to leave you behind; he just figures you've returned.

Dave Max was left playing pinball at a truck stop when the bus drove off. I think he was in his pajamas. No one even noticed he was missing until we were in the next town setting up gear and he phoned. One thing he learned is that truck drivers are legally not supposed to pick up extra riders.

> "If you get off the bus at night, put something on the driver's seat. That way I'll know by however many items are on the seat how many people are off the bus."–Our bus driver

Every tour our bus driver tells us this, but no one ever puts something on the driver's seat. The one time I did, it was early, early morning during an overnight drive. I took off my watch and left it on the driver's chair so he'd know someone was off the bus. He told me later that he picked it up and wondered why it was there. "I thought someone was making a comment about how long it was taking us to get to North Carolina."

> Frank and Martin's motto: "Never leave the bus."

BUS ETIQUETTE

Did I say bus etiquette? Yes, yes sweet traveler. Better to hear it from me now than miles and weeks from your home. I've given you some tips and some rules so you don't break your neck. To avoid breaking hearts and bruising egos, there is etiquette. As your tour posse gets bigger, there are things that become important to keep everything running smoothly.

Being On Time

This just keeps showing up, doesn't it? Be at the bus at the scheduled leave time. I realize this does not apply to many other events that involve time in the rock world, but bus time is real time. Bad and overused excuses for being late: "I was in the bathroom." "The cashier was really slow." "The alarm never went off." These may be true, but you are nonetheless late.

Often your driver has based his sleep schedule around a scheduled leave time. He's gotten up, showered, had some breakfast, and is ready to go. As he waits, he knows he could have had an extra forty-five minutes of sleep or already have been forty-five minutes down the road. Either way, you are inconveniencing your driver and compromising the safety of your drive.

> "Bus call is 8:00 AM tomorrow. If you plan to be late, bus call is 7:00 AM. If you plan to be only a little late, 7:30."–Ben, tour managing

We intend to be on time. What happens? A friend of mine and I agree that we need more time not at the *beginning* but at the *end* to finish our projects or get somewhere on time. We don't budget in those last ten minutes to wait for the elevator, buy that fried-egg sandwich, or walk through the parking lot to the bus. In New Orleans, there was a phrase: "I'll be there *for* four o'clock,"–not "I'll be there *at* four o'clock." It means you're there to see the clock strike four. You can be sitting in the front lounge as the clock ticks 4.00 pm. You'll be on time and someone else will be late.

For every minute we were late to the bus, we could choose to pay one dollar or do one push-up (girl or boy). We could also choose to do sit-ups, but it was five sit-ups for every one push-up.

> "Not to assign gender-specific push-ups, but what she did weren't even girl push-ups."

If you are late, pay up, fess up, bring blueberry muffins for everyone, and apologize. You'll just piss everyone off if you're always late. The tour may even decide to continue on without you.

> As we left Northampton, we left Ted in Brattleboro, Vermont.

Yes. Being left behind on purpose does happen on tour. Not often. But if you're not back at the appointed time, or if you're not in the lobby or on the bus when it's scheduled to leave, the tour manager will try to reach you on your cell phone and then may choose to leave you behind. You'll now have to make your own way to the next destination. Really. Hopefully you can cab to the venue or the hotel across town. Or you can talk your one-night stand into driving you to the venue across the state.

> Martin saw the bus drive by the bar window and yelled, "Stop that bus at all costs!" Inside the bus someone asked the driver, "Do you have directions to the hotel?" He answered, "I'm just trying to avoid the naked girl lying in the road." We looked out the front window and saw that a fan has taken off her pants and lay down to stop the bus. We opened the door and picked up three stray Poi dogs like the mother ship arriving.

Picking Up, Cleaning Up

Next to being late for the bus, leaving your stuff all over the bus is an amazing annoyance. No one thinks they are the messy one. Cleaning up does not mean the day you arrive home you get your stuff off this messy bus. If you peel a banana, can you not leave the banana peel on the windowsill next to you? Why would I want to lean my elbow into it later?

When you're finished with your beer or Coke, you could toss or recycle the can when you're finished, although I've never seen recycling on a tour bus. How many half-empty (or half-full, depending on how your tour is going) beverages must take up space on the kitchen table? Is anyone coming back for them? How long should we wait for the drink's owner to return before we throw it away? If the drink has fallen off the table twice while the bus is turning, I'm going to toss it. That's my threshold.

Storing Your Things in Your Bunk

You've got a whole bunk of your own to store your books and bags and hoodie and boots and laptop. Your bunk may even have a shelf to put things on. The couches in the front and back lounges are there for the musicians to use, not for backpacks and guitar cases to sit in. I know it seems a guitar is alive, but we are the living, they are not. And please can you not leave your dirty socks lying around? And yet you will.

> We picked up all the dirty white tube socks crawling all over the front lounge and hung them over lights, doorknobs, and in the microwave. In the morning, no one claimed a sock.

The day you have your own tour bus you can be as messy as you want, and won't that be fun? I guess you could try to talk your cook/masseuse into being your maid, too, but then you'd never get to sleep with her (see "Road Romance: Its Prevention and Cure," page 225, if you haven't already).

Choose Your Bus Guests Carefully

If you wouldn't invite the person into your home, do not invite him or her onto your bus. Friends or new fans are usually respectful of the bus. They're happy to see the inside of one and hang out and drink a beer with the band. (Inform them of the bathroom liquids-only policy.) But there will be a night or two when someone will inappropriately corner the lead singer or a friend of a friend brings a posse of five weird friends onboard. Or your guests may be more drunk than they appeared backstage.

> "Okay, it was nice to have you here, but now you've got to go."–Frank. A drunken girl tripped and grabbed onto the DJ rig set up in the front lounge and nearly pulled it all to the floor.

Bus Surfing

"Style and grace while in motion." Bus surfing is balancing while you walk on a rocking tour bus traveling 60 mph. You don't want to hit your head falling over into a cabinet. After a week, the only people who will enjoy your falling into them will be those wanting to sleep with you or get you to sit on their laps.

DRIVING OVERNIGHT ON THE BUS

The bus driver just gave us a weird lecture. I know he had a margarita this afternoon because he told me it was too big to finish, and now he just announced he hasn't had any sleep. And now we start an overnight drive.

To save money on hotel rooms or to arrive on time for your next gig, you'll drive out after your show. The bus will be your hotel for the night. These nights can be wonderful. There's nothing like a bus party. Eighty miles per hour through the night with your best friends, having good conversation and listening to great music.

There's Club Liz in the front lounge and the Star-Kissed Lounge in the back of the bus.

"They were in the back lounge and they had that glow about them. Well they found this R&B record with 'Just My Imagination' on it, and we must have listened to it six times, it gave them so much pleasure."–Kornell

When you feel done with the day and the night, you say goodnight and roll on into your bunk. Some novice travelers may have trouble sleeping on the bus. Bruce used to call sleeping on the bus "one hundred little naps." If you can remember a dream, you've gotten some REM sleep and you can't complain.

Dreams on the bus are weird. If you sleep deeply enough to have them, it's like you are picking up the dreams of the people sleeping in the cities you are driving through.

You won't be alone with your insomnia. It could be the swaying of the bus. If possible, switch to a lower bunk. It could be a strange half-dream that the brakes have gone out and the bus is out of control. (Possible, but very unlikely.) It could be mild claustrophobia. Really, the bunks will not collapse on you.

You may want to use your Rescue Remedy, Benadryl, Coffea cruda, homeopathy, or Ambien to sleep. Eventually you'll figure out what you need to do to sleep. Someone gave me a blue sleeping pill and even though I wasn't sleeping, I wasn't taking it. I was afraid that then I'd be asleep if there were a wreck. I realized I was choosing to stay awake to be safe. Drink some red wine, trust your driver, trust your life, and sleep.

Scheduling Tip: An overnight on a tour bus is so much easier than an overnight in a van. Still, it's not restful night after night. I think a tour should only schedule two overnight drives in a row. Not everyone can sleep in a moving vehicle. And not everyone sleeps the same hours. If your tour drives overnight every night, it'll be an emotional tour. Without sleep your band is going to become edgy and tired. The shows won't be your best, and your band will probably break up soon.

Stupid bumpy ride last night. Airborne in the bunk several times.

THE MORNING AFTER YOUR OVERNIGHT DRIVE

As the bus leaves the highway, the stop and start and turning corners of city driving may wake you up. You wander into the front lounge to take a look out the windows at the city. You may try to locate street signs so you can return to the Thai restaurant and Diesel store you've just passed.

Depending on what time you arrive in the next city, your tour manager may need to arrange for early check-in at the hotel. Let him know if you want to sleep in or be woken up to go into the hotel.

> "I want to sleep until I'm done sleeping. Can the tour manager not call through the bus at 6:00 AM, 'We're here. We're here?' I don't want to wake up or get up."

The tour manager can leave rooming lists and keys on the dashboard or front lounge table. An hour or two goes by and you'll wake up a bit disoriented. The bus is quiet. You might be alone for the first time on the tour. If there are no keys present, assume some of your bandmates have already taken them. You look out the windows and open the door and see no hotel. It can be oddly hard to find exactly where your hotel is. Hmm. Maybe the tour manager has left you a message on the front lounge table with an arrow:

"Sle'E'py heads, hotel is that a way."

So, now begins the rest of your tour.

4. The Day of Your Show

The day of your show you'll arrive at the next city in your itinerary. If there's time you might quickly check in at your hotel before heading to sound check. Some days you may arrive early enough to have a free afternoon to relax, find some food and explore the town. But other days the band will be scheduled to perform at a record store or will drive to a radio station for an interview and on-air performance.

HOTEL DWELLING

When choosing a hotel, you want one that is safe, clean, close to the club, and reasonably priced. Upon arrival you may find it not to be the right hotel for you. Some lodgings are just a step above residential hotels, offering AA and NA meetings in the lobby. If the front desk is behind bullet-proof glass, if there are mirrors on the ceiling, or what looks like blood on the walls, if the hotel clerk wants a TV remote deposit or a key deposit or wants to make Xerox copies of everyone's driver's license, you are at a sketchy hotel.

> The rooms aren't going to be ready until 3 PM. The front desk won't make them available as the maids clean them. And they want a $5 deposit for the TV remotes. And they won't let Heinz take a look at a room. So that hotel just lost thirteen reservations and we will have a hotel closer to the club.

You aren't going to be at the hotel for long but while you're there you don't want to get crabs or be robbed. If a hotel is not acceptable, the band will wait by the van or bus while the tour manager calls the club, the band manager, or the booking agent to find an alternate. Then he calls that hotel to check on availability before canceling the reservations at the first hotel. Hotel policies vary regarding room cancellation. At some hotels you'll have until 6 pm the day of the reservation to cancel while others require twenty-four hour notice.

Checking In

Check-in at most hotels is 3 PM, although usually you can check in earlier. If the band is driving overnight and arrives at the hotel early in the morning, the tour manager will need to call ahead to arrange early check-in. It's not always possible, but asking ahead of time, the hotel might give you your rooms as they are cleaned and become available. Leave the tour manager alone as he checks the band in. Let him enjoy the front desk hospitality while you:

> a) wait in the lobby and trip other guests with your baggage and instruments;
>
> b) wait on the bus for him to arrive back with keys and rooming lists;
>
> c) continue sleeping in bunk. Get your beauty sleep. Later, as you wander into the hotel looking for the elevators or your key, the front desk will usually know you are "with that bus" and may help you stumble through your request for keys, elevators, and a café.

We tend to hone in on other band people in hotel lobbies. They seem slow and dark. We must, too.

YOUR RESERVATION. It is very important that your hotel reservation be made under a standard and clear name. It could be the band's name, the lead singer's name, the manager's name, or the tour manager's name, but please convey the proper name to whoever is checking the band in. Otherwise, the front desk may appear not to have your reservation when you arrive.

DAY ROOMS. If you are driving out after your show, you might be checking into only two rooms for the day—the bus driver's private room (if you've got a bus) and a room for the band to shower, nap, watch TV, and maybe take a swim. Hotels don't necessarily like this piling of ten people to a room, so the tour manager will register two people and attach a list of everyone in the band. This way, if someone needs a key to get into the room, the front desk will know they're with the band.

I asked for a key at the front desk, but my name was not listed. I just needed to get in the room to put on some deodorant before going to the radio station. I told them I was with the band. "Oh, Poi dog Pondering. I love you guys. I've been watching you for years. You're incredible."

"And yet, you can't give me a key to get into the room?"

"Sorry, no."

ROOMING LIST. It's helpful if your tour manager has a rooming list ready to hand the front desk. This sheet of paper could look like this:

BAND NAME

ROOM LIST

DAY/DATE: _____

CITY: _____

DATE IN: _____ DATE OUT: _____

HOTEL: _____

ADDRESS: _____

TELEPHONE: _____

NAME	ROOM TYPE	SMOKING	ROOM #
_____	KING	NO	_____
_____	DOUBLE	NO	_____
_____			
_____	DOUBLE	NO	_____
_____			
_____	SINGLE	NO	_____

This simple piece of paper will avoid forty-five minutes of confusion with the front desk. Then, have copies of this rooming list made for each room reserved so band members can find each other.

Bellmen

Occasionally there will be bellmen at your hotel. They will see your pile of bags and might start loading all the suitcases and guitars onto their gold carts without your asking for help. If you don't want the service, just take your bags back. They may give you a bit of attitude, but that's just part of a staying at a reputable hotel.

"Wheels showing up on suitcases. Worst day of my life."–Bellman, somewhere

Hotel Storage

Usually the instruments stay in the trailer until load-in. As a safety precaution or if there's a radio show to play before load-in, the band may need to bring all the instruments and pedal boards from the trailer into the hotel. This stuff can be heavy and awkward to carry up to the rooms. Instead, ask if there is space in hotel storage. This is usually located right behind or quite near the front desk. Each item will be tagged and it'll cost you a tip of a dollar a bag to retrieve. If you have only one instrument stored, tip at least $2.

Your Room Key

The front desk will give you a key card or, on rare occasions, an actual key. Often you'll roll all your things up to your room, insert your key, and the door won't unlock. Try reinserting the key and removing it slowly. If that doesn't work, try removing it more quickly. Ignore the arrow on the card that tells you which direction to pull or push. Try to find a maid nearby. They'll often let you into your room. If you're out of luck, you'll have to drag your stuff all the way back downstairs, through various hallways, around the fitness room and the pool to the front desk to get another key.

> Our tour manager just told us to keep our room keys away from our cell phones. The front desk told him this may erase the code to open the room door.

Author Note: If you are staying two nights in the same hotel, often on the morning of the second day the key won't work. It's an inconvenience, but it's just how it is.

Requesting a Room Change

When you open the door to your room, you hope to find it peaceful and clean. Sometimes, though, it's not the room for you. If you find a crab, tick, or bedbug in the bed, you might want to change rooms (or hotels). Perhaps it smells of smoke or bananas. Perhaps it's the handicapped room without a bathtub and you'd like one.

> "I want a room with better art."

Perhaps it has a connecting door to the room next to yours and you can hear a whole family's conversation or a businessman on the phone. If you can hear them now, they'll be able to hear and complain about the party you'd like to have in your room later tonight. Maybe tomorrow you'd like to sleep late, and already you can tell that your room next to the elevator will be noisy with kids going to the pool in the morning.

It seems hotels often put bands in the wing they are still renovating. If you notice a sign at the front desk that says EXCUSE OUR PROGRESS, ask if the carpenters or carpet layers will be doing any heavy nailing or pounding near your room in the morning. If yes, request a different room.

We don't spend that much time at the hotel, but if the band is staying two nights or you have a day off here, it'll be worth the trouble to get a room you like. Then be sure to give your tour manager your new room number.

Your Hotel Room

The rooms are ready. Your tour manager has checked you in. The key to your room works and it's a fine room. You drop all your stuff to the floor and lie down on the bed. It feels good to stop moving.

YOUR ROOMMATE. Some musicians think they could tour forever if they had a private room every night. Usually you have a roommate or two. Hopefully your temperament and hours are compatible. Give your roommate some privacy in the room. Make an excuse to go out and tell them how long you might be gone so they can relax deeply.

> "Do you like it stuffy and hot and airless?" Howe came back to the room, cranky and tired like all of us.
> "Yes, I do."

THE BEDS. Who gets what bed? The person that gets up first should take the bed by the bathroom. That way, when they wander around in the morning it leaves you out of their shower and dressing path. And, the person who watches TV the most should get the bed across from the TV.

> When I came back from breakfast my roommate was on the phone, doing her nails, watching Jerry Springer, with her ironing all across my bed.

How often does the hotel wash the bedspread? We don't know. Some musicians pull it off the bed immediately to avoid touching it at all. But then you might not have enough covers to keep warm. (Use your leather jacket if necessary.) Sometimes you can pull the sheet all the way up and around the edge of the bedspread. There are so many things you can touch on tour that you wouldn't want to if you knew what had come before. Wash your hands often, take your vitamin C, and don't think about it too much.

THE TELEVISION. Not everyone falls asleep watching TV. Not everyone watches it all day long. You're on a paid vacation. You could leave your hotel room and take a look around Lancaster. Then again, I enjoyed every hour of the Countdown of One Hundred Greatest Country Hits of all Time (although I'm pretty sure it affected my show that night). And sometimes on a day off all you want to do is watch *The Silence of the Lambs* while drinking lots of cheap deli-tray red wine with your bandmates.

Stayed up late to watch a girls-in-prison-in-lingerie movie.

Then one night you'll turn on the TV in some average hotel you're staying in and the Grammys will be on. You wonder how that can be the music business and this traveling around in the van, putting on a rock show in a new city every night can be the music business, too. It's oddly depressing.

Grammys tonight. Alejandro called from his room every time some performer or presenter looked awful, sounded awful, or was great.

THE BATHROOM. A little bathroom etiquette: Before you take your shower, you might ask if your roommate needs to use the bathroom first. Then consider not dilly-dallying under the steam if someone is also waiting to shower. When you are done in the bathroom, think about leaving it as you found it. Sort of.

Author Note: After days and weeks of touring you will come to appreciate good shower pressure. Standing under an inadequate stream of lukewarm water will be more disappointing than you ever thought possible.

THE MINIBAR. Oh come on. Use only to indulge yourself when you can really enjoy indulging yourself. If you don't want to go out or the hotel bar is closed, take a look at the minibar price list and treat yourself.

"I'm going to have two Heinekens and some chips for $30 and never leave this room."

Incidentally, incidentals refer to the minibar. If you are in a fancy hotel on your major label's tab and you are told you have to pay for your incidentals, this means you pay for everything except for the room charges.

Last night some sweet man gave me a beer. Dave put it in the minibar fridge to keep it cold. Then we forgot it and just left it there. Does the hotel pay us for this service?

THE CLOCK RADIO. Before you go to bed, check that the clock radio is off. The maids may have accidentally reset it while dusting and it will go off at some ungodly early hour and you will cry. Sometimes it's just too confusing at the end of your night to read how this particular radio alarm clock works. You can simply unplug it from the wall.

THE TELEPHONE. Often your tour manager won't even turn on the room telephones. Unless your cell phone is broken, there's little reason to use it. If you need to use the room phone for outgoing calls, you'll have to go down to the front desk and give them your credit card. You'll need to dial 9 for an outside line.

If you call long distance directly from the hotel room phone, there may be a 35 percent surcharge. Be aware that 800 numbers, phone cards, and local calls cost a dollar even if the call doesn't go through. There may or may not be a sign on the phone telling you this.

YOUR ROOM NUMBER. Before leaving for sound check or for a bite to eat, memorize or write down your room number. When you return hours later you will appear slightly insane as you stare at the twelve buttons in the elevator unable to push your floor number. Or you'll get to your floor and not be able to remember which room is yours. If you can find a maid, they have guest room lists and may be able to find your name and room number. Otherwise it's back down to the front desk.

Room Service

The *idea* of room service is great. Usually it arrives cold, triple the price it should be, delivered by someone you hope leaves your room soon. Room service asks that you not leave the empty tray outside your room in the hallway when you're finished. Call housekeeping to come pick up the tray from your room. I'm sure you're supposed to tip them for this.

At some hotels you can preorder breakfast the night before. On an order form you check what you'd like and what time you'd like it delivered the next morning and hang it outside your door before 2 AM. Your breakfast arrives when you want it, not an hour later.

The Hotel Restaurant

At the average hotel, the restaurant is pretty average. It is, however, conveniently located. If it's a sports restaurant with six TV's playing, don't hope for much. At a nicer hotel they may pride themselves on a having an award-winning chef and menu. (The restaurant connected to the Hotel Congress in Tucson is not to be missed for breakfast, lunch, or dinner.)

Exercise Room, Pool, Hot Tub

There is so much nonmotion in travel. We sit in the van, or lie in the bunk, or lounge in the front lounge. Find the hotel fitness room. Your room key will let you in. Get on the elliptical cross trainer, swim in the pool, or soak in the hot tub–in any order you'd like.

After-hours pool and hot tub are not technically allowed. By the time you return from the rock show it's way after the posted hours of operation. Oh, if it were easy to sneak in it wouldn't be so memorable. "I want room numbers!" is not a serious threat shouted from a security guard at 2 AM to band members relaxing in the hot tub.

However, in the morning, the hotel may suspect you of stealing car stereos from the parking lot if you were caught sneaking into the hot tub the night before. The local police may suspiciously search the bus but won't find any stereos. They'll leave with signed CDs and T-shirts.

Hotel Shuttle Service

Ask if your hotel has a shuttle service. They may be able to take you into town to do your laundry, go to the mall to shop, or to a guitar store to buy strings, picks, and play a vintage guitar you can't afford. Often the shuttle is only available for taking guests to and from the airport. But sometimes it's for getting around town. The band may be able to reserve the shuttle to get to the venue. Ask what time this service stops for the night. (Usually, it's well before your show is over.)

TAKE A LOOK AT THE TOWN YOU'RE IN

You've arrived, checked in, had a quick shower, laid down on the bed, and looked over room service. After flipping through some TV channels, you've decided you'd like to see what this part of Annapolis or Ann Arbor has to offer. The front desk can give you a map and point out where to get breakfast or lunch. Oddly, they're really bad at suggesting good food or coffee, as if they don't live anywhere near the hotel or never, ever leave the hotel.

> The front desk has absolutely no suggestion where to get food or coffee. All they tell me is "At five o'clock everything closes." I ask for a phone book and look up Starbucks and take a cab there, hoping I'll also find food.
> –Western Illinois, out by the highway

But they can at least aim you toward the docks, or the old part of town where there are food options.

> We walk to get café au lait and beignets at Café du Monde. We are stupid from the bus ride, unable to decide anything. Finally the waitress who is used to handling distracted tourists asks for a show of hands. "How many coffees?" and our order is taken.

Find a Local Café

The best food is NOT by the highway, although you'll find the best diner breakfast at a truck stop. (If it's after 10 PM, often the *only* place to find food is by the highway. Order breakfast.) When you are able to, eat at a local place in town. Part of the joy of traveling is having regional food. Maybe you want an Egg McMuffin, but on another day visit a recommended local café. There is a good chance that in the same block you've got books, clothes, used records and CDs, and secondhand stores.

> We went to Dot's and had great biscuits and some strange huevos rancheros. Then to good coffee at Café Books while Martin rented us mountain bikes. We went riding along the river up in the mountains. Stupendous. We kept riding, looking at rock climbers and looking for mountain lions that the signs said were natural to the area.

While traveling in North Carolina or Texas the band would seek out barbecue. On Deer Island, Maine, we went down to the docks for a lunch of fish chowder, scallop stew, and crab stew.

> "That's what I want to see: a guy in a yellow raincoat walking up the dock with his catch. That's a fresh lunch."

While you're out having lunch in town you might enjoy a conversation with the owner. Invite him to your show. Invite the waiter (who asked you to come back to town and play on his record). Invite the French woman who owns a soap store. Put them on the guest list and give them each a "plus one." It's good for everybody. They get to enjoy a free show and the band has made some new friends.

"To Go" Tip: If you want some inexpensive food to go, stop at Whole Foods or a grocery store. You can make a salad or choose from the deli bar.

Good Eating Tip: A friend of mine told me, "I eat pretty well at home, but as soon as I go on the road it's hamburgers and french fries." A good starting point for eating well on the road is to seek out food that is food. Find food that has had the least amount of hands touch it, machines change it, or chemicals added to it. Patrice Sullivan, massage therapist and acupuncturist, on eating well: "What helps me when I'm on the road is just not eating too much dead food. Stay with live food, which includes fruits, steamed vegetables, lightly cooked vegetables, or even soups. Eat raw seeds, raw almonds as a daily insurance. If you start off with that you can eat a weird dinner and maybe get away with it."

See Some Sights

Travel can lull you into thinking you can't possibly get up off the bed, but you can. Every city has at least one thing that would be great to go see, even if you only have forty-five minutes until bus call.

> "How was the Rock 'n' Roll Hall of Fame, Steve?"
> "Imagine if the Third Reich mounted an exhibition of nineteenth-century Jewish culture."

I went to the Metropolitan Museum of Art and the Lee Friedlander black-and-white photo exhibit. I had two hours before sound check and was able to see a tender photo of the Count Basie Band late at night asleep on their bus. And a photo of someone's declaration of love written on a sea wall: "Every day I calls a phone to her. Every night I dreams for her."

Author's sightseeing suggestions:

- Nature: Hike in the Canadian Rockies. Don't try to pet the caribou, and keep your itinerary with you. The bus may have moved since you got off it and you may have to ask an alternative-looking waitress if she knows of a club connected to a hotel that a band you are in may be playing at this evening.
- Tourism: Go to the top of the St. Louis Arch. It will sway and you'll be claustrophobic on the way up and down. Run up the *Rocky* steps in Philadelphia.
- Rides: Take the ski lift up a mountain.

  > Thank God for the sky. If we could build in it we would. I took the ski lift up for the view this morning.

- Movies: See *Fargo* in Fargo.
- Culture: Go to a museum to get out of the 107-degree Kansas heat and watch a video installation called "Project Explosion" of things blowing up. Then have a late lunch at the museum café.

Sometimes there's no time for an exhibit, a movie, or a boat ride. You'll walk through town to find some coffee and take in whatever crosses your path. That's your sightseeing for the day.

> "It appears downtown Portland is sort of smacked up."–Heinz. I told him my favorite sign today was THE PLAYFUL NEEDLE. It was a knitting store.

> The architecture is incredible here; part house, part boat, and part barn. We stopped at an old cemetery. "Died at sea." "Lost in passage." "Died in passage from Kingston, Jamaica, to New Hampshire." It all gave me the chills.–Deer Island, Maine

Go Shopping

Shopping on tour is always encouraged–for yourself, for a loved one, or even a band member. You'll find clothes, boots, leather jackets, or hand-made pottery in all sorts of interesting shops. (I would advise against waiting until your last show in Springfield, Illinois, to buy that special someone a gift from tour.) I love buying things in different cities. I enjoy knowing I got some suede boots in Philadelphia, a lapis bracelet at a store in New York, a used copy of Hemingway's *A Moveable Feast* in Louisville.

> "I could just buy my way through tour."–Frank has two days off in San Francisco.

What if you're not sure about a purchase? The sixty-second rule applies. If you don't know if you like it enough to make a purchase in sixty seconds, then don't. If you still hesitate, ask yourself, "Is it foxy?" If yes, then buy it. I'm here to help the women on tour enjoy foxier clothes. Otherwise you'll notice the waitresses at the club and the women up front at shows are looking finer than you. This cannot happen.

> Film people always look more like movie stars than the musicians making a video shoot. I was just asked, "Are you with wardrobe?" I admit I was wearing my overalls.

The mis-purchase. It has happened. It will happen again. It doesn't fit the loved one. Or it looks weird on you in different lighting. Unfortunately, you'll be unable to return the item purchased as you will now be across a state line. It's a bit like gambling. Budget in some bad purchases. Don't' be too upset. Give it away generously. Let it go. Make another purchase.

Visit Old Friends

The tour may stop in a town where you used to live or where some of your friends have moved. Let's face it, you're not going to have much time to see your old friends though. And it could be you're just beat today and would love to take a long nap before sound check.

> "I used to call everyone I knew. Now I call just one."–Frank

Call one friend and put them on the guest list with a plus one. Tell them you'd love to have a drink after the show. Do you call your ex-lovers? If you'd like to. Why not catch up?

> "Why are girlfriends always worried about the ex, our ex? That's the one person you are never going back to."–David's ex came to the show last night.

It's possible your old friends will come to the show but you won't get a chance to see them. You didn't see them in the audience during the show. Afterward you look through the club. They left a note for you with the bartender. They have early-morning day jobs. Sometimes, though, the visit works out better than you expected. You call your friend. He invites you over to his house and makes a big salad, lets you check your e-mail on his computer, and you sit and talk on his front steps until it's time to get back to the club. The band enjoys meeting him and hanging out with him on the bus before and after the show. He gives the band parting gifts.

TAXICABS

You'll be using taxis to get around town, especially when you're on a bus tour. Decide on the band policy for them. Some bands have a "three to a cab" policy and will pay the fare to get band members from the hotel to the club and back only if there are three band members in the taxi. If you take a cab on your own, most bands won't reimburse the fare.

To get a taxi, you can phone the cab company or you can walk into the street and flag one down. Ask the front desk or someone who lives in this town what is the best way to get a cab there. Many cities aren't cab-hailing cities (Los Angeles, for example), and you'll wait a long time looking down the street for a taxicab in vain.

How to Hail a Cab

To hail a cab, stand in the street and raise your hand. It's okay to yell "cabbie" or whistle to get a cab driver's attention, but you don't need to wave a lot or jump up and down. Look for the cab that has no one in it or with lit numbers on top. That's the signal the cab is available, unless he's answering a call or choosing not to pick you up. If the NOT FOR HIRE sign on the roof of the taxi is lit, don't keep flagging him. There may be other people out on the street hailing cabs, as well. Whoever is closest gets it. Yes, even if you were there first.

Taxi Guidelines

1. Always get a receipt. This cab ride may be paid for by your tour. Turn receipts in for cash as soon as you can. If the tour doesn't pay for it, you can deduct the fare on your taxes.
2. Don't use the trunk, my sleepy traveler.
3. If you use the trunk, remember to retrieve ALL of your items. I've heard of a cab driver helping to remove things from the trunk and "forgetting" to get the laptop computer. I count my items. "I have

four–four things *into* the cab and four things *out* of the cab."

4. Cabs are not always available when you need them. In rural Iowa and places similar, taxis may not run after 10 PM or they might have only one or two cab drivers on duty. So, give yourself plenty of extra time if you're planning on taking a cab to the gig. At the end of the night be prepared for a long wait or a long walk home.
5. If it's raining or snowing in any town, good luck finding an available cab.
6. If the cab driver says it is $26 to the airport, hold him to the agreed-upon amount even if the meter is pushing toward $35. If he gets mean, pay the meter and no tip.
7. Never let a cab driver ruin your day.

Meet Your Cab Driver

Someone could make a documentary of cab drivers. They've been dreaming up ideas all day and you are now their audience (unless you've gotten the cab driver who doesn't stop talking on his cell phone). He may tell you his ideas about sex and religion and inventions and politics.

"It is okay to kill only if someone is about to kill you or if your spouse commits adultery."–Cab driver, Chicago.

My cab driver's name is Toussaint. His brother owns the cab company. His brother is 007-1. He's 007-2. Their phones ring the James Bond theme and their card says CHAPEL HILL TO ANYWHERE ON THE PLANET.

A cab driver in Chicago sang the whole "Climb Every Mountain" song to me all the way from Wacker Drive downtown to the gig at the Metro. It was beautiful and epic and aching. We stopped as he finished the song. "I am too old now. I drive a cab. But you are young. You must follow your dream."

PERFORMING AT ONE-STOPS

A one-stop is a CD distribution center. The official reason you play at a one-stop is that a salesperson at the one-stop takes telephone orders from record stores. If the person at the one-stop sees you play today and has a sense of your being a valid, creative artist and likes what you do, he or she may suggest your CD be added to the stores' order.

Who knew when you were writing those meaningful songs in your living room that you'd be playing them before noon for everyone working at the distribution center, including the stocking clerks, who are pleased to stop work an hour early and have pizza brought in for lunch, when you only want a really, really strong cup of coffee and no fucking Coffeemate. (What is this nondairy creamer and why is it, and whoever thought it was a tasty alternative to half-and-half?)

PERFORMING AT AN IN-STORE

An in-store is a five-song show at a record store. You may set up on a stage or you may be playing under very bright lights in the jazz or country music aisle. You could be performing acoustically under several microphones or amplified, like a club gig. Don't get precious about the sound and miking. An in-store performance is as rough and ready as a rehearsal or as casual as playing in the kitchen. You don't need hours to prepare. Grab your sunglasses and pick up your instrument.

If the record store and your label have failed to advertise the in-store performance, the only people attending will be shoppers who have no idea who you are who will look up briefly, with disinterest, while you sing. A well-run in-store will have a good amount of fans attending who are thrilled to see you, who can hardly wait to talk to you when you're finished playing. After your performance, the store will arrange a place for you to sign CDs and posters and meet fans.

If you ask for some good strong coffee, the clerks will usually know where to get it and will bring it to you. Your tour manager most likely can arrange for each of you to get a free CD or two. Keep a list of several CDs you'd like to own in your wallet, because you'll completely forget what music you've been meaning to buy. Thank everyone for coming. Thank the record store for being so cool, and hurry off to sound check. Take your spirulina, because you haven't had time to eat and you're getting spacey and hungry and not so nice.

A Quick List of Indie Record Stores for In-Store Performance
   1. Amoeba Music, San Francisco and Los Angeles
   2. Ear X-Tacy, Louisville, KY
   3. Easy Street Records, Seattle
   4. The Electric Fetus, Minneapolis, St. Cloud, Duluth
   5. Finders Records & Tapes, Bowling Green and Findlay, OH
   6. Good Records, Dallas
   7. Homer's Music & Gifts, Omaha and Lincoln, NE
   8. Kiel's, Lawrence, KS
   9. Lou's Records, Encinitas, CA

10. Mountains Music Espresso, Jackson, WY
11. Music Millennium, Portland, OR
12. Newbury Comics, Boston, Providence, RI, Portland, ME, and others
13. Park Ave. CDs, Orlando
14. Reckless Records, Chicago
15. Twist & Shout, Denver
16. Waterloo Records & Video, Austin

INTERVIEWS

While you are on tour, your manager may schedule interviews with the local paper, college paper, national magazines, or radio. These interviews reach many people and are worth preparing for ahead of time. Sometimes it's a phone interview. Sometimes you meet with the journalist in person. Sometimes you go to the radio station and not only have an interview but give an on-air or taped performance. On tour, we often get annoyed that there are interviews scheduled. They seem to eat up the very time we need for a warm dinner or to go to the Tibetan store and find presents. But the written interview or radio interview and performance will acquaint many people with your music and your band. This interview goes to many of the little towns you won't be traveling to. You hope it inspires people to come to your show or buy your CD and enjoy your music.

Scheduling Interviews

Interviews and radio shows are usually scheduled for mid-afternoon–before sound check. Avoid scheduling interviews or performances early in the day. It's hard for the lead singer to physically sing and hard on the band to make an overnight drive to get there on time.

> The tour manager announces bus call is 8 AM because we have early radio tomorrow. This is how it always goes. This is how you get three hours of sleep, starting your first night.

Designate two band members to whom the interviewer should direct his questions. Some band members are just more composed or eloquent than others. An interviewer wants to talk to the person that fuels the band, usually the main writer or lead singer, and another charismatic band member. Schedule not only a beginning time but an end time to the interview as well. More than once I've been trapped in an interview that should have taken twenty minutes and yet we were still there three hours later. You feel taken advantage of. You feel it could have been planned better. Your tour manager can help wrap up the interview by saying he's sorry to have to end it, but the band has to go to sound check now.

Prepare Yourself

Watch interviews of artists you admire. Pay attention to their answers. I saw Johnny Depp on *Inside the Actors Studio*. He was asked "Did you become friends with Marlon Brando?" His answer was, "What I learned from him was..." He didn't answer the actual question, yet he deftly led the interview.

Abra Moore, Grammy Nominated Recording Artist, on Interviewing:

"Interviewing is an art. Connect with who you are speaking with and focus on their eyes. It's an art that celebrities for a fact have studied and worked on for when they are in the public eye and asked certain questions.

"Be prepared, yes. I had homework. Literally, write down hundreds of questions that you think you might be asked and how you'd answer them, because you're going to be asked all kinds of uncomfortable things. You don't have to answer any of it. Not in any direct way. Stay focused on the goal, the subject of what you want to say. For example: 'How do you feel about being whatever?'–some uncomfortable question, something you don't want to talk about, an industry question. 'That's amazing, I was in Hawaii with these deep-sea turtles...' Just gracefully move away from it. 'So, how old are you? What age were you when you started this band?' 'Gosh, in college...' You go into another tangent. Or: 'It's amazing when you start...' You don't have to say, 'I don't want to go there.'

"You've got to put some thought into it beforehand. It's an art. Spin it back. You don't have to go into defense mode: 'I'm not this' and 'I'm not that.' You don't have to be all victimized.

"'So how was it when you left the label? How does it feel to be dropped?' You've already written it down for yourself so you can navigate. It's about what feeling you leave the interview with."

Predictable Questions

- How's the tour going?
- How did you get your name?
- You're from Austin, Texas. What's that like?
- You've been touring with [insert band more famous than yours]. How's it been going?
- How is this record different from your last one?
- How would you describe your music?
- What does this record mean to you?

- What was it like working with [insert producer or guest artist]?
- What are your musical influences?
- How do you write a song? Do lyrics or music come first?
- What CDs do you listen to? [You will forget . . .]
- What do you do when you're not making music? [You may not remember . . .]
- What's next for you guys? [You may not know . . .]
- Anything else you'd like to add? [Your record. The show tonight.]

Unusual Questions

- How does nature inform the music?
- How does the history of the band inform the music?
- How do relationships within the band inform the music?
- What was the pivotal moment that helped your creativity or career?
- When did you first feel divinity?
- When was there a moment when all moments afterward were different?

The interviewer may ask you about pop culture, other bands, or trends in music. As a creative musician, you may not know a lot about popular bands or a current trend. You've been busy writing and recording. The interview doesn't have to be all about music.

Art and Cultural Questions

Below is a list of things I wish I had talked about during an NPR interview in which I had little to say. It may help your interview if you have some of these at the front of your mind. Who or what is/are your favorite or least favorite of the following?

- Poet
- Fiction
- Painter
- Photographer
- Artist
- Film
- Musicians
- Songs
- Composers
- Athletes
- Cities

Interview Warning Signs

1. The interviewer may not have done his or her homework at all. He starts the interview with "I haven't actually heard your record yet, but I've heard really good things about it. Can you tell me about it?" This is demoralizing to the band after you've driven overnight to get to the interview on time. Don't get mad. Create the interview you want.

2. You can often tell when the writer has already written his or her story from a particular angle and is trying to get you to say things that support that story. You'll have to hold firm, not be caught up in the current.

3. You may sense that the writer is mischievously stirring up controversy: No, I'm not going to talk about how the lead singer has changed since he stopped drinking. No, I'm not going to tell you which band I'll play with if there is a conflicting date between the two bands I'm in. Out loud you don't disagree you just divert the answer.

4. It's probably not a good idea to let the interviewer speak to your family. Your family might be swayed to tell a band secret or announce an unannounced show in a most innocent way. It's not your family's job to know what to tell the press and what not to tell the press. It's yours. Family is off-limits to press.

Framing Your Answers

- Facts are elegant. Give the details of your story. Ground your answers in senses–the color, the temperature, the flavor, the volume. Give your anecdote a setting. "We were in the kitchen and he had on a miner's hat with the light."
- When making a point, consider using the "diamond method." Make your point. Elaborate with an example. Make the point again in a slightly different way.
- You can guide the interview. Have two or three topics or stories ready that you want to talk about. (See Abra Moore interview, above.)
- Even if you are asked, don't tell someone else's story–bandmates, famous people you're traveling with, anybody. They most likely want to keep their stories private and it's not your story to tell.
- Of course there are things to complain about on the road, but don't be a complainer. Don't speak poorly of anyone in public.
- Don't use this time as your personal therapy session.
- If the interviewer's questions piss you off or bore you, don't get all

bothered. Create the interview you want.

- Don't try to be clever and witty unless you are one of the truly clever people.
- Interview with some mystique.

> "We need to make good versions of ourselves. Then learn to fend for ourselves. The artists we love teach us how."–Patti Smith interview

Interviewing for Print

Provide the interviewer with a written bio of the band beforehand. It helps the writer focus the article and it helps the band convey what they're about. If you are being interviewed for a written piece, the interview may be recorded or the journalist may be writing things down as you speak. As he or she writes it no longer feels like you are having a conversation. There are pauses while your words are written down and again as the journalist forms the next questions. Let there be pauses.

Greg Kott, *Chicago Tribune* music critic, on interviews:

"One reason artists are artists in the first place is their social skills are not the best. This is their way to communicate. David Byrne feels most free to express himself onstage. Brian Wilson wrote teenage symphonies to God in his bedroom because he couldn't relate to the outside world in any other way.

"You may think of yourself as an artist, but you are also an entertainer. If you are going to get noticed and get people to write about you, you have to be entertaining–not only onstage but in the local paper. The totality of who you are as an artist includes telling your story, so hone your craft. It doesn't hurt to think about these interviews ahead of time. Don't just go in their cold.

"I used to hate the dog-and-pony-show aspect of Letterman or Leno. They tell the artists, 'You have to have three good stories. Come on here prepared.' Why can't they talk off the top of their heads? Think of it as if you were talking to your best friend at a bar, not a big daunting interview.

"The easier you make that writer's job the more likely you are to get favorable coverage and have people come back and interview you. It doesn't hurt to be friendly, entertaining, and enjoy the process. Ninety percent of these writers are talking to you because they like something about you. They are already on your side. The only way you can screw that up is being a complete asshole. And don't lie to the interviewer.

"If the guy is unprepared, or is an un-insightful bad interviewer, don't use it as an excuse to be incommunicative or surly. You can still use the interview as a way to come across like a person the listeners or readers want to meet. You have the ability to steer the interview like a blank slate. Use it as an opportunity. You are going to get some press out of it.

"Sometimes the story, your words, are going to get mangled. File it away. These are not all going to be positive. You can be aware of who does a good job and develop a relationship with that writer."

THE PHOTO SESSION. On occasion, the publication interviewing you will want to send its own photographer out to take your picture. You want to be a good sport and do what they ask. But you've got instinct that has brought you this far. Stay connected to it. If the photographer wants you to put on clothes you'd never wear, or hold a watermelon over your head or essentially not represent yourself, no.

If you are asked to wear makeup for a photo shoot (or for a TV show), don't let the makeup get out of control. You may feel uncomfortable with the amount being applied to your face. You'll be told it will make you look natural. And it might to a point. The truth is, as musicians new to publicity, sometimes we don't know when to keep true to ourselves and when to open up to new things. It's hard to stand up to people who have done this before–the record company, the fashion magazine, the stylist. Trust your gut, and it's okay to make some mistakes.

SHORT-LIVED PRESS. If the paper or magazine story comes out all wrong and you're misquoted terribly, well, it's too bad. It's going to happen. No one cares about it as much as you. Maybe you need to speak more slowly or more clearly in your interviews. Maybe you need to prepare yourself more for interviews. Maybe you won't interview with this writer again.

Unless you said you were more popular than Jesus, or confessed to not doing your own singing, or were hateful about another culture, these newspapers will be old in twenty-four hours. A week later you may be in a pet store and notice that the newspaper lining the bottom of a snake's cage with a snake curled on top of it is your band's photo and article (true story).

Radio Interview and On-Air Performance Tips
Your tour manager will call ahead to figure out what the band should bring to play at this particular radio station and to determine how many songs the station would like the band to play. The setup for radio is much like performing at the in-store. The band may be sitting in front of four microphones, squished in the DJ's control room, or may set up in a small studio,

using microphones, direct boxes, and pedal boards. It's a scaled-down performance. If the drummer plays, he'll use a small kit or maybe just one drum. The bass player usually won't be using his big bass amp but will bring a practice amp or go direct.

Radio is weird because it appears that we are all pretending to be on the radio. There's no audience and we don't necessarily know when we're off air or on air. (There's an "on air" light somewhere, but we don't know where it is or when it's illuminated.) The DJ might become mildly annoyed if the band is still talking and laughing when he clears his throat, lowers his voice, and begins his show.

Everything on the radio is audio. Speak into the microphone. Finish your sentences. Don't laugh into the mic. It'll make you sound kind of hysterical. The tone of your voice, the speed you speak, your breath, your laugh, are all a part of your radio interview. And remember to turn off your cell phone before the show begins.

> We went out to the Bronx to play on WFUF. Someone asked the DJ what her worst interview was and she said it was an international musician whose cell phone rang during the show and he answered it.

Jody Denberg, KGSR program director, on radio performance:

"If you're performing at the radio station, you want to do everything you can to come off great. You are speaking and playing for more people than may be at your gig. Don't be afraid to do everything you can to maximize your presence and presentation.

"Be sure to advance the date technically as if it were a regular gig. The radio station needs to know what you need. You can't just show up and expect them to have three DI's and five vocal mics. If they don't have the equipment you need, make sure they provide it, or bring it with you. Do what you can to get the sound the way you want it. You want to sound as good as you can on the air.

"Arrive early enough so you feel comfortable. Get water. Hopefully the person you are visiting will be doing the same thing. The DJ wants you to feel relaxed on the air, to be comfortable with him and think, 'This guy is cool. I can warm up to this interview.'

"The standard rules of etiquette apply. Don't be late. If you are, call to let them know. That way the DJ can say, 'Susan will be on the air today at 3:30.' And at three o'clock make an update: 'Susan's stuck in traffic up on Rundberg Lane and will be in just a little bit later.' It makes people feel like it's real.

"If there's not a mic screen and you're someone prone to popping p's, ask for one. Interviewing Yoko, there were no socks on the mic and I knew

I'd be popping p's and spending hours on pro tools getting rid of that. Andy, the engineer, found a clean white sock to put on the mic for me.

"It's very important to work the mic. The DJ knows how to work the mic and has himself sounding full and centered. If you are two inches off the mic, get right up on it. Ask the DJ what kind of mic. Is this omni-directional [don't need to be right up on it] or do you need to be close to it?

"Try to localize. If you went to a great restaurant or listen to a local musician, mention it. Say the things about the town that you think are positive. You are talking to and playing to the host *and* to the listening audience of several thousand. The host will be a conduit. Don't be real 'inside' with your stuff. Remember you are talking to a lot of people. Never say, 'Thank you, Austin.' When I'm on the air, I'm talking to one person and aware there are several thousand listening. You're doing both.

"Don't be afraid to offer up your information if the DJ is not doing a good job of it. 'We are playing tonight at 8 PM at Stubbs.' Give the exact time. 'I think there are tickets at the door.' Don't take it for granted that the DJ is good. Give your information. 'The song I just played for you, "From this Moment On," is from our new album.' There are ways to do things that are informative and not just blatant plugs.

"Assume people are tuning in and out and back in and they caught the last quarter of the last song. There is a way of saying the title and your info again. Reiteration can be subtle and not contrived.

"Remember the name of the DJ and even write down the station call letters. 'Thanks for having us on KGSR. I appreciate it.' You sound like you are in the know. People think, 'They are connected to my city. I want to see their gig or buy their record.' You are promoting a product or gig on the air and you are making friends with the city and each listener."

Station ID Note: After the interview, the radio station may ask you to record a "station ID": a five-second plug for their station. It goes something like this: "This is [your band name here], and you're listening to KGSR, Austin, Texas." They might ask you to say something specific or leave it up to you. You don't have to be a comedian. Simple is fine. You may need to write down the station call letters and numbers. These can be oddly hard to remember.

5. Show Preparation: 4 PM–8 PM

Late afternoon, at the time scheduled in the itinerary or day sheet if one is posted, the band will drive to the venue to begin preparing for tonight's show. The trailer has to be unloaded and gear set up onstage. Guitars will be played to check that the amps, effects pedals, and cables are working properly today. Direct boxes and microphones will be cabled, and lines from each are checked and labeled. Each band member will build a mix in his or her monitor wedge. The front-of-house sound person will have the band play a few songs to get a good mix in the main house speakers. The merchandise is set up and then everyone looks for dinner.

Author Note: The rock show does kind of start the minute you walk into the club. Dress the part. Arrive with some style. You can change again for the show, but don't come in wearing your shark T-shirt and sweats and then change dramatically into someone else for the show. You're an artist all the time. You don't want to overhear the house sound guys saying, "She was nice, but she looked better on the poster" about you.

LOAD-IN

Load-in to the club is usually scheduled at 4 or 5 PM. You drive to the venue and hope they have put a couple of orange cones out in the street to reserve a parking space for your van or bus as you requested. Then the trailer is unlocked and everyone unloads the gear and rolls it into the club. If the gig is on the second or third floor, you hope for a freight elevator. If there is none you hope for loaders.

If your band has asked the club sound guys to come in early because the band setup is so elaborate, arrive on time or they won't be happy and won't help you much. They usually start their day at 4 PM, so a 2 PM load-in is stealing part of their off time. At the end of the night, if they've done a good job and the show has gone well, you might tip them twenty to fifty bucks.

Tip from Howard Greynolds, Thrill Jockey Records: "Make it to the club on time and be courteous to the bartender, the soundman, and the promoter, as they will make or break your evening."

Setting Up

The drums and amplifiers are unpacked from their road cases and set up geometrically on the stage per your stage plot. On your first tours, you'll set up your own gear. Later, even if you have crew to do this for you, you may like to set up your own pedal board. Then you'll need power to plug it all in. If there is none near you, ask the house sound guy for power and he will drag a quad box (a square box with four places to plug in) over to your side of the stage.

Your band input list and stage plot should have already been faxed to the club. As stated in your technical rider, the house sound guys should have microphones, direct boxes, and cables already in place when the band arrives at the club. They probably won't be in place. The house sound guy may have even lost the stage plot with the input list on the reverse side. He may say it was never sent. No need to argue about it. Bring extras copies and simply hand him another. We all want a good show, and having a stage plot and input list will help to set up the stage correctly and quickly.

A Note about "Lifers": You may meet some really difficult, unhelpful, short-tempered people working at a club. It could be anyone from the owner to an overworked sound guy. The worst ones have been at this for twenty years and they know *everything* because they've been there for twenty years.

They'll tell you the DI you use is not top-of-the-line like the ones they use. They'll be overtly sarcastic. If you're a woman they'll tell you the club isn't open yet or ask which band member is your boyfriend. They most likely want to be onstage like you but have little musical ability, so the best they can do is make you feel miserable and inferior to their vast knowledge. Let your crew get into fights with them. Tomorrow you'll be gone from their godforsaken little world and they'll still be smack dab in their life.

Storing Empty Road Cases

You'll have to store the empty road cases somewhere. You can't just leave the dead cases out there on the dance floor in front of the stage where you unpacked everything. The club has done this many, many times before and will tell you where to store them. Stack your cases in one clearly defined spot so your band's stuff doesn't get mixed up with another band's. They don't want to take your things home and you don't want theirs. At 2 AM it's very easy for one of your techs to grab a guitar that doesn't belong to your band and load it into the trailer. Keep everything very separate.

Checking Your Equipment

Turn on your amp and play through your rig for a moment to check if everything is working today. Then shut off the amp and leave the stage. The house sound guys or your crew will be setting up microphones, stands, cables, and monitors around you. While they work, they don't want to listen to you play all your Steely Dan riffs for no one's pleasure but your own. Get off the stage.

If there's a problem with your rig–if you have no sound or a buzzing or crackling is coming from your amp–you'll need to track down and fix the problem.

1. If you have no sound, bypass every pedal and plug directly from your instrument into your amp. If it works, you know it's not the instrument or the amp or the cable you are using. One by one add a pedal back in. When it doesn't work again, you've discovered the source of the trouble.

2. If you have a loud hum or buzz coming out of your amp, most likely a cable isn't plugged in all the way or the ground needs to be "lifted." So, check your cables. If that doesn't quiet the buzz, switch the ground lift on your amp or DI. If that doesn't stop the hum, plug into a completely different power outlet or try putting a small gray ground lift plug on the end of the power cord of your amp. If you still have a slight hum, well, guitars are supposed to hum. Or someone will suggest it's the lights. Sometimes you just live with the hum.

3. If you have a crackling sound, it's probably a cable going bad. Go through each cable and shake it. When one crackles badly, replace that cable. It could also be that the cable insert on an effects pedal needs tightening.

4. There is one general all-purpose method to fix a problem that I learned from a Brian Wilson musician: "Turn it off. Turn it back

on. Everything may be all right." Sometimes electricity gets confused. Let electricity relax and collect itself.

What is broken one day will quite possibly work just fine tomorrow. But you never know about the day after that. The intermittent problem will often be not just one problem but several. Always pack extra cables and power supplies with you on tour just in case.

SOUND CHECK

At sound check the sound engineers will check that the lines coming from the stage are working and correctly labeled at the monitor desk and the front-of-house soundboard (guitar–channel 7, lead vocal–channel 8). If you have a crew, they'll do this before you arrive. If you've left the club after load-in, arrive back for sound check on time (within fifteen minutes of scheduled time) and be prepared to wait. You'll wait for the crew to finish line checking, and you'll wait for other musicians to sound check.

> While we are waiting for sound check I go watch the sunset. It kept rolling like orange red water in the sky, getting bluer and deeper and lovely.–Tucson

The monitor engineer will begin to create the mix the band needs to hear onstage and the front-of-house sound engineer will create the mix the audience will hear during the show. These are two separate mixes.

Ear Protection Note: If you wear molded earplugs during the show, put them in for your sound check. This is when the bad feedback may knock you over, and there you were with your earplugs in your pocket. (See "Volume and Ear Protection," page 157.)

Monitor Check

A monitor wedge is a speaker facing toward you supplied by the club. In it you build a blend of instruments and voices you'll need to hear to play a good show. If you are using the house monitor engineer, ask him his name and be very nice to him.

Although you've requested separate mixes for everyone, your monitor may be linked with someone else's monitor. You'll have your own wedge but will be sharing a mix with someone else. You'll have to hear the weird things someone else likes in their monitor at the level they like, along with what you need.

BUILDING A MONITOR MIX. Some bands create one mix at a time, calmly going around the band. ("John, what do you need in your monitor?" "Max,

what do you need in your monitor?") Some bands build mixes one instrument at a time. ("Who needs trumpet? Raise your hands.") Sometimes,
though, checking monitors is just chaos. Everyone talks and plays at once.
One musician may be playing for the front-of-house engineer while
another is playing for the monitor engineer. Having a strong presence
onstage–someone everyone respects, like the lead singer or a stage manager–usually keeps monitor check organized.

> "I'm glad you're not one of those bands that everybody shouts what they want
> all at once."–Monitor guy in Boston before our sound check. (But we are.)

If you don't know yet what you want in your monitor, here are some starting suggestions:

1. Kick drum and high-hat, especially if you're in a big echoing place.
   This will help you play in time when the sound is swimming in
   natural reverb and it's easy to lose the "one."
2. A chordal instrument like a piano or an acoustic guitar. This will
   help you play or sing in tune.
3. Lead vocalist, so you'll know where you are in the song. If things
   go wrong and the band gets lost, cue on the vocal. Wherever the
   vocalist goes is where everyone should go, and hopefully you'll
   arrive at the end together.
4. Yourself. Yes, you need to hear yourself to play well. But consider
   keeping it at a level that lets you also hear how you fit with other
   things going on. If you're always asking for "more me" in the monitor, your bandmates may give you shit for only listening to yourself.

ADJUSTING THE VOLUME LEVEL. The level or volume of each of the instruments you've placed in your monitor can be adjusted. Be succinct in asking for what you need changed during sound check and also during the
show. "Vocal–up. Vocal–down" is all that needs to be said. When the
adjustment is as you need it, signal "okay."

Volume is personal. Musicians may be disappointed if you want less of
them in your monitor even though they know it's about volume, not their
ability or how much you like them. Usually.

Author Note: Please don't ask for "the maximum 'me' before it feeds
back." Do you think there is some sonic barrier between your monitor and
the musician standing one foot away from you? We will all hear your "maximum" and it will become thunderously loud on stage as we compete to
hear ourselves.

ADJUSTING THE EQ. If the tone of your instrument or voice in the monitor is really weird, it will be hard to play or sing. You can ask the monitor person to make the sound warmer, brighter, less honky, or not so muffled. You can ask for more lows, mid-lows, or highs if you know this will fix the problem. Be ready for the sound people to start talking in this "k" language. "I've taken out the 5k and left in the 7k." You can admit to not knowing what they are talking about. They prefer we don't use their language, as we'll only misuse it. It's better to say to them "the vocal just sounds small." They will take pride in finding the right "k" to notch out and fix the problem.

Martin Stebbing, sound engineer, on understanding sound frequencies:

"Here's the layout. The 'k' thing is just an abbreviation of KHz (kilohertz.) Generally, anything over 1,000 hertz is referred to as 'k' or multiples of 'k.'

"Between 0 and 120 hertz would be low bass. This is where you're going to get the warm low feeling–a nice warm round bottom end. That's what we all love. It's the rumbly and the tumbly. Dance stuff likes that sub bass. 40 hertz down to wherever is the sub sub stuff. Human ear doesn't hear much under 40, but you feel it. It's the impact in your body. It's the throbbing, feel-good kind of thing that's so key to all dance music. It's driving home the beat, and it's warm and friendly.

"Bass is such a huge and powerful thing. It's where you perceive pop music, the kick drum, the beat. To a degree even the vocals–I put sub stuff on the lead vocal to give it more presence.

"Between 120 and 600 hertz, this would be mid-band. That's where a lot of the action is as far as defining stuff like voice and low-mid instruments. The male voice resides there. There's a phrase: Music is in the mids. That's what they're talking about. There's not too much detail, but that's where the meat of it is. If a musician says they want it warmer, raise the lower mids. If it's barky, it's around 250 to 350 hertz that you want to take out.

"Between 3k and 7k. This is where our hearing has the most hearing. 5k is the pain band. It's piercing and nasal and not very nice. If it sounds nasal, bitey, or harsh, it's centering around 5k, the pain frequency. Notch some out. If it sounds muffled, there are probably not enough frequencies from 5k on up.

"If something feeds back–that high frequency feedback–you can take those. They hurt, but they're not going to cause you to punch somebody. 5k feedback will make you want to punch someone hard and repeatedly.

"From 7k on up to 20k (we stop there, for the human ear doesn't hear any higher). This is the super-high stuff. This is the prettiness in cymbals. At a 600 hertz range, the mix would have no definition. Add between 3 and 7k and you get more definition. Add 7 and 7 up and it gives prettiness, definition, and shimmer."

USING IN-EAR MONITORS. An in-ear monitor looks like two hearing aids with wires coming out of them pushed into your ears. Many of the musicians you see performing during the Grammys or on live TV wear them. You'll need an experienced monitor engineer to build this mix. He absolutely cannot send ear-damaging feedback into the small speakers placed snugly in your ear canal.

Some musicians like in-ears because theoretically you can have a great studio-sounding mix in them and then sing or play better. Another reason to use them is that they work as earplugs, protecting your hearing. (See "Volume and Ear Protection," page 157.)

But, even if you get a good mix, you often feel separated from your bandmates who aren't using in-ears. If your bandmate leans over to tell you something during the show, you'll have to pull out your in-ear to hear him. If a fan yells something, you won't hear it. One solution is to set up a room mic so that you can also send some audience and stage sound to your in-ear mix. Mike Santucci, audiologist with Sensaphonics, who makes in-ear monitors, told me there is a new 3-D ambient in-ear monitor created so musicians can hear more of the room naturally. It's pretty expensive, though, at $2,000.

Front-of-House Sound Check

The front-of-house sound engineer creates a mix of the band that the audience hears in the house. Martin Stebbing: "What a band hears onstage is a weird reflection of sound. It might feel weird on the stage or it could feel right on the stage. What's happening in the room might be entirely different. Rely on your soundman to balance it right, unless you have some ecstasy-crazed loon who keeps pushing the sub bass to sub levels, rendering most of the audience sterile by the end of the night."

Author Note: The author would like to add that we *do* hear the sound in the house—maybe not entirely accurately—but we hear if we're absent, if we're featured, and if the tone is too trebley. Some musicians feel if the house is mixed well, they can do without monitors completely.

BUILDING A FRONT-OF-HOUSE MIX. Your front-of-house sound engineer will usually begin by asking the drummer to play. It's boring and tedious and loud to listen to the drummer sound check. Usually the rest of the band leaves the stage. Next, your sound engineer will add the bass. Then he'll look up and yell from the sound console in the middle of the room "Who else is ready and wants to sound check?"

When it's your turn it's useful to play high, play low, play something really loud, and play something he hears you play every night. If you use effects pedals, step on each so he can be prepared for the parameters of your stage sound and volume. Then he may EQ the sound a little, pan the sound to the right or left, or add some effects. He may have two instruments play at once to check the balance.

Once he's checked everyone individually, the band plays a song or two. You play your extremes—the most quiet song and the most loud. You play a song with the loop coming from the laptop onstage. You give him a variety of sounds from your show. Normally you won't play the song all the way through unless you're rehearsing it. Show-biz lore says you want to save the song for the show.

Author Note: The "whisper check" is the term we have given to a sly method of sound checking to get more of yourself in the house and monitors during the show. During sound check when the front-of-house or monitor guy asks a singer to sing, instead of singing in a full voice, they sing incredibly quietly, almost in a whisper. The front-of-house levels and monitor levels are set at this whisper volume. Then when the show begins, they sing with a full voice. The faders are set for a quieter voice. The singers have made sure their first entrance is incredibly loud. (The whisper check is possible with any instrument.)

ADJUSTING STAGE VOLUME. Your front-of-house sound engineer may ask you to turn your amps and monitors down. He may have a db (decibel) meter with him to show the band scientifically that the stage volume is as loud as a jet airplane taking off. It's not that the sound guy is a wimp. It truly is loud, and some clubs have a decibel limit of 100 or 103.

The other reason he may ask the band to turn down is that the stage volume may be overpowering the front-of-house mix. There isn't a sonic barrier at the foot of the stage separating stage sound and house sound. One will fold into the other, and they need to be compatible. Band members look innocently around at each other. "Am I too loud?" The rock answer is, "You're never too loud," but that's not exactly true.

Author Note: If a musician near you has his amp way too loud for you to play, ask if he can angle it more toward himself. Amps are pretty directional. He can still hear himself, and you don't have to be swallowed in his sound.

Rehearsing

You may use part of your sound check as a rehearsal. There may be new songs to run, mistakes from the previous night to sort out, or new arrangements to try. If there's an opening band checking after you, you could be considerate and let them have the stage and not rehearse on and on, taking their sound-check time.

Author Note: The order in which bands sound check is the reverse of show order. The first band to check is the headliner. The last band to check is the first band to play.

These little rehearsals can run late, so I highly recommend you bring your stage wear to sound check. As much as it appears you'll have three and a half hours to kill between sound check and show, this never happens. You'll be the one (along with someone else that you rarely hang out with) that has to cab quickly back to the hotel to get your sparkly show clothes.

Set Time Tip: Before leaving sound check be sure to ask and confirm what time the show is. You might think showtime would be a very set time, determined weeks ago. In reality, the showtime in the contract, in your itinerary, reported in the newspaper, and printed on the tickets may not match. Before you leave the stage after sound check, the official start time is declared. Your tour manager has confirmed with the club's production manager that your set will start not at 11 PM but 10:30 PM. Call your guests to let them know.

Lighting Design

There will be some kind of lighting for the stage. It may be very simple. At sound check there may be a lighting guy up on a ladder focusing lights and replacing gels. Talk with him about what kind of lighting you'd like on the band tonight. Tell him the mood you're looking for.

> "You are all going to have to pretend you don't hear me now, because I have to yell at the lighting guy."–Tom Verlaine show, Double Door, Chicago

I asked Mike Reed of Reed Rigging what lighting advice he can give bands going out on the road for the first time, probably without a lighting director. Is it appropriate to tell the house lighting guy how you'd like the lights to be?

"If the club has a lighting guy, that's what he's there to do. Rule number one for a lighting guy is to interpret what the band wants. He should talk to the band and get their ideas, get their input, figure out how they want to look. Your best lighting directors are theatrically trained. There, the actors are the show. Here, the music is the show and the mood and the atmosphere and the feeling is the show."

What colors are good or bad? Is green always bad?

"There is a lighting guy saying: 'Blue on the slow one, red on the fast one, and always light the money.' Green on a thing or on the floor is fine. Green light on its own looks terrible on anybody. It's how you use green. Green works best when mixed with something else. For instance, green and white look great together. (White light is clear, no color gel over the light.) Green and red make amber. So it's how you use green."

A lot of bands like a dark or moody stage. Any advice?

"My own belief is the singers and the band should be seen. How do you want them to be seen? I like sidelight. It's absolutely the best light to use in conjunction with front light. What sidelight does is it provides a rim. It rims the object. It separates the person from the background and they pop out. Any LD will tell you it's an enormously useful tool. I always look for side light positions to use.

"You need both backlighting and front lighting. Front only and you look like a cardboard cutout. But if that's what an artist wants, that's what you give them. A lighting guy has to balance what an artist wants and what the lighting guy thinks looks good. Lighting is extremely subjective."

Are strobes dumb? How often should light move onstage?

"There are two different kinds of motion–lights that flash on a beat and moving light that moves in time or on a beat. When I started there were no moving lights. All we had was to flash lights in time. It's what you do when you don't have a lot to work with. Personally I try to find a balance between gratuitous flashing and something interesting but not an extension of the kick drum.

"Strobes are great. Nowadays there's a data-flash strobe and you can raise or lower the intensity–do a single burst all the way up to many bursts. They are great for a highlight. I did lights for a fifties band and they were running around the stage and with the strobe on them they looked like they were running in slow motion. I can't imagine having a strobe on so long that it would affect anyone prone to epilepsy."

What lighting do you hate?

"Bad lighting? I saw a flamenco dance company from Spain. You couldn't see them. It's all about the feet and you couldn't see the feet. It's also about the hands and the body and they were doing this stuff where lights were overhead coming straight down and their faces looked like raccoons, their hands outside the beam, and you couldn't see their feet. Somebody read it in a book somewhere–awful.

"One last thing. There is a great book about concert lighting called *Concert Lighting* by James Moody. He talks about tour personnel, unions, road safety, cuing the music, designing the stage, and preproduction."

SETTING UP YOUR MERCHANDISE TABLE

During your sound check, your merch guy will be setting up your merchandising area. If you don't have a merch guy, you'll set it up yourselves either before or after sound check. The club already knows of a good spot in their club to put the merch table. Often it's on the way to the bathrooms or by the entrance or exit of the club. Everyone has to pass by it at some point in the night. The placement and lighting of your merch table is extremely important for selling merch. If it's too hard for the audience to see, to simply walk over to and pick up a CD, they'll probably just keeping walking to the bar or out the door with their friends at the end of the night.

> "People buy more merch the better the show. It's a euphoric feeling. They want to walk out with it."

Hang some of your posters and designated floor-model T-shirts on the wall behind the table. You'll probably want to create a nice display. Sticking torn pieces of silver duct tape onto the shoulders of a pink shirt to hang it from the wall simply looks bad. You can hide the tape or hang the shirts on hangers and tape the hanger to the wall.

Merchandise Tip: When ordering T-shirts, choose some tank tops and baseball shirts with a design that matches your CD. Plain old cheap extra-large T-shirts with your name on the front will fill your storage space unsold. In addition to offering CDs, T-shirts, and hats, you can also sell and sign a well-made poster for $5.

Should the band go out to the merch table to meet fans and sign CDs? Probably on early tours it's a good idea. But after you've traveled awhile, if you've done your job and put all your emotional energy into the show, going out is like bursting the spell you've just cast. That said, if you want to personally meet the audience and you feel it's right for you, of course you should.

The easiest way to keep track of merchandise sold each night is to write down the title of each CD and style of T-shirt you're selling. When one is sold, make a line under the item sold. Figure 8 is a sample merchandise settlement sheet to keep track of sold merchandise.

Merchandise/Venue - Settlement Sheet

Venue:		Date:
Address:		
City:	State:	

Venue Money:

CD	CD's Sold	CD Money
		TOTAL:

T-Shirts and other Merch.	Shirts Sold	Shirt Money
		TOTAL:

FIGURE 8

Your tour can be helped tremendously by merchandise income. Some bands sink this money directly back into merch design and production. Often tours use this revenue to pay tour expenses. But, if you've purchased the CDs from your record label, be sure to earmark a percentage of CD income to pay them back.

Your e-mail list can also be on the merch table. At each show, people who would like to be informed of upcoming shows or CD releases can write down their e-mail address. Encourage them to print. Someone is going to be reading this list and typing it into a computer. The later it gets in the evening, the weirder the handwriting gets.

BACKSTAGE

Backstage is the whole show-biz area beyond the stage. It's where performers relax and prepare for the show. The Vic in Chicago, and other old theaters like it, has a big backstage area underneath the stage with three dressing rooms, two bathrooms, and a shower, as well a catering area and production offices. Backstage may be so large that there will be signs on the walls and arrows on the floor directing you to the stage. At other venues, the backstage area may be the hallway by the stage or one narrow room painted black with a few old easy chairs and a couch.

Author Tip: Before you leave the stage at sound check, your tour manager may hand you a sticky all-access pass from the club. The club will want you to wear it. The adhesive will make a rectangular mark on your leather jacket or jeans that may be hard to remove. Often your tour laminate will trump a sticky pass so you can just put it in your pocket.

Dressing Rooms

The rock-club dressing room is often nothing but an unfinished basement (or broom closet) with pornographic or "philosophic" graffiti.

"Why, there's a penis on the wall."–Band member, first tour, Detroit

The room may be extremely small, with low ceilings, poor ventilation, and exposed and dripping pipes. The lighting may be way too bright or lit from a hazardous-looking thrift-store lamp in the corner. If possible, turn off the overhead fluorescent lights. The brightness does nothing to create a mood before or after the show. And you really don't want to see what that couch or carpet looks like in full light, do you? Often there's no bathroom, so you'll be standing in line with your fans out in the club asking if it's okay to cut in because you have to be onstage momentarily.

Occasionally the dressing room is fabulous. The Rave in downtown Milwaukee is decked out like a harem. The dressing room at the 9:30 Club in D.C. looks like a blue space ship, with blue bunks, blue couches, and an always clean shower.

Using Your Bus as Your Very Own Backstage Dressing Room

If you are touring in a bus, it will be parked outside the venue from the time you load in until load-out at the end of the night. It feels like your very small apartment is parked at the curb, so you can use it as an additional dressing room. While waiting for sound check or the show, the band can rest or watch a movie or change clothes. If the dressing room in the club fills up with friends of friends, you have somewhere else to go to relax.

You may want to keep some stage wear in a closet on the bus. That way you won't have to make your way back to the hotel to change for the show. And you won't have to dig through the bays looking for your suitcase, opening it up and choosing your clothes for tonight's show as your fans walk by.

Collecting Graffiti

Yes, most of the writing and drawing on dressing room walls is depressingly dull and uncreative. But occasionally these messages are worth writing down.

"Il y a des castors la bas (There are some beavers over there)."–Toronto

"What is a cowboy? Brains of a dreamer, the aspirations of a Casanova." –Scaly, TX

"What is a love letter? A bullet from a gun." (to paraphrase *Blue Velvet*)

"You think you're dead now? Wait 'til later."

"There's not a piece of my heart left big enough to be broken."–Utah

On a mirror in Northampton: "You look like you deal with it."

On the ceiling: "I'm so proud of you all."–Knitting Factory, LA

At the Seventh Street Entry, a smaller club connected to First Avenue in Minneapolis, many of the Great Lies of Rock 'n' Roll were written on the wall. (See "The 100 Great Lies of Rock 'n' Roll," page 249.) Outside the dressing room at the Double Door in Chicago, for no reason but mild entertainment, is a list of "Ham Bands"–over 500 band names altered to include the word ham. Examples:

Ham Halen

9 Inch Hams

Everything but the Ham

Ham & Dave

Blood, Sweat & Ham

Alahama

Hamoi Rocks

Pearl Ham

The Tragically Ham

Leonard Coham

Lindsay Buckingham

Fog Ham

Hamsta Rhymes

The club had to post a rule that says, "Please do not write down a ham band that's already on the wall!!!" But what are you going to do, read and remember 500 previous ham bands? Looking at the long list and the varied handwriting, it reminds me of the sort of writing that must be left on prison walls, a record of each night and a chronicle of the years.

YOUR DELI TRAY

"We'll give you the deli tray later. Too many rats in here to put it out this early." Yes, it's the old 9:30 Club behind the Ford Theater where Lincoln was shot. ("But besides that, Mrs. Lincoln, how did you enjoy the play?"– my favorite terrible joke.)

The deli tray you designed and requested in your hospitality rider and attached to your performance contract will arrive sometime around the time you requested. Thirty minutes before sound check is when you are hungry and happy to see it. Sometimes it's set up late in the evening, an hour before the show, when you are no longer hungry and don't want to eat.

Even though it's pretty much the same snacks every afternoon, a deli tray is a welcome sight. It gives the appearance that someone cares, someone cleaned up your little dressing room from the night before, someone hopes you don't go hungry and wishes you a good evening and a great show.

Depending on how important you are (number of tickets sold), your tour manager may have to politely demand the hospitality rider be fulfilled according to your contract. He may have to find the production manager, who will direct an employee to go out and buy some Red Bull or Goldfish crackers or a tray of cut veggies and dip.

Warning: Be sure to wash the fruit from the deli tray. The only time I was ever food poisoned was eating an unwashed apple from the deli tray.

YOUR DINNER

After sound check there's a pause in the show momentum as thoughts turn to dinner. Maybe the club is providing dinner or the promoter is taking you out to dinner. Maybe you are the opener on a national touring act and catering has made a fabulous dinner. Perhaps the club hands you a $10 buy-out and you ask if there's a Thai restaurant or a place to get some soup within walking distance. Maybe the club hands you nothing and to save money you make a sandwich off the deli tray.

Pre-Show Eating Tips: You want to have just the right amount of food before a show—enough to have strength but not too much so you're uncomfortable or drowsy.

"You can't be all contented and play rock 'n' roll."–Jon Dee, skipping the dinner entirely

Never eat rice close to showtime. It will expand in your belly and make you feel fat and full and stomachachy. If you eat rice, eat just a little and not with a carbonated beverage.

Dinner Provided by the Club

Sample dinner provision from a hospitality rider:

"DINNER: Will be served no later than three hours prior to artist's performance. There are seventeen people in the touring party, ten are vegetarians. Vegetables are not to be overcooked."

All through sound check you've been thinking of the dinner that will appear as soon as you're finished putting a distant echo of keyboard in your monitor. Instead of having to seek out an acceptable restaurant located somewhere between the hotel and venue, then waiting for your server to take your order, and then sitting with your bandmates with whom you have nothing left to talk about, you have "dinner in-house" tonight.

This may work out several ways:

1. Restaurant connected to the club. Sometimes you'll have to get your tour manager to track down someone at the club who will give you each a meal ticket. You hope there's seating available at the restaurant. Give the meal ticket to your waitress and order anything off the menu up to $15. Anything above that you pay for yourself. Tip on the full amount.

2. Club has a kitchen. You can order off of a "band menu" during sound check so the food is ready immediately after. This is usually a decent dinner, although band menus can be very limited. If you're hungry for something on the "regular" menu, order it and offer to pay for it. Sometimes they'll just include it with the rest of the band dinners. Be sure you tip your server, even if your food arrives in your dressing room later. It's easy to forget to tip since you're not at a restaurant seated at a regular table. If you don't tip, your band will be known as bad tippers and no waitress will appear the next time you are there.

If your sound check runs late, and you don't want to eat close to the show, the kitchen may let you order something for later.

3. Club gets dinner in big pans from restaurant nearby. It could be Thai food or ravioli, chicken parmesan and a pan of salad. It doesn't look that appetizing in the long aluminum pans, but it may be delicious. Or not.

> Dinner arrived after sound check. They brought us one pan of fried chicken and one pan of barbecue ribs. That's it. No sides. No bread. No cole slaw. Two meats.

4. Club owner's dad prepares feast. Playing at the Art Bar in Baton Rouge, the club owner's dad invited us over to his house for an incredible Cajun meal.

5. Club owner's friend loves the band and brings food to the club.

> He reveals containers full of freshly boiled crawfish. We'd seen them alive in a basket on the sidewalk earlier with a steaming pot beside them. Life and then not life. The band is pulling them apart. I have a guilty vegetarian taste and they were good.

6. Promoter takes the band to dinner after sound check. If the locals take you out to a restaurant, pay attention to what they are ordering. They've been here. They know what's good or what to stay away from. Keep an eye on the clock. With a big table full of people, this dinner may take a long time. It may run right up until showtime. But the lead singer is with you and the show won't start without him.

Professional Catering

On the big tours where the venue is called a shed (which means arena on the far side of some city), walking to a restaurant will mean trooping through miles of parking lots. The tour hires professional catering that travels with a kitchen. They make breakfast, lunch, and dinner for the crew and band.

Dinner was ready every afternoon at 5 PM when we were on tour with the Dave Matthews Band. I think more than one band member fell in love with the caterers. It was the only tour I've been on where I never got a stomachache. Something as simple as knowing when and where dinner would be served each night takes a level of stress out of the road. And a freshly made delicious meal is always welcome.

The Record Company Dinner

Your label may invite you to dinner. Or a label that would like you to sign with them may make reservations for dinner at a very nice restaurant.

"I guess I like pasta; I like macaroni and cheese."–Record company dinner at a fancy Italian restaurant

This may be the first and only time in your life you see a *tip* that is bigger than what you earn in a month. Try to schedule this dinner on a night off. It will be rich, opulent, and leisurely. Why hurry through a $100 bottle of wine?

The lead singer will be adored by the president of the label or the head of A&R (who is going to be fired next week but doesn't know it yet). Bandmates are left happily amongst themselves or maybe they're seated across from the college radio guy (who will one day be an A&R guy).

Yes, yes, order another expensive bottle of wine. Savor each entrée. This will be one of the best meals you've ever have. Let me remind the novice record company diner that you don't have to eat *everything*, and you probably don't want to ask for a doggie bag. If you have a show within an hour, too much good food will make you feel really dopey onstage.

If you have an early-morning videotaping the next day, I am here to gently remind you of the food hangover. You may not care at this moment, so go ahead and polish off the asparagus and salmon hors d'oeuvres, the basil capellini marinara, crème brûlée, and fourth glass of merlot. The trouble with a food hangover is that it makes you look puffy and dark circled. A food hangover strikes both genders. However, one may be more familiar with concealer or a cucumber mask.

Dinner on Your Own

Sound check is over. You're starving and there is no pan of pasta or meal ticket for you to eat at the club. Hopefully there's a deli tray to snack on while you decide where to go for dinner. You want a restaurant within walking distance with quick service that's fairly inexpensive. The club may be able to give you a few recommendations. If you don't want to wander the streets, the bartender or the production manager may have a stack of menus of places that will deliver.

VEGETARIAN DINING. If you are a vegetarian, finding good food on the road is tough. Although cheese is what most of America thinks "vegetarian" means, eat sparingly. Our sound woman was keeping a tally of all the cheese sandwiches she had on tour. She wondered if she had to include all the ethnic variations of the cheese sandwich: pizza, quesadilla, lasagna, cheese omelet, quiche, nachos, cheese enchilada. It's all a cheese sandwich. And it can be hard to digest, especially if you're sitting in a van all day.

I've had a cheese sandwich on stale French bread. I guess tour has begun.

If you're near a university, you may be able to find a Thai, Indian, Italian, Middle Eastern, or straight-up vegetarian restaurant. Some even serve fish. You'll find soaked and cooked beans and fresh vegetables. Soups will be homemade, mashed potatoes will be real. You'll get a mixed green salad instead of white lettuce. (If you ask the waitress what's in the salad and she answers, "Why it's lettuce, dear," that means iceberg and you're not at a hippie restaurant.) If your restaurant options are few, you can order a "salad on a bun" at Subway. With cheese, of course.

GET SEPARATE CHECKS. If possible, get separate checks when you all go to dinner together. I don't know what law of higher mathematics applies, but you will always pay more than you owe when it's all on one bill. Somebody always pays less, so you will always pay more. And if it's a sushi dinner with sake you will pay *a lot* more.

> The damn group-check sushi dinner again. Never works. You wind up owing $36 for miso soup and four pieces of California roll. –Portland

If someone suggests, "Oh, we all had about the same thing. Let's just split this five ways," agree only if it's true (or you feel flush and generous). If you only had an appetizer and one glass of wine, ask to look at the check. Then pay for what is yours and add a bit more for the good of the group.

6. The Night of Your Show and the Morning After

Once doors are opened and the audience let in, the night begins. The opening band plays while you make a set list, choose what to wear, and prepare yourself for your show. Then it's showtime, and you're propelled to another dimension. Afterward you may want to decompress privately or you may like meeting fans and friends immediately. The after-show party commences and may take you to another club or a fan's house or hotel room. Before you disappear into the night though, you'll need to pack up and load out of the club. Depending on your tour routing, the bus may need to drive out tonight to get to the next town or you'll grab a few hours of sleep in a hotel bed.

GUEST LIST AND BACKSTAGE PASSES

During sound check, a sheet of paper will have been circulated for you to write your guest list names on. If I'm not sure my guests will be able to attend, I put them down anyway. That way I don't have to add them at the last minute. The club and your tour manager don't like it when you add a name twenty minutes before the show.

Write your initials after each name. The amount of complimentary tickets available to the band is written in your performance contract. Clubs are usually pretty flexible about the number of comps until you've pushed it too far. If they want to start taking names off the list, your tour manager will come find you and ask you which of your guests' names can be cut. Then you've got to let your friends know the guest list was too tight and they were bumped off.

At smaller clubs your guest can easily come backstage. At bigger venues, they'll be need a pass of some kind. Let your tour manager know which pass your friend should have to get them past security:

1. All Access (all access all the time)
2. After Show (access to backstage *after* the show)
3. Guest List Only (no backstage privileges)

Let your guests know that tickets and passes in their name will be at "will call" (the box office complimentary ticket line) or on a typed guest list at a table by the door. There may be several guest lists–one for the club, the promoter, the opening band, and the headlining band. If your friends are asked, "Who's list are you on?" tell them to give the band name–not your name.

Very often guest list names and passes get all screwed up by the time they get to the box office. The person with the list doesn't find your guest's name and begins to doubt she is even on the list. The club has heard it all before. Tell your guest to persevere and not give up. Hopefully the name will be found deep on page four, misspelled and written sideways. The ticket taker will check off your guest's name and hand her and her "plus one" their tickets and passes to allow them backstage. Often the backstage pass indication may have been lost as well and she'll be let in but won't have a pass to come find you.

FIGURE 9

If there's a problem and your guest's name isn't found, have her ask for the tour manager or send someone to find you backstage. She could try to call your cell phone, but if you're in the club you'll never hear the call. At the end of the night when you check your messages after the show, you'll hear her stressful message. She's standing outside the club and can't get in. Is there anything you can do to help? And you thought she just didn't bother to come.

SECURITY

Depending on the size of the venue, there will be security posted at the door of the club, in front of the stage, and by the door of your dressing room to keep you and your things safe. They aren't hired to be pleasant.

I make a point to say hello to security when I go past them into the backstage area. I'd prefer to feel friendly with the somber person sitting on a bar stool by the closed door rather than adversarial. And if I lose my pass, they might remember me and let me back in.

> "So, go to the south side entrance to the security booth and tell them you are here to unload. I'm sure they will be very nice to you."—Field Museum show

During the show they might stand with their backs to the band, facing the audience to "protect" you. After the show, when you've been clearly visible as part of the band and have just played the show of your life, they still might ask for your pass before letting you go into your own dressing room.

At the very end of the night they can be very tough on the crowd as they clear the club. Fans who are waiting to talk to you may be rudely and loudly told to leave. Have a meeting with the club if security is notoriously hard at this venue. You've just created a mood and an experience for the last two hours. Do fans need to be pushed around by security now?

Author Note: Despite security, more than one dressing room has been robbed of leather jackets, backpacks, and purses. I had a thick stack of laminates (collected from many tours) stolen one New Year's Eve. I had my entire purse (with saved-up per diems inside) stolen the last day of a tour. And I had money stolen from my wallet by one of our own crew who had a heroin addiction. When you leave the dressing room to go to the stage, hide things behind or under a couch or hand your manager your wallet for safekeeping.

CONCERT PHOTOGRAPHY

Bands often don't even think about a photographer taking pictures at the show until someone from the club runs into the dressing room moments before you take the stage and says something like, "Cameras are okay but no flash?" It sort of feels out of your hands, but it's not. (Note: If you invite a photographer to a larger venue show, he or she will need a photo pass to be allowed in with his camera and lenses.)

I asked rock 'n' roll photographer Matt Carmichael about rules and restrictions he's encountered when shooting concerts and his photographer suggestions for bands:

"Restrictions tend to be about time and distance. The general rule is three songs only (usually the first three songs) and no flash. We've had things like thirty seconds of one song and thirty seconds of the next song. We could only shoot the Red Hot Chili Peppers the seventh and eighth song, but then the publicist lost track of where they were in the set so we all just guessed and were sent out there whenever. It just shows how arbitrary it is.

"Increasingly, it's all about putting us photographers farther and farther away. One of the Smashing Pumpkins only wanted to be shot from one side. So there was literally a piece of tape on the floor we could not cross. Sometimes it's security reasons. If there are a lot of crowd surfers you're occasionally in the way and the band wants you gone. So some bands say, 'We're using the same space in front of the stage. We need to get you out of there.' You get to a stadium show and you're put forty yards from the stage, back by the soundboard. No matter what size lens you use you're only going to get a head-to-toe shot.

"It's helpful for bands to remember photographers are not your enemy. We're trying to make you look good. All the photos that bands grew up looking at–Jimi Hendrix lighting the guitar on fire at Montreux and Jim Morrison writhing around–those don't happen in the first three songs.

"You probably fell in love with rock 'n' roll looking at Johnny Cash flipping off Jim Marshall, the photographer. All these shots young bands have in their heads were taken by a photographer allowed to shoot them. And the more you restrict us from doing our job the less we can make you look good while you do yours.

"Bands think of their image–stage backdrop, clothes, light. Let that be captured for all the people who aren't there at the show who you want to have there next time.

"We're only there for a few songs. Be nice to us."

THE OPENING-BAND EXPERIENCE

Playing an opening slot with a headlining band is a great opportunity. Opening bands don't get paid much. It could be $50, $100, $250, or $500 if you're playing a big venue. It could be a "buy-on," in which you actually pay for the opening slot. But your name is advertised in the paper with theirs, so it raises your credibility. It looks like you might be friends with them. You'll be playing for the early arrivals to their show and hopefully gain more fans of your own. And you learn a lot about touring. You learn by watching how they do it. You learn by their techs yelling at you. "Camper Van Boot Camp" is what Bruce used to call being the opening act for Camper Van Beethoven.

An opening band is chosen for a variety of reasons. You might be hired because you'll set the right mood for the night or your sound is compatible with the headliner. You might be hired as a favor from the headliner's label to your label or booking agent. Perhaps the club just needs somebody to entertain the people who come early to talk and drink. You may simply be chosen because you're a solo artist or part of a duo and easy to get on and off the stage.

"If you're an opener you get spoiled with big crowds, good sound."

The Opener's Sound Check

You load in to the club as scheduled. Your sound check time comes and goes. The headliner is still checking. They rehearse a song or two. The singers are disagreeing with the band leader. The drummer and percussionist are telling a story about last night. The headliner seems to have no awareness that you'd love to get a sound check and probably need one more than they do. They may not even notice you are all standing there with your drums and amps and guitars spread out on the dance floor ready to move it all up to the stage when they're done. Truth be told, the headliner doesn't really believe you're any good until you actually play. If you are any good they figure you'll tough it out like they did when they were the opening act and didn't get a sound check.

Once the headliner is done checking and the stage is yours, you'll be setting up around their band gear. The headlining band's stage crew might be willing to move their pedal boards, but usually the amps and drum kit are staying right where they are. Be respectful of their stuff. Don't roll your heavy amp over one of their guitar cables duct-taped to the floor. (Pick up the amp.) Don't touch or move any of their equipment, ever. Ask their tech if something can be moved even a little bit.

"Hey, the gang's all here."–Tech, as we're loading in to the Great American Music Hall. "Hi, I'm Dan. Do you need a hand with anything?"

Moments later we realize this is not a tech but Daniel Lanois.

The house sound guys will be doing your monitors and front-of-house sound if you don't have your own sound guys. Sometimes you can hire the headliner's monitor person to mix your band. He'd probably love to be doing front-of-house sound for a change.

The headlining band may have taken so long to get off the stage that you may not get a sound check at all. You set up your stuff as the doors are opening and then look for your dressing room. If the headliner is famous, they may have taken all the dressing rooms. Usually you'll get the smaller one with some apples in a bowl and a six-pack of some domestic beer that nobody drinks. (It's okay to take this six-pack to the bartender and ask him to swap it for a beer your band likes.)

> The famous band has to have both dressing rooms–not that they use them. They've got the backstage and they've got their bus. So we sit in the office until the show is over.–Tippitina's in New Orleans

Showtime for the Opener

There may be only an hour between the end of your sound check and your show. You're the early band. If enough people aren't in the club at your scheduled start time, you may be asked to start a little later. Showtime is rather flexible in clubs. If you start late, ask the club if they still want you to stop at 10:00 PM or if you can play your whole fifty-minute set.

At bigger venues, showtime usually isn't so flexible. If you're the opener for the Dave Matthews Band at Red Rocks outside of Denver you'll start at 7:30 PM and end at 8:15 PM. You don't want to be late for your own show. If one of you goes back to the hotel after sound check, you may want to keep in mind the tremendous traffic jam caused by fans driving to the very show you are a part of. If you didn't plan for this you may find yourself stuck in concert traffic. Your band's start time may come and go while you're still in the cab on the freeway. Your bandmates are standing up in the dressing room thinking of songs they can perform for thousands of people without you. Whether you get there or not, your performance time will end at 8:15 PM. (This is a true story, and the lead singer hopped out of the cab, ran through the parking lot, pushed through security, and the show started only ten minutes late.)

As you take the stage, it may feel like you're walking onto someone else's stage. You're surrounded by the headliner's gear and in the gaze of mostly their audience, who may holler out their name. You can see people sitting with their arms crossed who don't bother to clap. Each night we were on tour with Dave Matthews he would give away his own entrance by walking onstage with us at 7:30 PM and introducing us as his "good friends." When I thanked him for this, he said, "Well, it dispels the cynicism."

I watched a solo opening act walk onto a stage—one man and a guitar. The audience was not there to see him. He took his time. He looked out at the audience, smiled, and stamped his foot forward like he'd accepted a dare to step over a line and say "mine." The audience loved him for it.

If you didn't get a sound check, it may be hard to hear yourselves during the show. There may be unsteady feedback and barely a vocal in the monitor, yet for some reason you've got a snare drum so loud your eyes water. The mix in the house may sound different than your usual show. There is a sound engineer trick to not give the opener full house volume. They'll explain that they keep the opener volume down so the evening has some headroom, has somewhere to go. It's also a way to make the headlining band sound more powerful during their show, now that every piece of sound gear is at full throttle. Push on through whatever bizarre thing happens. Give what you've been giving every night. You are probably doing better than it seems.

Play your strongest songs in the back half of your set, closer to the start time of the headliner's show. That's when most of the audience will be arriving. It's also when the headliner may have a moment to hear you play. Until then, they've been busy doing an interview or getting prepared for their own show.

When you're scheduled to stop playing, please end your set. If you're not wearing a watch, ask the monitor guy to signal 'two more songs' so you can end your set with the songs you like.

The Opener Backstage

Despite what you may perceive, the way to help your career is to rock hard and be nice to everybody. Don't beat up the club for five cases of beer. Stay out of the headliner's way. Don't invite twenty of your friends backstage to drink all the headliner's beer.

The headlining band will have a good-looking deli tray. You peer in their dressing room and see strawberries and fresh juices, French bread, cheeses, grapes, and chocolates. Traveling as the opening band with Robyn

Hitchcock, his entourage saw us eying their deli tray, which they were tired of. They'd seen this stuff every night for months. We were hungry. They were happy to invite us to come in and take anything we wanted (except the chocolate and red wine, as I remember).

Some of the famous performers you'll meet won't be so nice. This is something to watch and learn from. When you're the headliner or a famous performer, you don't have to implement this star treatment:

- Don't look [the artist] in the eyes.
- Don't watch [the artist's] sound check.
- Don't walk past [the artist's] dressing room on the way to the stage even though it's closer—no, you've got to walk all the way around.
- Everyone has to clear the hall before [the artist] walks down it.

Sitting in with the Headlining Band

The headliner may ask you to sing or play one song with them during their show. They'll love that you're able to bring backing vocals or a string line or percussion part that's on their CD into the live show. Don't ask to get paid for this. Love it and put it on your resume. They may hire you later to go on tour with them.

Be aware your bandmates may not all be so happy for you. If you have one main band leader in your band, he may be annoyed that he is paying you and yet the other act is getting the use of you. Make sure to give a little extra love to your own band to soothe any abandonment or competitive feelings.

Being around Famous People

The headlining band may be famous or their friends may be famous. If you're traveling as an opening band or performing at a major festival, you'll start recognizing famous artists or celebrities backstage. This may be the first time you are this close to fame.

> We were onstage and I looked left and there was Ethan Hawke in a baseball cap. It was like there was an Ethan Hawke movie playing stage left.
> —Irving Plaza, New York City

You feel like the universe is acknowledging you in some way, as if the band is on the right path to fame since it's there in front of you.

> I was standing stage right and the door opened and there was Perry Farrell wearing a big straw hat and then the door closed and he was gone.
> —Lollapalooza, Thievery Corporation stage

You want to know how to be relaxed and calm amongst the famous. Everyone is oddly drawn to them. So first, ignore that weird magnetic pull. You're interested to meet someone whose music or movies you admire, but in a way that feels like normal human behavior. If you're introduced, talk about something other than the fame, because once you start being a fan, they'll respond to you like you're a fan. It's how the exchange works. And never ask for an autograph. We are equals here, sort of.

> "Why would I sign your cello? I haven't even heard you play yet."–Michael Stipe, Athens

GETTING READY FOR YOUR HEADLINING SHOW

About an hour before showtime, everyone slowly gathers up from wherever they are and returns to the venue to prepare themselves for the show. You need to be backstage a minimum of thirty minutes before the show during the set changeover. On rare occasions the show is moved up thirty minutes, and where will you be? A set list has to be made, stage clothes chosen for the show, and even if you aren't aware of it, you have your own rituals that you'll want to go through to feel performance ready.

Author Tip: Before you disappear after dinner into a quiet cubbyhole of a distant dressing room, tell somebody where you are. That way if your bandmates don't see you in the dressing room before the show, someone knows where to find you and can go wake you up.

Making Your Set List

Your performance contract will specify your set length–usually seventy-five or ninety minutes. You can often play until curfew, but two hours is plenty long. More than that often seems too much, too bulky, to unwieldy, like you didn't craft your show. If you figure each song is about five minutes, your set list will have between fifteen and eighteen songs and four encores to choose from. Yes, not all your songs are five minutes, but when you add in talking, tuning, and audience applause, it'll work out to about five minutes a song.

There will come a night when a band member suggests that the band can just wing it without a set list. Override this impulse and make a set list. Some of the worst shows I've played are ones when the band thought a set list wasn't needed. The show never gathers steam and doesn't take off. When you have a set list, there's not so much lull between songs.

Some bands change the set completely every night. Dave Max got so tired of making a set list each night that we decided to play the songs alphabetically. (Fun and memorable, but not a seamless show.) You could play your new record from start to finish, but this poses problems. While it works well on CD, it doesn't necessarily translate to the stage. You could think like a DJ. Does the end of one song flow into the beginning of the next? Are the songs in compatible keys? Some bands have groups of songs—mini sets—that work well together and then will insert other songs that compliment the mood of the night.

A Note about Segues: You don't want your show to just be song stop, song stop, song stop. Segue some songs together, that way the energy of one just rolls into the next and rolls into the next. There's a theater saying: "Walk into the applause." Begin the next song before the applause stops. (Unless a quiet room is the perfect beginning for your next song.)

How do you make a good set list? The first three songs are your launch into the show. These songs welcome and warm up the audience that just got home from work, drove across town, parked, dealt with security, and found a comfortable spot in the room. You can start quietly and get bigger and then lift off. Or you can start with a bang and then back off and crescendo in again.

"Some shows you need to come out swinging."—Frank

Two-thirds of the way through your show is a false climax. Then, back the energy down and give the final three songs a fireworks finale. Some bands like to end with a huge explosion and then for the encore drop to a sweet caress to say goodnight. May everyone in the room go home, make love, and wake up tomorrow to the sound of your CD that they purchased after the show.

Selecting Your Stage Wear

Dress up for the show if you feel like it. Decorate yourself. Watch artists who inspire you. What are they wearing? What colors? Is the fabric coarse or smooth? Does their outfit seem to be inspired by another era? Another country? Is it close to their body or flow out from them? Don't copy what this artist does, but notice how clothes can be an extension of their music and their stage persona. The clothes you choose may help you access and express another part of who you are.

"Do you want to look just like the audience? People want to see the success, to see the mystique. Think of Loretta or Tammy Wynette. The country people know. They are the same as their audience and then they add the rhinestones and silk."

Change and explore what you wear just as you change and explore your music. Let a friend choose a shirt, a dress, a scarf, or some jewelry you'd never pick out on your own. As far as color, white makes you look bigger and helps you show up onstage. If you wear black, you'll blend in with the back curtain or a dark stage. Whatever you choose, feel at ease in your clothes or change into something else. Ingrid Bergman once said, "elegance is comfort." That is my best clothing tip.

Author Note: Take off your watch and your laminate and your sticky pass before walking onstage. These bind you to earthly things like time and space.

Choosing Pre-Show Music

There will be some sort of music playing in the house before your show begins. Usually it's a CD the house sound guy threw on between sets. It might be awful. You can choose to create a thirty-minute mood that your show will drop into. It could be a CD of an artist you love. It could be your bass player's instrumental side project. Or you could make the perfect pre-show CD. This CD could include a song that signals to the band it's time to have a show. On an early tour, when we heard "The Girl from Ipanema" we had four minutes to get to the stage.

Getting a Massage Backstage

Sometimes there will be a masseuse backstage. A friend of the band might offer to bring his massage table, or the festival you're playing has hired a masseuse for the artists. This is very generous, but be careful how you time this. It feels great to have the tension pounded out of your shoulders or kneaded out of your neck. But stop all massaging thirty minutes before the show. There's a certain amount of tension you're familiar with in your body, and after a massage you'll be floating. If you float to the stage, you'll have a strange show. A relaxed body with a very sharp mind is a good balance to have for a show. Give yourself thirty minutes after the massage to recover your wits. Plus, you'll have massage lines on your face from the headrest. It takes at least fifteen minutes for those creases to ease back into smooth skin.

The Countdown

It's helpful if a member of the crew announces in the dressing room when it's thirty minutes, fifteen minutes, and five minutes until showtime. ("Five minutes, Mr. Sinatra.") We've borrowed this countdown from the theater. There, the stage manager lets the actors know how much time remains for them to get into costume, put on makeup, or otherwise prepare themselves. It lets everyone know that all is on schedule, and it prevents you from being surprised when someone says "Showtime!" and you still have to put on your boots or go pee.

Sometimes the start of the show is pushed back because "there's still a line of fans around the block" waiting to get in or the opener's contract states they can play a full hour and not thirty minutes like the tour manager thought. If the crew let's you know this as soon as they know, you'll avoid being all primed and ready for the show only to have to wait and pace around for another forty-five minutes or go through some of your pre-show rituals a second time.

The Band Changeover

The opening band has finished. There's now thirty minutes to get their gear off the stage and get yours in place. Your crew (or you) should have the stage rock-ready so your band can walk on, plug in, and start the show. If your amp, pedal board, and mic stand were moved, they will be returned to their marked spot on the floor. Make sure amp and pedal settings haven't been inadvertently and radically changed during the move. Any cable unplugged after sound check to save on batteries should be plugged back in. Amps turned off should be turned back on and set on standby. If gear isn't ready, the show begins with a stutter as the problem is sorted out and the audience watches and waits. Ideally, you want to roll onto the stage and use the crowd energy and your own to begin the show.

Pre-Show Rituals

How do you prepare your mind or body for the show? Some artists meditate. Some artists like to talk, entertain, tell stories, or play guitar for everybody backstage like they're winding themselves up before they hurl themselves onto the stage. Some artists want absolute privacy an hour before the show. You never know who will walk by and say something that might unravel you. Then there you are onstage trying to shake the comment. You might watch a little of the opening act to get a feel for the audience or the room. I suppose you could have a cigarette in the alley outside the stage door now that many clubs are nonsmoking. Try to avoid having last-minute rehearsals of a song. You'll only confuse yourselves remembering which chorus is a double chorus. It'll be fine.

It often feels good to start moving, engaging your body so you feel fluid as you step onto the stage. If you're a singer, do some breathing or singing exercises you've learned along the way. You're warming up your body like you'd warm up the car on a cold winter day. Warm up the engine, the steering wheel, the leather seats. Warm is better than cold before you play. Cold feels like fear. Cold feels nervous. You want to invite the audience to get in a warm car and take a ride with you.

Some bands like to meet in a circle moments before walking onstage to acknowledge "we're with each other." A quick gathering is good, but if there is clapping or chanting that only a few people are into and others think is pretentious, stop the circle.

Getting to the Stage

It may be helpful if your tour manager walks the band to the stage. That way you get there on time and together. (Sort of together. One band member will be at the bar and one will have already made his way to the other side of the stage but no one knows he's there and everyone wonders where he is.) Backstage corridors might be dark and you may have to navigate stairs. Your tour manager can light the floor for you with a big flashlight. Or if you have to walk through the audience he can lead you through the crowd.

Often, you'll reach the side of the stage and wait. Is someone introducing us, you wonder? Are we just walking up? Is the front-of-house sound engineer ready for us? The house music ends and then starts up again. Then somebody has to pee and then someone wants to get a drink. You look at each other. You peer into the house. You ask the drum tech what's up. He doesn't know. Your front-of-house sound guy should give you a signal when he's ready to go. When he's ready and you've got the lead singer, it's time to walk onto the stage.

One Last-Minute Tip: As you walk toward the stage, relax your eyes, relax your tongue, relax your throat, relax your face. Breathe and relax your heart and relax your stomach. Lift your heart up and out. Now walk onstage.

THE SHOW

Playing your show is the reason you left home. It's what you've traveled all these miles to do. The preparation and hard work invested is now returned to you for the next two hours.

On the best nights, a show takes on a life of it's own. It rocks. It's raw and truthful. It digs deep and soars high. A bad gig feels like the show is at your feet, crumpled on the floor. It never stands up. Each effort seems self-conscious. The band and the audience want no part of each other. Maybe they blame each other for the show's failure. A rough show is often the result of bad preparation–poor promotion so nobody comes out, rushed sound check so now the sound onstage is so bad you can't lose yourself in the songs, or you've driven too many overnight drives in a row so now you're exhausted and can't shake your mood or your drug of choice to medicate your worn-out body alienates you from your mates. But you play like the band on the *Titanic*, because no matter how bad it is, it's not that bad.

> "I was looking for the good things. There's one. There must be another one coming."–Kornell tells us after a rough show

> "The performer has to win onstage. The crowd has come to see it."–Axl Rose

Stage Fright

The moment you first walk onto the stage and look out into the room is an odd one. You're onstage, but the show hasn't started. You may be nervous. Your breath may be fast. Palms sweating. Your knees are shaky. The familiar clichés are true. That nervousness under your skin is fuel for the show. Without it the next ninety minutes might feel like a Sunday afternoon watching an old movie. Invite the adrenaline on in. If it's overwhelming you, imagine breathing down out your feet and down into the stage. Breathe out your hands into your instrument.

Usually nervousness disappears and transforms into a sort of reckless passion once the show starts. Your muscles know how to do this even if your mind is ragingly unfocused. Look your bandmates in the eyes. Listen to one melody and answer it.

Trust all the shows that have come before tonight. They worked out just fine (for the most part). Stay focused on your bandmates playing next to you–the drummer playing drums like he gives massage, the cellist who makes you laugh, the distorted guitar that you love. You don't really need to think about the 17 or 1,500 or 30,000 people you're playing for. Listen instead to the tones you're creating and this song that you love.

> "If you just feel it, you can never fuck up."–Howe

Peggy Firestone, psychotherapist for many artists and performers, says, "Do you recognize how selfish fear is? What happens when you're afraid onstage? Are you generous? Do you give to the other players or to the audience? Can you feel that fear is closely related to excitement? Move the fear down your back through your adrenals into the kidneys and around to your belly and let it radiate up. This is the performer you can't take your eyes off of."

Still other performers suggest owning your place on the stage first and then open up to each other. "Make the stage your own," whatever that means to you.

> "Act like you've been there before and you're gonna be there again."–Max quotes Tom Landry

Musicianship

When you perform you've got to be better than in rehearsal. You've got to be show ready. You want to know your lyrics, and parts, and your instrument so well that the confusion of stage sound, stage lights, and stage nerves won't shake you.

> We felt confident tonight onstage. *Confidence*. Such a good word.

The band needs to rehearse enough to know the mechanics of the song instinctually, to be able to play it without thinking. If you rehearse too little, the song can go to pieces. There's a saying that "one show equals ten rehearsals." There is nothing like the laser focus to "burn it in"–to really know your parts.

There are probably millions of musical tips to give. Number one is this: Express something and express it completely and deeply. Play what matters to you and play like it may be the last notes you'll ever play.

> All you can do in this life is show who you are. It will take you to the right place.

> "Loss and redemption. It's all loss and redemption."–Jon Dee

Then, listen to the other players. Let somebody else express something. Respond to what you hear. It's a conversation. Doing this will also help you lose your stage fright.

It's fine and encouraged to stop playing sometimes. Give yourself some space. It doesn't have to be continuous sound. What happens when you stop? You'll wait until you hear something to play and then start again.

Decide to play something deliberately different. Go where you have no idea where you're going or how you're going to return.

Never try to recreate a great moment. It can't be done. If last night you played a great solo that everyone congratulated you for, you can't recreate it. Instead, think about what you did or thought right before the great moment.

A Note about Showboating: Showboating is essentially showing off. It's upstaging the song and the other performers by drawing extra attention to yourself. I used to just hate the predictable things showboating performers did to impress the audience—play high, play fast, hold the high note a long time. A vocal coach once said to me, "What harm is it? Some of the audience comes to be thrilled by that—to be taken by this larger-than life performance. It's interesting gymnastics but it doesn't move the soul."

Develop a radar for any performer around whom you begin to doubt yourself or feel insignificant. My jazz teacher in college, Professor David Norman Baker, told us very shy beginners, "Any famous performer that makes you feel small, he's not so big himself. The best players will be so generous they'll make you better. They are good enough and secure enough."

Author Note: You probably don't want to be drunk or really high while you're onstage. Your bandmates may notice your excesses before you do. Our tour manager decided to hold the liquor until after the show. It would be sitting on the table of the bus like a cake, like a dessert.

"I can always tell when he's been smoking pot because he's far away onstage."—Frank

What's a Musician Thinking, and What Are They Saying to Each Other?

What goes through a musician's head during a show? Sometimes it's just matter-of-fact: "Okay, we're coming up to that solo part and then everything goes up a step." Sometimes it has nothing to do with the show: "I hope some chips are left after the show and a beer, a good beer." Often thoughts are all over the place: "I hope Kornell comes over here and does the four corners with me." "Is Frank ignoring me?" "Why did the keyboard turn up for his solo and then 'forget' yet again to turn back down?" "I *love* this drumbeat. I've got to turn around and let El John know." "This is my favorite part of the song." "Do my cheeks look fat when I play the violin?"

Occasionally during the show, a band member will walk over to another and say something in the middle of a song. The audience sees this but doesn't know what is being said. Even the bandmate only half hears the words because of stage volume. It's oddly theatrical. Josh, our stage tech, told me, "I always wondered what you guys say to each other onstage." (*Author Note:* If you yell directly into someone's ear, it will hurt their ear. Either close their ear and yell or yell past their ear, not directly into it.)

What is being said depends entirely on the show. You could be teasing your bandmate that your solo beat his. It could be that the lead singer wants to skip the next song listed on the set list. It could be sorting out a personal problem from earlier today.

"Why do you hate me?" Dag looked at me, held up his hand, and started counting on his fingers before grabbing the next power chord.

As the show evolves, the raw emotion, the sheer volume, and the lights hypnotize you into a realm of feeling. Your thoughts become less as you're inside this language of music. You may check back to reality to make sure you don't trip over a pedal, or to unwind a knotted-up cable, or to check the set list for what song is coming up next. . . . and then you are transported again.

"Excuse me, I just played the solo of my life—was anybody with me on that? Excuse me, Frank, about a minute ago I played a solo that took me to the next realm and what I want to know is, did anybody hear that?"—Adam, after the show

Making a Monitor Adjustment

At sound check you had your monitor sounding exactly as you wanted. Since then, an opening band may have performed and the knobs on the monitor board didn't get returned to the exact spot for your mix. It's possible the instruments you've chosen to put in your monitor may have turned up and now they're way too loud. Or the whole stage is rocking on adrenaline and the level of sound you had in your monitor is now completely drowned out by the volume onstage. A monitor adjustment needs to be made.

Most likely you'll want more of yourself. You look to the monitor engineer and gesture. The communication to the monitor guy is all gesture. He has headphones or a cue monitor wedge next to him so he's able to hear exactly what you are hearing in your monitor. All he needs for you to do is point at whatever instrument or player you need changed and then point up or down. Remember to signal okay when the adjustment is right or he'll keep adjusting.

If the problem is critical or you can't get the monitor person's attention, you might have to leave your spot onstage to talk with him. But this is a last resort, as you've had to break from the show. Tell him succinctly what you need. He doesn't need to know that "earlier the guitar was so loud that the vocal was missing but now it is sounding better but what would really help—" Stop. Simplify. "Kornell up, loop up, keyboards down."

If your monitor has gone out entirely, point at it and make that knife-across-your-throat gesture that means it's cut, it's gone, it's dead. Most likely the monitor has come unplugged and the stage techs will track down and fix the problem. (If it's come unplugged he'll probably shoo the audience back away from your monitor wedge and tell them to get their drinks off the stage and please don't lean onto the monitor and unplug it again, and then hand them their coats that shouldn't be over your monitor muffling the sound.) If it takes awhile to get the monitor back on, remember that you've probably played in rehearsals without a monitor mix. It can be done.

We all get emotional about our monitors. Monitor guys know this. If you start asking for picky little monitor adjustments, they'll pretend to change it and look back up at you as if to ask, "How's that?" They haven't changed a thing. Sometimes asking for a monitor adjustment is asking for some attention. And your monitor man just gave you some.

Volume and Ear Protection

Why does it get so loud onstage? Some musicians love to bathe in their own sound. Others like to have just enough volume so they sing or play more strongly. It gets very personal and very emotional. Never, never, touch someone else's amp to turn them up or down.

> "Dynamics? I'm playing as loud as I can!"–Dave Max says this is the oldest joke in the classical-music world

STAGE VOLUME. Tone and volume and expression all go together. There's an eternal quest for tone. You'll find what you like, tire of it, and search again. Volume is often a component of your tone. There's a certain amount of volume that gives you the tone you desire at the level that expresses you.

> "It's not as loud as it appears to be on the loud songs."–Dag tells me during the show.

A band always knows who plays too loudly onstage every night. This person probably doesn't know it. The problem is, other musicians turn themselves up to hear over the loud person. Add show adrenaline and you've got a stage so loud nobody can hear anything.

I asked audiologist Mike Santucci why musicians like it loud onstage: "The emotional and physical correlate to volume in any music," he says. "It pumps your adrenaline. When things get loud it affects us physically–increases adrenaline and heart rate. It's a natural rush. People like that rush. It's like driving a Harley."

The solution to having a quieter stage isn't simply for the band to "turn down." Not everyone will, and there you are. The answer isn't "turn up," either, because it's not volume you need but definition of sound. Maybe there is no solution. Wearing molded earplugs can help define the sound and also protect your hearing. (See "Mike Santucci, audiologist, on Hearing Protection," page 158.)

FRONT-OF-HOUSE VOLUME. The band onstage may not realize how loud it is out front because the mains (main speakers) are in front of them. They have control over stage volume, but the front-of-house soundperson determines the decibel level in the house. There is a certain level they need to create an emotional and effective show. Some bands require in their technical rider that the club be capable of 103–110 decibels or the gig is off.

If the sound person is losing hearing from being at this too long, the mix may sound bright or brittle. This is because we lose the high end of our hearing first. To compensate, the sound person will add more brightness than is necessary.

HEARING LOSS AND PREVENTION. No one wants to lose his hearing. We're musicians. We love sound. To protect your hearing, you can wear squishy earplugs, but they'll muffle the sound. They're more effective for watching a show than playing a show. Some clubs offer them for sale behind the bar for a dollar or two.

You can be fitted for custom earplugs that are molded exactly to your ear canal and sound much better than the squishy ones. You can choose a 9-, 15-, or 25-db filter. If you need to sing, you'll have to get used to the sound of your voice in your head or pull the earplugs out a little bit.

MIKE SANTUCCI, AUDIOLOGIST, ON HEARING PROTECTION:

"Musicians come here [Sensaphonics] from all over the world, and there's some hearing loss from some very famous people and they're regretting it. Musicians come to me and say, 'I've already ruined my hearing.' I ask them, 'Is it gone yet?' They answer, 'Well, no.' I say to them, 'If you lose your hearing completely, then where did the quality of your life go? It's going to go down and there is nothing you can do about it for the rest of your life.' If I can get musicians to grasp onto something and protect 90 percent of their hearing . . .

"There are two time-exposure scales, and there's controversy over which one is correct. OSHA [Occupational Safety and Health Administration, the agency governing safety in the workplace] has a safety criterion based on how many decibels and how many hours exposed. The more the db, the fewer hours you can be in it. At 90 db it's safe to be in it for eight hours. That's 90 db 'A weighted.' 'A weighted' is a different scale than 'C.' Every front-of-house guy has his db meter on 'C.' At 'C weighted' it looks like you can handle more.

"Every time the volume goes up 5 db you cut your safety exposure time in half. So, if it's safe to be in 90 db 'A weight' for eight hours, at 95 db you get four hours. If people follow that stringently–it's all military and industrial tests–you still lose some hearing.

"In Europe it's a 3-db exchange rate. At 88 db you're safe for eight hours, 91 db for four hours, 94 db for two hours. According to the European scale you're safe for seven or eight minutes on a rock stage. We'd give up.

"Tinnitus is noise in your ears. Other things can cause noise in your ears. You could have too much caffeine, earwax, ear infection, brain stem disease, or exposure to loud sound. Think of ringing as an irritant like a runny nose for your whole life. The ringing is an irritant; 1.8 percent can't tolerate it. The others that get it don't think about it.

"I'd tell young musicians, see an audiologist as the number one thing. Get a hearing test. Get a base line to know 'here's where my hearing is now.' This gives you choices. Come back every year or two. The best thing is to wear personal hearing protection–custom plugs with the filters. Putting a Plexiglas shield around the drums is really more for shielding microphones. It may help protect the drummer, but it reflects sound back to the band.

"Hearing loss is permanent. There's no surgery for it, no medicine. It's a horrible thing. Don't let anybody tell you otherwise. Those big guys that like it loud, when they come to me they're upset. They get in a group of people and can't hear. And if they can't hear, they can't participate. It's too hard to concentrate. You answer inappropriately and others think you're high. It makes you look like an idiot. I saw a famous musician on Jay Leno one night. Jay said to him, 'You're going to need a shopping bag to get all those Grammys home.' The guy answered, 'Oh yeah, I had to take my wife shopping all right.' Musically, maybe you can get around hearing loss. Socially, you'll never get around it."

Stage Banter

You'll develop your own style for talking to the audience from the stage. You may tell stories or you may let the music speak for you and say nothing. If you're unsure what to say, play two or three songs, then say "hello" or "thank you" to the audience. Three songs later, you could tell a story or briefly introduce the next song. Trust your song. You don't need to tell the audience everything the song is going to tell them. Before the last song, thank them and maybe introduce the band. When you're done, say goodnight.

If you ask, "What's up, [city]?" or "Is everybody having a good time?" or clap your hands over your head trying to get everybody to clap, it just signals you're unsure onstage and don't quite know what to say or do. If you announce you've got CDs and T-shirts for sale in the back, you'll interrupt the mood of your show with commerce. If your merch is well placed, the audience will find it. And although you might work as a bartender when you're at home, you don't need to encourage your fans to tip the waitresses and bartenders.

Author Tip: You may want to know how to correctly pronounce the city you're in.

Large-Venue Tip: The bigger the audience, the slower you need to talk. And the slower their response will be.

Being Introduced

I like when musicians onstage are introduced for a reason—before a song they wrote, before a song where they are featured, or because they just rocked a great solo. Otherwise, being introduced can be a showstopper and uncomfortable for the one being introduced. You're happy for the acknowledgment, but what do you do at that moment?

> "It's the pinnacle of self-consciousness. We all wish we had some gesture, like pointing to the ceiling to God, so there was something we could actually feel comfortable doing at that moment."

Author's picky editorial: It's probably time to retire the Buddha, thank you, *namaste* hand gesture onstage. It's the one where your hands are praying at your heart. You're not a monk. You're not in a yoga class. You've been introduced as a musician onstage. Find a way to acknowledge the applause that feels comfortable to you.

Do you introduce your sound guy, monitor guy? Perhaps, yes, if it's been a great night or if it's the last night of a tour. But introducing the lighting guy, sound guy, everybody, well they aren't out there creating a relationship with the audience . . . you introduce one, you've got to introduce everybody. It'll bog down your show.

Weird Things Happen Onstage

Once the show begins, everything that happens onstage is good. Really. (Well, it should at least be perceived that way.) During your set, gear may break, mistakes will be made, and unexpected things occur. You may have to pee really badly. Or you'll get your period. Or you might be hit by a broken flying drumstick.

El Paso was sight distance to Juarez, Mexico. Did that have anything to do with all the problems we had? Wily little devils. Cables exploding, power loss on stage right, Alejandro couldn't breathe and had to take a break. Jon Dee filled in by singing and tripped on his pedal and fell back into the drums. But we would not fail. It was odd, not evil, just little traps of trouble.

PROPS FAIL. You may be using fog, fancy lighting, video, or a confetti cannon. All have the potential to fail or perform quite differently during the show than they did at sound check.

We walked out onto the stage of the Aragon Ballroom in Chicago in overabundant stage fog that had gotten ridiculously thick. We blindly felt our way, searching for our amps and instruments. Our only hope was to find the little red or green power lights on each of our amps. The brand new bassist was the last to find his instrument–still looking as the drummer counted off the first song. All we heard was, "Wait, wait, wait, I can't find my bass," from a foggy corner of stage left.

> "Stage fog is like an uncooperative stage prop," I said to John Convertino as we watched the fog float up and off stage left, missing the band entirely.–Urbino, Italy

GEAR BREAKS. Your gear that worked perfectly at sound check and has shown no sign of trouble for weeks will suddenly decide during the show to stop working.

> "I don't know why it's acting up now. Now that it's worked its way into my life."–Dag's new pedal broke

It's hard to track down what the problem is. The pedal? The cable? The power supply? The jack? How do you sort this out in the middle of a rock show? Remain calm. Let the tech run around with cabling wound around his shoulder and neck. He doesn't know what's wrong either, but his job is to look efficient, and having a cable ready looks like he knows.

Our stage manager, Matt Morrison, advises, "Check that cables are plugged in all the way and haven't been accidentally pulled out. Make sure each pedal is getting power. Then stomp on each to make sure the light comes on." If you still have no sound, bypass all pedals. If that doesn't help, get a new cable from the tech.

Author Note: As the problem is solved, the tech probably shouldn't tell the band member that it was their fault something didn't work. Let's be happy that the technical breakdown is over and the show can go on.

ELECTROCUTION. We call it "getting shocked," but it's electrocution by another, kinder name. Your crew should have sorted this out already at sound check so it doesn't happen to you. But then, mid-show, you're touching the strings of your guitar and you put your lips to the microphone. You get a shock like a snakebite on the lips. If it's really bad you might see an arc of blue light and the lights dim. Supposedly you just flip the ground switch on your amp and it'll be okay, but for the rest of the show you'll stand far, far away from your microphone.

MISTAKES. Most mistakes can be faked through. Half the band goes to the chorus and half the band continues into the bridge. Everyone onstage knows it, but the audience probably doesn't. If the rhythm section and the singer can find the same place, the song may survive.

Your front-of-house engineer should be pulling faders to try and mask the song that's falling apart onstage. Trust him or her. Stewart Bennett, sound engineer, once told me, "If I'm doing my job, you shouldn't think about me. All you think about is the stage."

> Everything I could imagine going wrong did. Videos failed. Singers went one way, the band went another; major key over minor key. The loop was two bars behind us. I just trusted Martin to pull faders, hiding the mess.

The Audience

The audience is truly a part of the show. You're all standing with each other in one big room responding to whatever is happening. Some cities seem more or less responsive than others.

"The steel industry has really taken it out of these people."–Dag

Regional Audience Myths: The northern audience is quieter than that of the South. The South is more enthusiastic than the North. Big cities are less impressed than smaller towns.

An audience isn't completely anonymous to the band. The audience is what you're watching, although you can only see the first four or five rows of people. Beyond that you see shapes and shadows. You notice if someone yawns or holds up a cell phone. You can see people singing lyrics, or trying to. If someone brings a harmonica and plays along with the band, you will hear it.

The people in the front often try to get your attention and talk to you. (Um, there's a show going on here, and I can't have a conversation just now.) Also, if we're wearing in ear monitors we can't hear anything but the monitor mix of the band in our head.

Sometimes a person in the front row will hand you something.

Sometimes things are thrown to the stage. These items can include:

- A room key wrapped in a note with a phone number and room number
- A CD of a band (Really not a great idea. We rarely get around to listening to them.)
- Lacy panties (Yes, it does happen.)
- A piece of paper with a song request
- A lengthy note that the owner of a restaurant you used to love and frequent but now closed is here and wants to see you after the show
- A hat
- A beach ball (They come slow motion through the air to the stage. We're part of the chain, so we send them back out into the audience. It probably feels good to have something physical come from the stage, but we're not at the beach and I always think we're going to trip on them or they'll knock over a guitar or mic stand.)
- One dollar bills
- A tray of drinks; nice, thanks!
- Half-cute, half-drunken girl who wants to dance with the lead singer during a song about his mother dying of cancer. Let your crew know ahead of time how you want to handle this. Poi dog Pondering used to let the girl dance one song or a half a song. Then the stage manager would gently escort her off.

> During "Castanets," the cowgirls got up onstage and danced–short skirts and cowboy boots.–Continental Club, Austin

FAINTING OR FIGHTING. Standing close to each other in a tight, hot club, your fans may faint. You can see when someone gets overheated up front. Their face gets pink and flushed or completely white. Their eyes get watery and have no focus. Happiness has left their face. Offer them water. They are about to pass out.

I've never seen a full on fight in the audience, although you can see it gather up if it's crowded and people are bumping each other. Gestures get faster. The crowd steps back. There's pushing. If you see this happening, you have some power from the stage to calm things. Charlotte asked the crowd to "introduce yourself to your neighbor." Frank asked those in the back not to push forward. Choose to play a very calm song to settle the room down. Have the techs hand out water.

HECKLERS. We call people who yell stuff hecklers, but they're usually just bossy fans who've been drinking. Usually what they yell isn't negative, it's just disruptive. And often we can't quite hear what someone yells. You hope it's positive.

> Someone yelled, "We love you, Paul." Except, Paul isn't here. He doesn't even play in the band anymore. And then they yelled for "Big Constellation." We had just played it.

Yelling for "Free Bird" is sort of funny again because it's such an old cliché. I suppose the band could cue up an iPod and play "Free Bird." No one has really heard it in a while. It's actually quite lovely.

TALKERS. The band wants to play their songs. The audience has paid to get in and wants to hear the show. The band hates to have to shush the people who are talking. I watched a singer look directly at a group of talkers and play quieter and slower, quieter and slower until they noticed and stopped.

Author Note to Talkers: When you go out with your friends of course you want to catch up. But once the show starts, wrap it up or go somewhere else far, far, far from the stage.

Playing an Encore

There is the show and there is the pretend goodbye and then you return and play the last two or three songs. Unless it's been a horrible night, the band always wants to come back to play the encore. When the band leaves the stage they have an adrenaline-fueled minute in the hallway or in the dressing room. Some band members grab beer or water. Someone has to pee. Several are quickly deciding what to play for the encore and want get back up to the stage before the applause stops.

> We left the stage before the encores and got locked out of the building. An audience member heard us banging on the door and let us back in.

If the audience applause sounds half-hearted or is dwindling, the band can choose not to go back out. The audience has to hold up its end of the encore bargain.

During the encore, you may want to invite a surprise special guest onstage to play a song with the band. You've played your show. Now you may want to add something completely unexpected. It can be a treat for both the audience and the band to have another guitarist or singer bring their presence into the song and the stage. The right guest is fabulous. Even if they don't know the song well, it's still fun. The wrong guest may want to stay on for too many songs or doesn't know when to step back and let the band just do what it does. If things are getting weird with your semi-famous guest, give him a hug and say into his ear "Fantastic! We're

going to do this last one on our own." Then end the night the way you'd
like to.

Choosing Post-Show Music

If you feel like the show is complete ("That's it. We're done. We can't
top that."), tell your stage manager to signal the house sound guy to put
on the after-show CD you've chosen. You've spent the last two hours
creating an emotional experience. Don't destroy it with some god-awful,
terrible music now. The right music will complete the show. It will
escort the audience, the band, and the club into the remainder of the
night.

THE AFTER-SHOW PARTY

The show is over. You've played an encore or two. It was either a fabulous
night or not. Rarely do we all agree on what kind of night it was.

You'd like to have a beer or a drink and let your heart rate return to normal. In your dressing room, there might be a tub of beer and one red and
one white bottle of wine. Hopefully the opening band and their friends
didn't finish all your refreshments before you got offstage.

> The bartendress says we can have whatever we want at the bar. It will be
> on Wally's tab. I don't know who Wally is, but I think he's a great guy.
> —Champagne Urbana, after the show

Dressing Room Privacy

It's up to the leader of the band to decide what the backstage policy is
immediately after a show. Some bands like to keep the dressing room clear
for fifteen minutes to wind down with each other privately; to have a
quick after-show postgame wrap-up without witnesses. The band is in
another dimension after performing and perhaps isn't ready to talk just yet.
Maybe you'd like to change clothes and drink some of the good beer
before your guests and their friends drink it all. Some bands are okay if fans
just come blasting backstage even before the encore is played. Let your all-
access guests know what the band prefers.

If the backstage area has two rooms, consider having one for band
only, that's not accessible to fans. Valuables can stay there. Any band member who isn't ready for the after-show party and wants to just chill out can
relax there privately.

Meeting Your Fans

After the show you may meet some of your fans. They will have been enjoying your show and drinking for several hours. They may be unusually open.

> After the show a girl came up to Matt Fish and said, "We had eye sex, didn't we? Do you want to make out in the bathroom?"

They may not remember seeing you onstage at all.

> "Did you play tonight?"

They may have bold opinions and want to tell you how your set should go or why your record sucked or how you should play at their friend's club or how you should smile more.

> "I bet my boyfriend $5 he could make you smile."

> "Why did you kick [insert ex-band-member name here] out of the band?"

Hang out with people you enjoy. When you return to this town, it will be nice to see them again. Don't give too much of yourself to the drunken fans that won't remember the conversation tomorrow.

If a difficult person needs to be removed from the dressing room, find your tour manager. He should be very gentle with them. You don't want to piss off a drunken fan. But you also would like him to leave.

BACKSTAGE DREAM ETIQUETTE:

- Do not monopolize the lead singer or anyone in the band.
- Don't drink all the beer. Don't even take any until it's offered to you.
- If you're drunk, ask your friends to take you home now.
- Please hold up your end of the conversation.

> His friend was a little tipsy but nice. She had a martini glass in her hand and I asked her, "Is that a cosmopolitan?"
>
> She stumbled over to me and said, "Well, actually, I'm in nursing school."

Compliments and the Worst After-Show Compliments

Learn to accept a compliment about your show. Accept it thoughtfully—as if no one had said this to you before. If a fan tells you it was a great show yet you think it was horrible, simply thank them. There's no need to tell him or her how it was awful. Don't take away the experience they just had. Occasionally the compliment is unintentionally insulting or off the mark. We fondly remember these as the worst after-show compliments:

- "I can't tell you how great that was."–Steve Goulding made this one up.
- "How long you been playing, roughly?"–Evidently Bob Wills was famous for this.
- "I used to play cello until the grade school burned down. Burned all the cellos, seven violins, and most of the trombones." –Backstage in Houston
- "My grandmother plays the cello."
- "Great drumming. You were a great drummer. Don't ever quit."– This was to our bass player
- "It's too bad you're overlooked."
- "Your violin sounded like a viola."
- "You were very technically proficient."
- "Where'd you go to school?" "IU at Bloomington." (One of the top music schools in the world.) "That's okay; I went to a state school, too."
- "You really dug yourself into a hole with all those pedals, but you found your way out at the end."–to Matt Fish after his Jimi Hendrix cello solo
- "I told my husband, 'She looks scrawny enough, but I bet she'd beat me in a fight.'"
- "I love you guys. Are you in Wilco?"
- "You were great. Don't ever quit. What band were you in?"

Signing Autographs

Asking for an autograph is usually an acceptable invitation to have a five sentence conversation with the performer. It's a pleasure, and it's surprising the first time someone asks for your autograph.

> "I took a taxi to sound check and some people were already in line for the show. Some guy flips out a book and asks for my autograph while people look on and wonder. I wonder, too."–Lounge Ax, Chicago, dead of winter

Sometimes a fan asks for an autograph to impress his friends that he was backstage and met you. Sometimes it's a desire to be near the energy that was just onstage. And sometimes, someone feels a real and deep connection to you and your songs. Take the time to give an autograph. Look in the person's eyes. Ask his or her name. Write it on the CD and then sign your own.

A black Sharpie fine-point permanent marker is the best pen for signing autographs. The ink shows up well on posters, CDs, dollar bills, breasts, and bellies. It writes easily so your hand muscles don't cramp up. Have the tour buy a box of them or ask for them in your rider, because they disappear.

Accepting Presents

Occasionally someone at the show has a crush on you or simply enjoyed the show so much they want to give you a present. Often it's their own jewelry. If it seems too valuable and you sense they'll regret their gesture in the morning, thank them and decline. If they absolutely insist, you could say, "I'll hang onto this for you, but next time I see you I'm handing it back to you." Regarding gifts of brownies and cookies: a fan won't likely poison you, but they may bake a lot of pot in those cookies.

GETTING PAID

The top two rules of getting paid from Chris Von Thies, head talent buyer, Direct Events, Inc.: "First, have somebody sober settle. Second, never leave without getting paid."

There is a finesse to being paid accurately. The club has done this a million times. Soon you'll want an experienced tour manager settling for you. But early in your career you're most likely on your own. It's a good idea, upon arrival at the venue, to meet the person who will be settling with you. Discuss when and where the settling will take place to make sure there's no confusion at the end of the night.

Then, at the scheduled time, take your contract, calculator, and settlement sheet (Figure 10) with you into the production office. If it's been a good night there will be stacks of cash on the desk. Sometimes there's so much money you feel it's not polite to look at it.

> "You can't cheat a drunken promoter." Heinz says the promoter was the most drunk he's seen anyone in a long time. "He threw a wad of money at me and said, 'Count it.' He gave me too much."

Contract Expenses

If you have a straight guarantee, you'll be paid the guarantee and off you go. If you are being paid a percentage only or a guarantee plus "85 percent of the gross box office receipts after all approved and documented expenses and a promoter profit of 15 percent on expenses," it can be tricky,

Settlement Sheet

date
venue
city
capacity
attendance

box office

category	price	sold	comps	gross
advance				
dos				
dos 2				
total				

summary

gross

tax

adjusted gross   *Notes*

expenses

promoter profit   *Support*

total expense

net after show expenses   *Deal*

band %

guarantee   *Club Info*

artist earnings

less deposit

less cash recvd   *Promoter*
                                                       Rep@Settle
balance due   *Specific Night Info*

check received   # -

final

date
venue
city

FIGURE 10

especially at bigger venues. Look carefully at the Contract Expenses page
of your performance contract (Figure 11(b)).

HIGH ROAD TOURING

Phone:
Fax:

DEAL MEMO

Offer #
Contract #

Artist:
Date(s):
Venue: Great American Music Hall
859 O'Farrell St.
San Francisco CA 94109
USA

Purchaser: Music Hall, LLC
333 11th Street
San Francisco CA 94103
USA

Contact:					*Signatory:*		*Contact:*
No of Shows:	1	*Showtime(s):* 9:00 PM			*Production:*		
No of days:	1	*Onstage:* 9:00 PM (approx)					
Load In:		*Curfew:*					
Sound Check:		*Age Limits:* All Ages					
Doors Open:	8:00 PM	*Set Length:*					

Tickets:

Quantity	Price	Comps	Deducts	Description	Totals	Ticket Surcharges:
600 @	$			GA		Phone:
						Remote:
						Box Office:

GP:	$	*Capacities: Building:*	600	*Merchandising:*	*Ticket Sales:*
Tax:		*Per Show:*	600	*Merch [BuildSell]:*	*On sale date:*
NP:	$	*Total Tix:*	600	*Merch [ArtSell]:*	*Ads begin:*

Scaling Notes: General admission, partially seated club show
Deductions: $1.00 per ticket, facitlity surcharge
Terms:

Deal Notes:
Additional
Provisions: Contracts are due at least one month prior to performance.. Waiver on all merch fees for recorded product has been granted.

Other Artist(s):

Payments:

Full payment to artist on night of show. All overage monies are due Artist immediately following the performance herein via cash only.
Notwithstanding anything to the contrary in this agreement, Artist's settlement on the night shall be in cash only.

Page 1 of 2

FIGURE 11(a)

HIGH ROAD TOURING   Phone:
                                          Fax:

DEAL MEMO   *CONTRACT EXPENSES*

ARTIST   Contract #
                                                    Issued:
Showdate(s):
Venue:

Tickt Price(s): $
Venue Deducts: $
Tickt Surchrg(s): Phone: Remote: Box Office:
Capacity: Sellable Cap:
Gross Potential: $ Taxes: Net Potential: $
Purchaser:
Note:

EXPENSES   *Mark to the right of the variable denotes amounts used in agency estimates and deal calculations below.*
                $ Amount   Description   *$ Amount   Description*   *Artist Guarantee:* $

Ads Nat	Permits	
Ads Local	Phone/Fax	
Ads FlyPost	Piano	
Ads Radio	Police	
Ads Leaflets	PRS	
Ads Poster	Rigger	VARIABLES
Air Travel	Runner	Rent Guarantee
Backline	SecPvt	Rent Cap
Barricades	SecT-sht	Rent % %
BoxOff	Setup	Rent [ph]
Catering	S&L	Tkt Cmsn % %
ChairRent	Spotop	Tkt [ph]
Cleanup	Spots	Tkt Cmsn Cap
DressRooms	Staff	Insur % %
Electrician	Stage	Insur (ph)
Elecpower	Stghnds	Credit Card % %
EquipRent	Stgmgr	Credit Card [ph]
Firemen	Txprnt	Credit Card Cap
GroundTrans	Tksell	% %
HseExpl/Nut	Tktake	[ph]
Hotels	Towels	Total Variables 0.000
Immigration	Venue Hire	Total Fixed Exp: $
Ins Liab	Ushers	ESTIMATES
Ins Cancel	Utilities	Break Even $
Loaders		Break Even Units
Meal buyout		Break Even %
Medic		
Misc		
Monitors		
PayTx		
Parking		

                            Subtotal Exp $

Deal Notes:

FIGURE 11(b)

Most of the deductions will seem reasonable although surprising if it's the first time you've had to pay them: local ads, box office, catering, insurance, medic, stagehands, production techs. Some of the expense deductions you'll wonder about. "PRS" stands for performing rights association, like ASCAP or BMI, that needs to be paid. "Sec T-shirt" means T-shirt security. Jackson Haring of High Road Touring told me, "T-shirt security is different than uniformed security . . . football players from the state university." "S&L" stands for sound and lights. Jackson: "If the promoter goes into a room that doesn't have sound and lights, he'll need to bring them in."

The headlining band and opening band guarantees and the expenses are totaled and then subtracted from the take at the door. The amount left (if any) is split between the bands and club by the percentages agreed on in the performance contract.

Chris Von Thies advises: "As an artist settling your own shows, be smart about it. If you're doing well enough to command a decent guarantee, to settle with a real promoter, it's a big step. When you settle, it's best to be smart about it. Ask for receipts and verification that this money was used for these expenses. If there's no proof at settlement, if the club doesn't have receipts, you don't have to accept the expense. Good tour managers will squeeze as much money as they can out of any given club. They'll go through each expense item line by line."

Example: If the club is deducting $800 in towels as a show expense, you'll want to ask to take them home and also ask the club to produce a receipt for $800 of towels.

Padding

Some of the expenses will be padded–made to look more than they are. Chris Von Thies: "There's a certain amount of acceptance of padded expenses. It's hard for the promoter to document the advertising expenses in multiple markets of radio, TV, print. How do you put a price tag on graphics people that put time in that you can't document? Some of those pads are justified. It's not that the promoter wants to be a bad guy. Those expenses are there, but there's no way to document them."

Reduction in Guarantee

If you're being paid a guaranteed amount but the audience wasn't as big as hoped, the band can accept less. Chris Von Thies: "I've never not paid somebody, but I have asked for money back. If you want to play at a venue again it's nice to give even a small gesture if the night didn't do so well. If you have a $2,000 guarantee but you give back $250, it's a gesture to the promoter. You have expenses and the club has expenses. It's nice to meet somewhere in the middle. It's called a reduction in the guarantee."

Cash or Check?

Ask the club for payment in cash. They may want to give you a check. Hand it back to them and ask if there is any way they can turn it in to cash. Brad Madison from Mongrel Music urges, "Always get paid in cash."

There are exceptions. Chris Von Thies: "If a big band tanks with a $40,000 guarantee, I'll say to them, 'Here's five grand in cash and here's a check. We'll tell you when it'll be good.' You want to play at a reputable club with a promoter or club owner that you know and can trust so that check *will* be good. But when you're traveling from point A to point B you can't always do that. You need to fill in the date and you roll the dice. On the other side, if the promoter doesn't know the artist, they are taking a gamble as well. It's all a gamble really."

Buy a locking zip bag to keep the tour money in. Use this cash to pay tour expenses rather than putting expenses on a card. If you are accumulating too much cash, turn it into a money order and send it home to management.

TOUR ACCOUNTING

You'll knock on your tour manager's hotel room door one night. He's in his boxer shorts having a beer, watching TV, with tour receipts spread out all over the bed. He's doing the tour accounting. He knows he has to do this at least once a week or receipts get lost and information becomes less clear.

Every tour manager has a different method of keeping track of income and expenses while on the road. Some simply throw all the receipts from the day into an envelope, put the date on it, and let the manager at home sort it out at the end of the tour. Some are instructed by management to keep a very current, accurate accounting of road income and road expenses using Excel or QuickBooks.

Weekly Income Report					
Beginning Date:March 30					
Ending Date:April 6					
Date	City	Venue	Total Cash from Promoter	Net Merch Income	Misc Cash Income
03/30	Bridgeport, CT		940.00	435.00	
03/31	Kutztown, PA		1,150.00	280.00	
04/01	New Brunswick, NJ		1,150.00	25.00	
04/02	Off				
04/03	Washington, DC		2,500.00	280.00	
04/04	Aston, PA		1,350.00		
04/05	Reading, PA				
04/06	Durham, NH				
		Totals	7,090.00	1,020.00	

FIGURE 12

Figure 12 is a weekly income report. It shows the date, city, venue, show income, and merch income for each night and a total of each for the week.

Weekly Tour Report		
Beginning Date:		
Ending Date:		
Envelope #	Item	Amount
1	Airfare	-
2	Auto Rental	-
3	Auto Expenses	-
4	Bus Driver Fee	-
5	Bus Expenses	-
6	Equipment Maint/Repair	-
7	Fedex/Messenger	-
8	Hotels	182.98
9	Local Transport	-
10	Per Diems	315.00
11	Production	-
12	Telephone/Fax	-
13	Tips	-
14	Truck Expenses	89.00
15	Tolls:	17.05
16	Advances:	-
	Total Expenses	604.03
	Cash from Show Income	7,090.00
	Cash from Merchandise Income	1,020.00
	Misc. Income	
	Float to road	435.00
	Total Income	8,545.00
	Balance Forwarded from Last Report	903.01
	Less Expenses	604.03
	Less Money to Office	7,665.00
	Balance Forwarded to Next Report	1,178.98

FIGURE 13

Figure 13 is a weekly tour report. This is the tally of the expenses and income for the week. Some of this money will be sent to management. Some is kept to pay for next week's tour expenses.

Author's big tip about your tour income and taxes: When you get home, go to your bank and open a tax account. Throw money in there for taxes (perhaps fifteen percent of your earnings) that you will have to pay come April 15. You don't want to see a $4,000 tax bill that you can't afford. And if you sort of ignore your inability to pay year after year, you're going to have an expensive mess to sort out when it catches up with you.

PACKING UP AND LEAVING THE CLUB

It's been a great night. Everyone lingered until the last. But now the club guys say they're sorry but it's time for you to leave. Everyone still lingers.

> Alejandro has been buying us Petron. If he can't drink, he'll order for us. Someone comes in and says the only thing that will get us to leave the bar: "Your bus driver is out front."

Thank everyone who helped you out tonight—the opening band, the monitor guy, the lighting guy, the sound guy, and your hospitality person. If he or she has been especially helpful, you can tip them. Tip your bartenders. They probably poured you free shots.

> "My brain is not as drunk as I appear to be." The bartender sent us a tray of seven-layer shots.—Baton Rouge

The two people at the club whose names you might want to remember for next time: the house sound guy and the owner/production manager (and maybe the bartender, although bartenders and wait staff seem to be short term). On the next tour, when you arrive back, it'll be a bit like seeing old friends. And on a long tour that's a happy thing.

Take water, drinks, and good snacks from the deli tray. It does seem wasteful that the club tosses those vegetable trays at the end of each night. But unless you are the band that has a juicer and wok with them and your cook can make stir fry and carrot juice before giving you a quick massage, leave the veggie tray at the club. Take only the food you know you'll eat. You'll be very happy to have your bus well stocked.

> "Now this is how you properly leave a club." He stood in front of us and every pocket was full of fruit or beer.

Your tour manager may be able to talk the club into another case of beer. Chris Von Thies: "You want the artist to come back. You do as much as you can to make sure they have a good time and the fans have a good time. If the artist is having a good time, it trickles down. There's no point in the production guy arguing with a tour manager over a bottle of Jack. If a bottle of Jack will make the headliner happy, will make this guy's night, give it to him."

LOAD-OUT

If you have a crew, they have been packing up and loading the bus or trailer while you've been enjoying yourself at the bar. If you don't have crew, you'll pick up your beer or whiskey drink and pack up your pedal board, put the cover over the amp, and roll your stuff by the other road cases ready for load-out. You loaded in. Now at the end of the night you load out.

The club will have loaders to help your band load out if you've requested this on your technical rider. Still, every band member should be a part of load-out. It's good for morale. Everyone knows who helps and who doesn't. Even if you don't lift the heavy amps, carry the smaller gear. Later your crew may do all this loading for you. They'll slap letters and numbers on the amps and road cases that specify what bay and what order each piece goes in— rather than making up a new pack each night, like we do now.

THE FIVE STAGES OF LOADING THE TRAILER:

1. Everyone agrees it's time to load out.
2. Two guys are loading and two guys are off somewhere else.
3. The bass player leaves to get some food.
4. Three guys are gone and you're at the van by yourself.
5. You call home on your cell phone. "This is fucking shit. I'm so done with this."

Author Note: In extreme temperatures, bring the instruments (especially the wooden ones) into the hotel at night. An ice storm in Nashville cancelled our gig, and we left our instruments in the trailer. It seemed like they would stay warm together like sled dogs. They seem to be warm-blooded when we're holding them. Fortunately, they made it through the icy night just fine, but cold will crack wood so bring them inside.

"Radio Pack": If a radio show is scheduled before load-in tomorrow, you'll have to adjust the normal packing of the trailer and separate out the instruments and pedal boards to be used. If not, half the trailer will have to be unloaded tomorrow to find a keyboard.

Load-Out Robbery

During load-out, *always* have a spotter watching the gear piling up outside the trailer as others go inside to get more. If you are approached by someone who is talking a lot, keep an eye on that gear. Don't be distracted. This is how magicians make things disappear–make you look over here while something is actually happening over there.

It's best to have more than one person watching the equipment. Why? If a thief grabs a guitar and runs off, your one spotter chases him, leaving the rest of your gear vulnerable to his thief friend. If you have a second spotter, the gear is still watched.

Load-Out Injury

Musicians and crew get hurt during load-out. There's a little drinking, a little lifting and twisting, and muscles get pulled. Fingers get banged. A rolling case may roll down a ramp into the merch guy, who happens to be at the end of the ramp folding shirts back in the box. Take your time. Pay attention to how you lift. Know what is too much for you and ask for help if something is too heavy or awkward to carry. Always wear shoes when loading.

THE AFTER AFTER-SHOW

The tour manager will let everyone know when the van or bus is leaving the venue to go back to the hotel. If you decide to continue on to the next bar or a party at someone's home, you've left the force field of the tour and are on your own.

> "I was having trouble forming complete sentences. I didn't think I should be going to a party."

Your new friends may take you to an Al Capone hangout or to hear a great DJ. You'll get to see something besides the club and the hotel. Just be in your bunk when the bus rolls in the morning.

> "I've seen how these harmless adventures turn into epic odysseys."
> –Tequila in San Antonio.

Going to Another Club for One Drink

Will the party reemerge at another bar or should you go home? If you choose to continue on into the night, the next bar may be simply be a "drinking bar" or may be a unique place in the underbelly of an old city.

> We walk deep into the French Quarter, by the graveyard or catacombs of Jackson Cathedral to the absinthe bar John had found earlier. Carried

glasses of absinthe back for the crew, sipping them as we walked down Chartres, past Jackson Square, past a couple of friends arm in arm puking —one night of Mardi Gras winding down and a bus party starting up.

The band has discovered and informed me that if I apply for a job at the gentlemen's club next to the hotel they'll all get in for free.

Going to a Party at a Fan's House

Bar time may end and a group of fans may invite you to come back to their house for a party. Often these parties don't work out. And definitely don't agree to drive to a party thirty miles away. You may arrive, find no party, pick up someone's dog, and drive thirty miles back to the bus party.

> "If you can't hear it as you're coming down the street and there's no one making out on the front lawn, you know it's not a party–just five people sitting on a couch, smoking some pot, and looking at each other."–Max

It has happened that the hostess at your party drugs the band's tray of drinks. We're not sure why. You may leave the party, start walking in what you hope is the direction home, sit down for a moment by the river, and suddenly it's dawn and you're waking up under some bushes.

> "I went to this totally great party and wound up passing out by the river."
> "That's funny; so did Susan. Thank God she wasn't alone." (A road romance was almost busted.)

How Will You Be Getting Home?

There comes a time to say goodnight to this party. The person who drove everyone here probably shouldn't be driving, although maybe she's asked you to spend the night.

> "She got into the tequila. Her face was a little red and her eyes were going two directions and she asked me, 'Do you need some help getting into bed?' I turned her down."

Our bus driver gave us his advice: "If you can't brag about it, don't do it. Be proud of what you do."

You'll have to find your own way back to the hotel. Do you have your itinerary with you? If not, did you note the correct and full name of today's hotel? It's a Holiday Inn, but is it the Holiday Inn Lakeside, Holiday Inn Airport South, Holiday Inn Airport North, Holiday Inn Downtown, Holiday Inn Outer Drive, Holiday Inn Inner Circle? You need to know which Holiday Inn, don't you? Is it safe to walk?

> I start to walk back to the hotel. There's a man peeing on the sidewalk. Our box truck drives by and I flag them down and hop in with Martin and Matt.

If you think the hotel is too far away to walk, is the cab company still open to take you home? Will it take an hour or two for the cab to come get you?

Dag Juhlin Tip: If the cab company is closed or the cab has not arrived despite repeated calls, you could call for a pizza to be delivered. When it arrives, bribe the driver with cash, CDs, or free tickets to your show. He may agree to carry musicians back to town with him.

Bus Party

If the party has moved to your tour bus, keep track of your guests. Don't allow them to wander into the bunk area without you. Convey the "liquids only" policy of the toilet. This also means you can't throw up on the bus.

> The party at Club Dread went until 4 AM, when it moved to the bus. From the parking lot the bus must have looked like a cartoon bus rocking back and forth. At 8 AM I went to the room to sleep for an hour and a half.

The Hotel Bar

The hotel bar may close early. If you're lucky to find it open, it's often quiet enough to talk, with a fine selection of beverages. And, you don't have to navigate anything but an elevator and remember your room number to get home safely.

> "Susan, get your ass down to the bar. I just ordered ten shots of tequila."

The Party Room

Someone's hotel room will be designated the party room. Unless you have no need to ever sleep, can drink ceaselessly, enjoy smoke and guests who spend the night, you'll probably offer your room only occasionally. Someone fills the bathtub with ice and beer. Someone brings leftover chips and salsa from the deli tray, and someone sets up an iPod. Sometimes it's just the band unwinding. Sometimes there are new friends. And when you're ready to find your room, it's as easy as weaving down a well-lit hallway.

Finding Late-Night Food

Often there's a search for food late at night. After the gig, especially if you decided to skip dinner, you'll be hungry. Your fans or friends or the club owner may be able to suggest a late-night place that might be open after your show. Most restaurants stop serving at 10 PM. On rare and wonderful occasions, you may meet a restaurateur who loves the band and would "be honored" to have you all come over to his restaurant. He's going to keep it open extra late to serve you an incredible feast.

The hotel restaurant and room service are probably closed by now. Often the *only* place to find a restaurant open after 10 PM is by the highway. That's fine if you're driving out that night, but if you're spending the night, the front desk may have some suggestions. If all they have is a Domino's menu, look in the yellow pages to find Chinese. Or you could stop the Chinese food delivery guy in the hallway and ask for a menu. You know they deliver. He tells you it's good. It's your last option for the night.

SLEEP—HAHAHA

Sleep. There is none on a rock tour unless you've got a three-day drive across the country, and even that is not restful. It seems like every night is a late night and every morning is an early morning.

Nobody goes to sleep until 4:00 AM. I should just quit fighting it.

It might be your inability to fall asleep on a moving tour bus. Or the tour schedule doesn't schedule in sleep. After a late-night show, you have to get up early to drive to interviews or radio shows in the next city. If you get four hours of sleep a night you'll be able to navigate stairs and road cases and cables.

I was too sleepy to tie my shoes and form words.

After a while only those on tour with you will seem to understand what it is you are trying to say. Store clerks may seem cold to you. Waitresses won't understand your order. You will feel safest and clever only with those on your tour.

"I wanted tomatoes in eggs; not tomatoes in pancakes."
"Oh, we wondered about that."–Waitress

You'll find yourself avoiding well-lit rooms and close-up looks in mirrors. Know that your eyes are bright with stories and memories and mountainous thundering shows. Under your eyes will be a deep valley of no sleep.

"Do you ever scare yourself looking at yourself?"–Luke, at the end of our marathon all-night all-day drive

You'll grab a little sleep whenever and wherever you can. It won't be a clump of eight hours in a hotel bed. It'll be a little in the van, a little after load-in on the floor of the dressing room before the show. You may even close your eyes during the show and have a quick little dream.

"I learned how to sleep anywhere. And to quit being so precious about light, the space, and the shape I have to curl up in."–Abra

SPENDING THE NIGHT IN YOUR HOTEL ROOM

If you have an early-morning bus call, you may want to skip the hotel bed entirely. Take a quick shower. (There are theories that because shows are so emotionally purging, we should take a shower at the end of the night to wash not only smoke and sweat from our skin but all the emotion that was released during the show.) Gather your things and head directly to your bus bunk. In the morning you might wake up when everybody comes onto the bus, but you can stay cozy in your bunk through this bit of commotion and then continue sleeping.

If you decide to sleep in the hotel bed, there are a few things you can do to help you and your roommate have a good sleep in the hotel room. Bands are often going to bed when the sun is coming up and when the rest of the world is waking up. Barricade yourself from this early world as best you can.

1. Find and hang the DO NOT DISTURB, QUIET, PLEASE, or ZZZZZ sign outside your door. If you forget to do this, clean towels and sheets will come by at 8 AM, and that's all the sleep you'll get. If there's no sign, make one on some hotel stationery, tear a hole in it, and slip it over the doorknob. So very, very, important.

2. Turn off your cell phone. Mute the ring or shut the phone off entirely when you plug it in to recharge it. The alarm may still work on your cell phone even if the phone is turned off.

3. Apply your sensory deprivation devices. Put in your squishy earplugs to block out the sounds of whoever gets up at 7 AM. Use your Tempur-Pedic eye shade to keep it dark in your eyes.

4. Arrange a reasonable wake-up call and have a backup. Negotiate the time of this call with your roommate. If you're both quick in the morning, it can be twenty minutes before leave time. Use two alarms—the hotel wake-up call and another alarm, because one will fail. If your wake-up call is your tour manager calling to see where you guys are, you'll race out of the room with no shower, perhaps forgetting your day bag or rings (which you meant to place in your boot) and face a bus of nicely showered and breakfasted travelers. Head to your bunk immediately.

   > "Is that yawls' bus that's leaving?" The Phoenix Hotel called Dag's
   > room this morning shortly after he returned from the bus party.

Sometimes you'll wake up to unexpected maintenance—drilling, pounding, or a fire alarm. Why weren't you forewarned so you could have changed rooms? And why would a hotel try out the fire alarm at 10 AM on the day you can sleep late? When you call the desk to complain, they will not give you a discount or say "I'm sorry." They will tell you that you already have a discount and fire alarms are required to be checked at 10 AM. This will be as far as you can negotiate, and you have ended that night's sleep. You might be up in time for the free breakfast buffet.

HAVING BREAKFAST THE MORNING AFTER YOUR SHOW

Breakfast is personal. Some completely skip it. Some will lose sleep to have it. Often it depends on how late the night went the night before and if there was a decent dinner. At some point on tour you'll have the debate if breakfast is necessary or even good for you.

> Matt Fish tells us today that if we eat breakfast our metabolism will be faster all day and we'll actually lose weight.

Breakfast at the Hotel

You could look over the expensive yet delicious-sounding room service choices and decide to treat yourself. You may wait a long time for room-temperature toast and scrambled eggs to appear. If you preordered breakfast by placing the order form outside your room door before 2 AM, it will arrive right on time this morning. There's no waiting. Chances are good that the meal will still be warm. You can stay in your PJs and slowly wake up.

If you prefer a free breakfast, you may ride the elevator down to the lobby in search of the breakfast room with cold cereal and toast. Complimentary breakfast can be absurdly early–often packed up or locked down by 9:30 AM–and pretty bad. In Europe, complimentary breakfast is incredible–a buffet of hard-cooked or scrambled eggs, smoked salmon, fresh-baked bread, butter, yogurt, fruit, muesli, tea, and strong coffee. Most U.S. hotels won't offer anything like this, but often you can make your own waffle, and that's entertaining.

If there's a restaurant at the hotel, you may find a rough-looking bandmate already seated. He may tell you to avoid the breakfast buffet. He tried it and isn't sure the eggs are real eggs. (Sunday buffet brunch can be an entirely different story with biscuits, strawberries and kiwis, and omelets made to order.)

Author's Breakfast Tip: If you are told "Breakfast is over; lunch only," order a fried egg sandwich on toast. Often the waitress will agree to your sandwich order and the kitchen will make it, even if it's not on the lunch menu.

Breakfast in Town

Someone you met last night may have highly recommended a breakfast place in town. If you wake up early enough and are still interested, you might look for it. There's a chance you'll be recognized the morning after your show, so you may want to take a shower, wake up a little, and dress better than you feel.

> We stop at the Lakota on 9th on the way out of town. I'm wearing my Poi dog T-shirt and the waitress says she loves that band. Did we get to the show last night?

It's nice to find your bandmates already there, especially after a late night.

> "I blame you." I point at David sitting with Alejandro. "I'm sorry about the Southern Comfort." David greets me and buys my coffee.

Having breakfast at a local café gives you yet another feel of the city.

> We're at Tallulah's in, oh, somewhere North Carolina. Grits, fried tomatoes. Not a rock club, not a gas station or convenience store, just some normal folks looking at us.

COFFEE

Coffee deserves its own section. It provides so much comfort on a tour.

> "It's amazing coffee hasn't been outlawed."

It briefly overrides the pain of a hangover. It may wake you up enough to drive.

> "I'll have the 300-mile coffee."–Cellist says every single day to a new waitress

When traveling by bus, you may not want to bother with coffee in the morning. You'll be all wired and wound up in an enclosed area. Wait until you arrive in the next city, and while your crew is setting up your stuff, a nice little excursion is to find coffee. Pick up an extra double mochachino for your tech or sound person.

> We found the Sir Real Coffee Shop. It's out here next to the Christian Book Store and the Video Lingerie Store.

Do we go to the "unbeatable for what you need when you need it" Starbucks or do we venture into all the other Café Whatevers? If you've got the money to burn, support the local coffeehouse. If the coffee is awful, just find a Starbucks on the next corner and get a cup of good strong coffee.

> "Having Starbucks coffee in Vancouver is like shopping at the Gap in Paris."–Bandmate in Vancouver, having Starbucks

HOTEL CHECKOUT

The daily sheets posted in the front lounge of the bus and backstage will state when the bus is leaving in the morning. Usually this leave time is well before 11 AM checkout. (However, if you have a short drive to the next city or if you're driving after the show, your tour manager may request a late checkout so everyone can get some extra time to relax.)

Before your tour manager checks you all out of the hotel, band members need to go to the front desk and pay for any incidentals (room service, minibar, movies, or phone). He wants to see a $0 balance on all the rooms. Tell the front desk which specific charges you wish to pay or simply pay for all the room charges and hope your roommate will reimburse you. You can still hang onto your key, go get breakfast, and come back to the room to brush your teeth.

Author Note: If you look around your hotel room and it's clearly the morning after a good party was had in there, you can leave the maid a tip. She is going to have to do a lot of extra work. No one will know if you leave her some money. It's not required. It's just a kind gesture.

Bus Call Tip: You may want to arrive early to the bus before the bays fill up with suitcases. If you're the last one there, you may have to pull out three or four heavy bags and rearrange them so yours will fit.

> Leaving the hotel, there was a man in a suit, out smoking a cigarette in the parking lot. "Artists are the creators of the world. I should know. I am one." Who was that guy? Tom Waits?

LOST AND FOUND

You're going to lose stuff on tour. You'll leave it behind at the restaurant, the dressing room, or your hotel room. Or it drops out of your pocket. Or it gets stolen. You sometimes don't know where it went or when it went.

> Tour loss: the singer/percussionist lost $700 from a breast pocket . . .

Idiot-check is the very intentional "one last look." Look where things aren't easily seen. Get a flashlight and shine it between the dark stage curtains and black monitor wedges. Check behind and under chairs, couches, or the merchandise table. Look to see if anything is hanging on doorknobs, or off the back of a chair, or caught in the bed covers. Look in the shower. It's amazing what you have left after you have everything packed.

> "I've lost so much on this tour. I've got to remember to bring stuff I can lose. At least it gives you a reason to shop, because you've got to get more stuff."–El John

If the tour is still in town, you'll go get your missing book or backpack that was left behind. If you left it at the club you may have to track down the production manager to open up the building. If you're already underway, thirty minutes down the highway before you notice you don't have all your things, don't ask your tour to turn around. Call the hotel or the venue and arrange for them to mail the found items to the hotel you'll be at in a few days or directly to your home.

GETTING REVIEWED BY A MUSIC CRITIC

Reading a review of your show is both exciting and frightening. It's an acknowledgment that you're worth writing about, but what if it's bad? No one knows the band's weaknesses more than you. If it gets pointed out publicly it's painful. If the critic is just flexing a literary muscle and perhaps hasn't even seen the show, it feels like a cheap shot or like someone is being clever at your expense.

You'll remember those bad reviews–the one that put you in the wrong column of "those who rocked and those who did not" (although you were in great company), the one that said you sang "woefully out of tune," the one that said your show lost its way. You'll also appreciate the good ones–the one that said you "saved the day" or the one that called your record "mighty fine." Be prepared for the songwriter and the lead singer to be singled out, followed by the band member with the next most charisma. The looked-over band members may begin to feel unfairly left out.

Author Note: Do critics not know that the band is going to be sitting in the dressing room reading this review together? It gets uncomfortable reading a comparison between each other, or praise of one and disdain of another. And never read press before your show. Whether it's good or bad, it'll be rattling around your head while you're onstage.

If the same critic continually misjudges you in press, you may write him one time. If he's incorrectly reporting the simple facts of your show (the number of new songs played or the style of music you play) you may inform him of the facts he missed and then criticized you for. Develop a relationship with a music journalist who seems to understand your band and appreciates the risks you take.

Q: Why do music critics go to heaven?

A: They're on the guest list.

Q: What's the difference between a critic and God?

A: God doesn't think he's a critic.

Greg Kott, *Chicago Tribune* music critic, on what a good show is:

"As a critic I appreciate an artist who is on a journey and a search for the self–their essence or real personality. An artist who has a clear sense of what they want to be and how they want to present themselves is going to have the most successful show. It becomes apparent to everybody what they want to accomplish.

"I'm looking for a real powerful spontaneous expression of personality. It is bursting to come out and can barely be contained. They are not like anyone else. They could only be themselves. This translates to everything: the song, stage, band, show sequence, covers. The bands that generally rise to the top in terms of presentation and critical acclaim have thought about every aspect. Not just, 'I've written these songs and now I'm going to play them.' Gimmicky stuff makes me angry as a reviewer–that it's being done for only commercial reasons.

"The artists I respect are the ones who love what they are doing. It is clear that this person would want to be no other place on earth. They love this music and communicating in this way. This is the whole reason to start a band and get into this–being in love with this music. Either you have it or you don't. Don't be afraid to express that. Let it shine through. I believe every word because you believe it. Don't be shy about it. There should be a joy about it. If you love it, let it come through. Express that love."

7. Other Types of Shows

Traveling around the United States, playing your show one night at a time, city after city, rock club to rock club is the staple of touring. But there are other types of shows to be prepared for, each with its own unique factors.

SIX OTHER KINDS OF GIGS

Here are six other kinds of gigs for which the preparation, venue, parameters, and purpose of the show are different enough from the typical nights you'll be playing that they need to be mentioned: a summer festival, a college gig, a private party, a benefit, a music conference, and the New York City gig.

Performing at a Summer Festival

At a festival you'll most likely be playing outside on a covered stage. The weather can be a factor. It could be Texas hot and you're not used to such heat. Let yourself lie down after load-in or sound check to recover. It may have rained the storm of the century all day, but when it comes time to play, if there is no lightning and no danger of electrocution, the show will go on.

We played while watching people sitting in the rain watching us.

Often you don't get a sound check or monitor check. Your crew will throw the gear up in the twenty-minute changeover between bands. The promoter will announce your name and then your show begins. This is fondly known as a "festival style" sound check.

The sound will be bad at first. Your front-of-house soundman should bring up the rhythm section and the lead vocal first. Everything else he can fill in as you play. Performing outside has a different sound to it. Without concrete walls, a ceiling, or a back wall to contain it, the sound seems to float away. It's not just you. The sound waves don't rebound back. Placing more of your own vocal and more kick and snare in your monitor may help you hear yourselves onstage.

Your set time may be scheduled during daylight. Instead of moody club lighting with a darkened audience in front of you, everyone is well lit. The band isn't used to playing in bright light. The festival audience—wearing cutoffs, hats, and sunglasses—is so very visible. They'll want to talk to you while you're quickly setting up or during the show more than any other audience.

> "Remember us? We saw you in Boulder. It's our wedding anniversary. We love you."

Your set list may be shorter than it would be for a night at a club. You want to choose the right songs, songs that represent you and engage the festival crowd. There's a feeling that it's got to be all loud, fast, and epic songs and no quieter ones. Yes, a crowd wants to feel good and to party. But an audience responds to a beat. Keep the pulse strong and you can play a balanced set.

Backstage there may be one big artist area with small curtained-off cubby holes for each band. Hospitality will be abundant. If the festival is at higher altitudes, oxygen will be provided, which is quite nice. (*Author Note:* Drinking alcohol at higher elevation will affect you much more than at sea level.)

At the festival, you'll get to see a lot of performers you might never think of buying tickets for but are incredible: Red Hot Chili Peppers like a force; Loretta Lynn dressed like Cinderella; Björk, incredibly feminine; and Tammy Wynette.

> We arrived in Nashville last night and our passes let us get backstage to watch Tammy Wynette offer a moment of silence to Conway Twitty, who died today. Then she sang "How Great Thou Art." She ended her show with "Stand by Your Man" for Conway. It was one of my top ten touring moments.

Make sure there is a plan in place regarding when and how the band will be leaving the festival. You can request an early van for those who want to leave immediately after your show and schedule a later van for those who want to watch other performers. Even with a van scheduled, those who decide to stay longer may be stuck on a hill or mountain outside of town, waiting and waiting for the festival van to return. It could be 2:30 AM before another van is available to load you all back to your hotel. It may be freezing cold and you've been at this damn festival since noon.

Festivals usually pay a guarantee and include dinner and lodging. They will arrange your transportation to and from the airport and from the venue to your hotel and back.

> The girl driving us from the venue to our fabulous Marriott six-pillow hotel rooms told us about West Virginia: It's completely in the Appalachian Mountains. There are black bears and mountain lions, and an hour south of Charleston it's really poor, all coal mining.

Make sure your driver has had a few hours of sleep and non-drinking before getting behind the wheel of your airport-bound van in the morning.

Playing at a College

A college gig usually pays a good guarantee. And you'll have a stop in a college town with a concentration of good shops, well-made inexpensive food, and strong coffee. The stage may be temporary risers set up in a hallway, a cafeteria, or a cement valley outside. Your backstage area is in a classroom with chalkboards, chalk, and student desks and is a long, long walk from the stage. The college won't provide alcohol. You'll have some only if your tour manager thought to purchase it earlier. Beer must be poured into paper cups ("cups only" policy). Coeds will have made pan lasagna for dinner and will be serving it in the teacher's lounge.

Sound Engineering Class 101 may be helping with your sound this afternoon, so sound check may take longer than normal. There may be feedback. Wear your earplugs.

Playing a Private Party

The private party could be an elaborate birthday party or an art installation. It usually takes place in a rented hall, a private club, a dance club, a warehouse, or a backyard. The "stage" may be a wraparound porch. Sometimes an open space is converted into a club for a night. If the host hired proper sound, light, and stage companies the show will run fairly smoothly. If not, the night isn't so easy. Power may not be close to the stage. The lights may interfere with the sound. The people running the show may be tense trying to pull it all together.

A private party sounds like a fine idea. It pays well. Maybe the host fell in love with his future wife at one of your shows and *loves* the band. Maybe the performance is part of an art opening or special event and it'll be an interesting night. But being the entertainment for a party can also be demoralizing. You'll be welcomed and people will be happy you're playing, but you're not the reason everyone is attending. The band is not the center of attention.

At your own shows you're booked to express who you are. At a private party you're hired to entertain. There's an inherent problem. The host may want to tell you how your show should go. "Start with something up-tempo." If you play a quieter song someone will tell you to "pick it up a bit," and if you get expressively loud you may be asked to turn down so they can talk. Or the host may join the band onstage for most of the night (although he *is* a famous Chicago Bulls basketball player and it *is* his birthday).

As there are no paying guests, the host may pay you with a check that can't be cashed until the next morning, so the band sleeps on the bus in the driveway of the ranch where the party was held. Accept the private party only if it helps finance your tour or the independent making of your record.

Playing a Benefit

A benefit is the gig you play to raise money for someone in need—a non-profit organization, an uninsured musician, disaster relief, or any cause that needs money. If your band is doing well, it might be time to donate a show. The more popular you get the more benefits you'll be asked to play. Your band might want to discuss how many benefits you'll play per year or what causes are important to you.

Benefits are often well run. They're usually put on at a rock club that already knows how to put on a ten-band show. The organizers of the event will be very thankful you're playing. Also, benefits aren't always entirely unpaid. Sometimes you'll be paid $100 each to defray some of your own costs.

Performing at a Music Conference

Playing at a music industry conference is usually not a paying gig. It could be a Triple A radio conference, South by Southwest, North by Northeast, or CMJ. Your band will be seen and heard by those involved with the music industry attending, which might be radio programmers, rock journalists, or record label personnel. Like the festival gig, usually there's no sound check, but you may gain new fans and you'll get to see some bands you normally wouldn't.

One of the biggest music conferences is South by Southwest in Austin, Texas, held in mid-March every year. To apply, upload your electronic press kit to SXSW.com by November and the conference rejects or accepts you by February. You'll be given a forty-minute time slot. The band has a choice to be paid $100 for their performance or to be paid in wrist bands, which enables you to see other bands playing. If you go, book other gigs on the way to help pay for the trip.

Greg Kott: "Don't go down there thinking, 'This is our big break. We're going to get signed.' Go there to have fun: for the love of playing in front of an audience. You may have a terrible slot, at a club nobody comes to. You may think there will be talent scouts and critics. Well, the worst-case scenario is you will drive from Chicago to Austin [twenty hours] and play forty minutes to seven people at a bar. I've seen it happen. But if you think it's worth it to go to meet some people, learn some stuff about the 'business,' and see the festival, okay."

At the festival there are so many bands and so much hype and self-promotion, it can be overwhelming.

"It hurts me a little bit." Matt Fish said the most honest thing I've ever heard about SXSW.

The best approach is to enjoy your showcase and then let the wide selection of music available inspire you. In the span of one night you might see a mariachi band, Brazilian jazz, German drag cabaret, a pop band, Public Enemy, and the Waco Brothers.

Michael Corcoran wrote in the *Austin American Statesman* during SXSW weekend:

"Being in a band is a ridiculous pursuit. This is what I was thinking when I was driving downtown Friday and a group of guys with mop-top hair and skinny black jeans were posing for pictures in front of the bat sculpture on South Congress Ave ... I imagined what they'd all be doing in ten years and rocking out wasn't an option. Every year at SXSW there are bands that everybody is buzzing about and almost all the members are at this moment selling real estate or working the milk steamer or stewing in their bitterness and checking the mailbox for random residual checks.

"The truth is that SXSW is not about discovery, but about recharging. ... The Kings of Leon were absolutely amazing, a powerful engine that roared for all of us who want more out of life, at least during these four days when we're not as hip as everybody else. Being there at Stubb's on Friday afternoon was being at the hippest place at SXSW at the moment, which is really what it's all about."

Author Note: If you are accepted to play a showcase, book another gig or two at a non-conference venue while you are there. These are usually well-attended daytime shows in a parking lot behind a coffee shop, a Mexican restaurant, or an art store.

The New York City Gig

A New York gig is always both exciting and stressful. And it poses some unique touring difficulties. Simply finding your way through tunnels and traffic and parking is a feat. Everyone wants to know New York City, but most young musicians do not.

> We took the Holland Tunnel in and then essentially slid right off the other side of Manhattan, failing to take a left turn onto Hudson that we never saw. Suddenly we're on the Manhattan Bridge. Two vans, two illegal U-turns, and we're back in Manhattan.

At the gig you'll feel the presence of the music industry and pressure yourself to play your best show—a sure way not to. Here are some New York tips.

BOOKING A HOTEL. A good rate in New York City is anything under $200. (There's a city tax and occupancy tax as well.) Google "cheap hotels NYC" and see what you can find. Bands have stayed at the following:

> Off SoHo Suites, 11 Rivington Street
> Holiday Inn Midtown, 38 Lafayette Street
> Union Square Inn on 14th Street
> Red Roof Inn, 6 West 32nd Street

TUNNEL RESTRICTIONS. I asked Maggie Wrigley from the Bowery Ballroom and Mercury Lounge about any tunnel restrictions. "No trailers in the Holland Tunnel. Thirteen-foot tall or less in the Lincoln Tunnel is the height restriction. Look up Port Authority of New York for current restrictions." She says bands are always calling her stuck at the tunnel and having to reroute into the city.

> We took a tunnel in. Why is it wet in there? And can we not talk about what a drag it would be to die drowning in a flooding tunnel as we're driving through one?

BUS RESTRICTIONS. Your tour bus can drive into the city and park by the venue, but there may be noise restrictions. Irving Plaza: "You can't have the generator running here at the club. It makes a lot of noise. You could get a noise fine." Without the generator there is no power, so no lights, no heat, no A/C, no stereo. Often it's easier for the bus to head out to New Jersey after load-in. You'll have to grab all the things from your bunk and the bus closet that you'll need for the afternoon and evening.

STREET PARKING. Overnight street parking for your van is a long shot. There are many restrictions posted. Gloria Winter, a musician's personal assistant in New York, says, "There are a lot of street cleaning restrictions, and they vary by neighborhood. You're okay on Wednesdays. They don't work on Wednesday. There's no standing between 7 AM and 10 AM for traffic. They mean it about fire hydrants—ten feet on either side. The only coin a parking meter will take is a quarter. Nothing else will help you. For a quarter you can park for ten minutes or it could be a half hour. If you get a parking ticket in midtown it's $115. Residential, $65."

Maggie Wrigley suggested a secret spot: "We usually tell bands to go down and park on Forsythe and Chrystie streets below Houston. Those are open zones—no space restrictions and no meters. A bus or a van and trailer can park there."

PARKING IN AN OUTSIDE LOT. Often vans are too tall to fit in the parking garages, so you'll find a parking lot. As a safety precaution, park with the back door of the trailer up against a fence or wall so if the door was pried open, nothing could be taken out. Gloria says, "Outside parking lots will charge an extra $10 for oversize. It's usually $25 overnight. On the far West Side at 35th and 10th Avenue there's a twenty-four-hour outdoor lot."

TAXICABS. You'll be able to hail a cab easily unless it's raining or snowing. Cabs are less expensive in NYC than in most U.S. cities.

LIMOUSINES. A limo holds only six people comfortably and is awkward as hell to get in and out of. Crouch and glide. Keep your butt down. Inside there may be a complimentary minibar, a TV, and a DVD player. People in passing cars will try to peer through your tinted windows. They want you to be someone famous who will perhaps see them and invite them into the limo, into your fabulous life, maybe marry them, or offer them a contract and a lot of money for something they don't even do (the limo fantasy).

CAR SERVICE. The really rich and really famous don't take limos. They have a car sent around. Your car will be a black and shiny vehicle with leather interior. If you have a lot of band members, you may want to order a car service instead of hailing a cab to get you to the hotel or the airport. Call the service yourself. If the hotel arranges it for you, the price is higher.

PERFORMING ON NATIONAL TV SHOWS

Okay, this can be fun, and it can scare you to death–the *Late Show with David Letterman, Late Night with Conan O'Brien*, the *Tonight Show, Saturday Night Live*, or *Austin City Limits*. Except for *Saturday Night Live* and *Austin City Limits*, these are one-song shows with a camera lens as big as your head inches from your face. The man holding it appears to have one real eye and one camera eye. And he doesn't say anything. He just keeps moving the camera closer to you.

> I'm flying to New York to play *Saturday Night Live* with John Mellencamp.
> If I make it too big of a deal it will be impossible to play.

The Musician's Union

Network TV is a union gig. You have to be a member of your musicians' union and *have your card on you*. Your crew can help set up, but they will be limited because there are union stagehands who have to plug and unplug and move things. Often these stagehands are ornery and impatient. Their bad moods and fixation on breaks and clocks seem so not rock. It isn't rock. It's TV. Don't let it get to you. You are visiting their stage. Without having to go to a million homes, you can be broadcast into them. And you'll be paid for this.

Rehearsals

There's a rehearsal for sound and a rehearsal for the cameras. Your own front-of-house soundman can't touch the console but may offer clear, direct suggestions to the union sound person you are required to use. Often TV mixes are just dry vocal and drums. Ask for what you like. Remind them you'd like to be able to hear whatever instrument you're looking at.

During these rehearsals, the studio is cold. Once the show begins and the lights come on, it warms up a lot. Being cold can make you think you are more nervous than you are–and you will be nervous. And you will be cold. In your nervous coldness don't ask your tour manager to demand a new thermostat setting. You're a guest on national TV. Put on a sweater and enjoy the whole unusual experience.

Make sure instruments are tuned and then tuned again moments before you perform. The cold of the studio may cause the instrument to go sharp during rehearsals. When the lights and heat are turned up for the show, instruments may go flat. If it's cold in your dressing room, leave your instrument near the warm stage so it will already be warmed up for the show. And then tune it again.

Makeup, Hair, and Clothes

> With JCM playing the *Late Show with David Letterman* at the Chicago Theater. It's calmer than *Saturday Night Live*. Not as scary this time. Older ladies are backstage to do hair and makeup.

Hair and makeup artists will be available at the television studio. Men in the band are made up to look healthy under the bright television lights. Backstage and close up they'll look a little like a puppet or a newscaster. If they choose no makeup, they'll appear very pale on TV. The makeup artist will ask the women in the band what "look" you are going for. Have an idea to help them. Otherwise you may wind up in the bathroom trying to take off half the makeup.

Bring clothes options. You want to wear something you are extremely comfortable in; probably something you have worn onstage before. Avoid solid white or a bold print.

Performing the Song

You'll be playing one song you have played hundreds of times (except for *SNL*, where you'll play two and ACL where you'll play 60 minutes). However, if it's too long for your allotted time, you'll be asked to shorten it, which will be a bit panicky to figure out and to remember on the fly. Make a cheat sheet and place it on the floor in front of you if you need to.

The difficulty of a one-song show is you don't have the luxury of five songs coming before it to warm up to the stage, to the audience, or to each other. Your concentration and energy need to accelerate (zero to eleven in two minutes and thirty seconds), which isn't difficult as you'll be flooded with adrenaline.

Sitting at home watching these TV shows is so relaxing. The first time you play national TV, when you're actually on the set performing, the cameras, bright lights, and precision timing of everything can make you dizzy.

If you get nervous, trust your fingers. Trust your muscle memory. You've played this song before. Listen to the sound. It's your friend. It's taken you this far. Just bring to the stage what you've been doing every night. Show who you are.

Performing on *Letterman, Conan,* and the *Tonight Show*

The late-night talk shows are taped around 5 PM. While you wait in the green room for your turn on the stage, maybe your A & R person from the label will come visit you and be encouraging. The live audience helps it feel like the sort of show you are used to. Still, walking onto the stage with very bright lights and rolling cameras about to send you into millions of homes can feel like you've agreed to jump over Niagara Falls. It's big and it's unstoppable. There may be a catastrophe. It'll be fine.

Afterward, the band can go back to the hotel, drink champagne, and nervously watch the whole show at 11:30 PM. Your performance will be the very, very last thing, and there will be so many commercials before you play that you'll be sure the band has been cut.

And then, there you'll be. Some of the band looks great. Some look terrified and unnatural. You'll hope for more shots of you but not too many. There will be weird camera mistakes. During the guitar solo you'll see the background singer. During a drum breakdown you'll see the keyboard player's hands. If the band is any good at all, the host will come shake hands after you play.

Performing on *Saturday Night Live*

During the day there will be a sound rehearsal and then a camera rehearsal. At 5 PM there is a complete show with a live audience. At 11:30 PM it's the actual "Live from New York, it's *Saturday Night!*" show. With all these run-throughs it may be hard to remember where you last saw your instrument. Did you leave it onstage or is it back in the dressing room up a flight of stairs?

The first song will go by really fast. Then you'll wait through the rest of the sketches to play the second song, which feels easier than the first. Afterward, call your family from your dressing room. They were watching back home.

Performing on *Austin City Limits*

Austin City Limits is taped on the University of Texas campus. It's a very well-run show. Load-in is in the morning. Everything is set up and line checked. You'll design a sixty-minute set, although only thirty minutes of it will usually air. There is a break for lunch, and when everyone returns the band runs through the whole sixty-minute set for sound and again for camera angles. Then everyone relaxes in the dressing rooms that an intern will help you find. The makeup artist will apply makeup that you'll need cold cream to take off later.

At 8 PM the show is performed in front of about three hundred people who are pleased to have gotten tickets and be out of the Texas heat. It's a concert, but it's also a taping. Press on through any mistakes. If something goes wrong you can replay a song at the end of the show. Immediately afterward you can watch the taped show on a big-screen TV. The band may suggest other camera shots or sound adjustments.

PERFORMING ON LOCAL TV SHOWS

Sometimes the early-morning news shows invite bands to come by and perform. This is really early for a rock musician—to arrive at a television studio at 6:00 AM is early. It's so early it's actually a late, late, night. Bring several outfits to choose from. Sometimes they'll do your makeup; sometimes they don't bother, so if you want to wear lip gloss, bring your own.

The set looks much like a theater set of a news show. There are fake walls held up by wood planks, a lot of electrical cabling stretched across the floor, and except where it's very bright, it's dark. Be quiet. Move slowly. As you walk through huge partitioned rooms, you don't want to trip over a cable or sound baffle or walk onto a live broadcast.

The assistants often get cranky with bands because they don't know where to stand while waiting and often end up right in the producer's way.

There's no stage. You'll be set up on the floor at the far end of the room. There's usually not a live audience. It's just the newscaster and the camera crew. (You might be able to read the teleprompter, which is entertaining.) Sometimes it's just three cameramen and a guy with a clipboard and an earpiece. Musicians need to rally for this sort of performance. Remember the camera operators have lived life. The man with the earpiece has been in love. They are doing their jobs, but they are also listening to your songs. Play to them.

The band will be asked to play one song early in the hour and one song at the end. The producer may also ask the band to perform "bumps" in and out of segments—ten seconds of a song before going to a commercial. The last song the band performs may get cut off as time runs out. It's possible to guide these shows so you feel respected. Yes, it's great to be on TV and be seen by many people, but you want the band to be presented well. Ask yourself how a famous band you respect would handle this. Would they play incidental music in and out of segments? Would they allow their hit song to be cut off? Your manager should communicate the band's parameters to the TV producer before agreeing to be on the show.

FLYING IN TO PLAY A SHOW OR START A TOUR

There comes a day when your band will be flying to a gig. You may be flying to play one song on national TV. The band may be flown to San Diego to play a private party. It could be you are flying into the Pacific Northwest to start a five-show mini-tour.

Making Your Airline Reservation

Book nonstop, direct flights when possible. It's easier, safer, and quicker. Some airlines will charge you a tax just for touching down in a city.

If you book the flights early, they'll be less expensive. If that's not possible, Southwest Airlines and Jet Blue have fairly low last-minute fares even if you're booking one-ways. Sign up for frequent-flier miles and then book on that airline as often as possible. The miles do add up, and then you've got a vacation flight in your future.

It's possible to request seating where you are most comfortable. The bulkhead seats in the very front have the most legroom as there is no seat in front of you. Your bag has to go overhead and your tray is between the seats. The emergency exit rows in the middle of the plane have more leg and knee room than the other seats. However, for safety reasons some don't recline. If you are seated here you agree to help people in an emergency—to open the big emergency window and help people exit through it. The seats in the back of the plane always seem crowded and claustrophobic to me. But they are the "survivor seats," as Matt calls them. You're most likely to live through a crash if you're in the back of the plane.

Packing for the Fly Gig

If the band is flying in to play just one show, bring whatever heavy things you want. You only have to move your stuff from the airport to the one hotel. If it's the beginning of a tour, pack economically. Most airlines allow two checked bags (Southwest Airlines allows three). If you go over the weight limit of fifty pounds you'll have to pay $25 or more depending on the extra weight.

Flying with Your Instruments

If your instrument is too big to fit in the overhead bin, loosen the strings, wrap T-shirts around it, slap a FRAGILE sticker on the case, cross your fingers, and let it go onto the conveyor belt. You may have to sign a waiver of the airline's liability. At the destination city you'll pick it up at "oversized baggage." If the instrument arrives cracked, smashed, or broken, the airline may reimburse you a small amount. And now where will you find an instrument to play for this tour? (Is there a playground full of monkeys back there beyond the airline counter? Jumping on instruments, playing softball with them?)

> Matt's cello arrived in Cleveland with a crack running the entire length of the back, directly over the sound post. It doesn't look as bad as Alison's smashed cello on the flight to Minneapolis. Unbelievably, an hour before the show he called a woman who was willing to bring her $40,000 cello to the club for him to play. Now we have to figure out what to do the rest of the tour.

Soft bags and acoustic-shaped guitar cases are allowed onboard if they fit in the overhead bins. Sometimes the agent will stop you and have you gate-check the instrument. You know it fits easily in the overhead, but it looks big to her. Your instrument will then be hand carried underneath the plane to ride with the baby strollers. At the end of the flight, wait in the gangway for the instrument to be handed back to you.

Check-in and Security

Traveling in a big group there's always a group check-in vs. individual check-in debate. Most tour managers think it's better if you travel as one big posse and check in fourteen bags. If there's an oversized bag/group check-in counter, then checking in as a group is fairly easy. If you're standing in the regular line with other passengers, the group check-in clogs things up and slows everything down for you and everyone else. It's more efficient if you each keep track of your own two bags from check-in to baggage claim.

Security rules keep changing and vary from city to city. You could check TSA.com before flying. In addition to removing metal items as you go through the screening, you have to remove your shoes, your jacket, and your hat. Laptops need to be put in a gray bin. In some cities, security will boss you around like you are recently out of prison; in other cities security will be calm and helpful.

Flight Delays

Flights get delayed often. Wouldn't you rather be on the ground than in the air, circling and bouncing in "weather"? While you wait, you probably don't want to disappear deeply into an airport bar or magazine shop. The flight may leave sooner than expected and you may not hear the announcement and miss your flight. This used to be good for free flight vouchers, but not any more.

If the flight leaves late, you'll usually make your connecting flight. The pilot can make up some time in the air and the airlines build some buffer time into the flight schedules.

Fear of Flying

> Landing bumpy and foggy. I hope our wings are hot and hold no ice. I
> always prepare to die (a bit) whenever I fly.

If you are a nervous flier, pull out the Rescue Remedy or Xanax you packed and take before you get on the plane. If you are prone to claustrophobia, sit in an aisle seat near the front of the plane. You probably don't want to talk or think about famous plane crashes you remember. The smaller airplanes bounce around more and seem less safe, but a flight attendant once told me the little planes are actually safer than the big ones because they have more maneuverability.

> This airplane travel is nerve-racking. Adam's eyes are big and stony. I bet
> his palms are wet.

Finding Ground Transportation into the City

The hotel you are staying at may have an airport shuttle. Call them and they may come get you. Perhaps the promoter is picking you up. If not, while waiting for your baggage (crossing fingers that all pieces made it safely) ask at the information counter about ground transportation into the city.

Of course what you want is to take a taxicab or a taxivan, but often the fare is expensive, so you check out your other options first. There are cabstands in major airports. You can't just wave down the first cab you see. You'll have to wait your turn in line.

Your may decide to rent a van to get into town or to start a regional tour. The airport car rental place may be a shuttle ride away from baggage claim. The tour manager and two band members will go rent the vans while the others wait with the gear.

If one or two band members are flying in separately from the band, they could take a Super Shuttle if it's offered. These blue and yellow vans are oddly old, sticky, and not so clean, but they cost significantly less than a cab. If you aren't in a big hurry and don't mind stopping where six other people need to stop, this is an option.

Arranging Backline

For the fly gig you are going to have to arrange for "backline." Backline is the heavy gear that is expensive to fly–amps and drum kit. There are shipping companies like Rockit Cargo (RockitCargo.com) that are very good at transporting musical equipment. Maybe you could hire a friend to drive your gear in a box truck across the country to meet you. Or you could rent backline. You'll fax the promoter your backline requirements (Figure 14). Make sure your performance contract clearly states what gear you need, who will pay for it (club or band), and if they expect cash or credit card upon delivery or at the end of the night.

Alejandro Escovedo Orchestra 7 Piece Band
Backline Requirements Nov 2007

MA: Bass
1- SWR bass amp (500 watts)
1- SWR 4 x 10" bass cabinet

AE: Guitar
1- 50 watt Marshall amplifier (w/no master volume)
1- 2 X 12" Marshall speaker cabinet
1- Fender Vibrolux

DP: Guitar
1- Marshall 50 combo or Marshall 50 watt half-stack OR a Vox AC-50 PLUS
1- Fender Super OR Deluxe or Twin (in that order)

HM: Drums/DW or Sonor Drums
1- 20" x 16" kick drum (no hole in front head)
1- 10" & 12" toms (with REMO coated Ambassador heads)
1- snare drum
1- 14" floor tom (16" optional)
1- Djembe
2- cymbal stands
1- snare stand
1- hi hat stand
1- drum throne
1- DW kick pedal (5000 or 9000 series)
1- 8' by 8' drum carpet

BS: Cello 1
Amp: 1 SWR bass amp (500 watts) with four 10" speakers

MF: Cello 2
Amp: 1 SWR bass amp (500 watts) with four 10" speakers

SV: Violin
Amp: 1 Fender Twin

Miscell aneous
- 5 guitar stands
- all speaker cables
- we are bringing our own vocal mics (Audix OM5)
- both guitar players have pedal boards with built-in DIs
- cello has a pedal board with DI
- violin has pedal board with DI
- 2 chairs without arms for cello players

FIGURE 14

Jet Lag

Jet lag (or soul lag) is the beat-up feeling you have after a long flight. Maybe it isn't possible for your cells to be shot across the country at five hundred miles per hour and all arrive at the same time. It takes a while for all of you to catch up. Jet lag can claim even the most responsible victims (those who don't drink six little bottles of red wine on the flight).

To help get over jet lag, drink one glass of water each hour you're in the air. Avoid alcohol unless you're fear of flying is too great. Set your watch to the new time. When you get to your hotel room, take a long, warm shower.

TOURING IN CANADA

It may have been easy to go to Canada as kids with your family, but entering the country as a touring band is more difficult. You'll need to start preparing weeks before you cross the border.

Passport, Carnet, and Work Permits

You are required to show a passport at Canadian customs. The band will also need a current and accurate list of all gear going across the border, called a carnet. Gil Gastilean, tour manager: "You should always have a list of equipment reflected in a tech or tour manager equipment checklist. For example: 1. Telecaster (blue), 2. Jazzmaster bass guitar (red)."

The band will need to get work permits to perform and earn money in Canada. Yvonne Matsell, director of North by Northeast Music Festival and talent buyer for the El Mocambo in Toronto: "Work permits must be obtained by the first club on the Canadian leg of the tour. For the club booker to get these processed they must be provided with each band member's date of birth, Social Security number, and address and signed contracts for each club date before they can file the paperwork with the Canadian authorities. This needs to take place at least two weeks before border crossing.

A work permit costs $450 (Canadian) per band and covers all the tour dates. If your routing takes you back and forth across the border, you can reenter on the same permit as long as all the dates have been filed the first time.

If any of your band members are non-American, without a green card, then the procedure is more complicated. That band member has to apply at the nearest Canadian consulate, and this is a much longer process.

When the work permit processing has been completed you'll be provided with a work permit number to quote at the border or a copy of the permit papers will be faxed to you. Time is of the essence in getting this paperwork done. Who pays for the work permit is usually negotiated between the booker and the agent. Clubs do not want to pay as it is yet another cost that they struggle with."

Bringing Merchandise over the Border

There is a big tax you'll have to pay on merchandise coming into Canada. Unless you feel confident you'll be selling a lot of merchandise, ship the merch to your next U.S. destination before you enter Canada.

There are ways to bring some in without paying the tax. You can count the merch as promotional items with no value, thus no tax. You can roll up some of your band's T-shirts and stuff them in pillowcases, making it look like dirty laundry. You can divide some CDs and T-shirts between bandmates, so it looks like these are gifts and not meant to sell. Most touring musicians suggest just being honest at the border and paying the tax.

Yvonne Matsell: "Some bands decide to take the risk of not declaring their merch when crossing. However, you run the risk of having your merch impounded by customs if they decide to search your vehicle."

Going through Customs

Experienced tour managers suggest customs is easier if you go through in the middle of the night. Some even have favorite or less favorite crossing points. Usually you'll choose the most direct crossing to get to your gig.

Yvonne Matsell: "Very important: get rid of anything that should not be in your vehicle (e.g., drugs) well before you cross the border."

There are actually two stops. First, you'll stop at U.S. customs, which is typically fairly easy if you're a U.S. citizen going into Canada. They'll usually just ask what your business will be in Canada. Then you'll pull up to the Canadian customs. They'll ask the driver several questions—nationality of everyone, the purpose of your trip into Canada, and how long you'll be staying. Don't offer more than the question asks.

Gil Gastilean, tour manager: "Please listen and do not ask questions back. Be polite. Be attentive, and there should be no problems." Since the border guards are looking for drugs, illegal immigrants, terrorists, and thugs, and you are simply a band trying to play music for some Canadian fans, you'd think it'd be simple enough.

Customs officials may ask their questions and wave you on through. Or they may direct you to park and will either come onto the bus or invite you into the immigration office. You're not allowed to use your cell phone at immigration. You'll sit on plastic chairs under fluorescent lights listening to the interesting Canadian "o's" and "eh's" as you eavesdrop on the unlucky people in front of you in line. What could they have done to be so silent and so detained? (*Author Note:* Evidently the "eh" comes from Scottish immigrants.)

If you have any outstanding warrants or are a drug felon they will discover you at the border. The band will go on and will no longer have a monitor engineer, who was put on a bus back to the States with an outstanding marijuana conviction of some sort.

Yvonne Matsell: "If anyone in your band has any past convictions or a DWI, don't even think of trying to cross the border. You won't get in and will come up as a 'red flag' any other time you attempt to cross. If a DWI has been taken care of then everything is fine. I believe it's called a 'Ministers Permit' that is needed to clear things up to cross the border."

> "They turned us away at the border. The driver had priors. We don't know for what." Four hours later: "We're still here at customs. We just got done getting the full soul search. They took us all apart. Ran dogs through the bus."

Finding Canada

More than one band has had trouble finding the actual road leading into Canadian customs or out of customs into Canada itself. Maybe it's all this interrogation. It makes us nervous.

> "After they cleared us, we got back into the van. There were all these signs saying EXIT, and we followed them and wound up going back over the bridge, back into the States and had to do it all over again. Luckily they recognized us and didn't give us any problems getting back in. So now we're finally on the other side."–Phone message from Canada.

And another band on another Canadian tour couldn't find their way either.

> We can't find the road to get into Canada. Circling, backing up, and turning around. Finally from the back of the van someone asks calmly, "Has Canada moved?"

Author Note: Once you arrive in Detroit you may think you're almost in Toronto, but you've still got to go through customs inspections and then have good four hours to drive. You've got to budget in more hours than you might think.

Canadian Currency

If you're to be in Canada for one night, don't bother changing any American money into Canadian currency. Often you can use your

American dollars. You'll be given change in Canadian. If you are staying longer, use an ATM to withdraw what you think you'll need. On your return, only paper money can be changed back to American currency. Currency exchanges won't accept any coins.

Author Note: To mail a letter or a postcard, you'll have to use Canadian postage. The U.S. stamps that you've got in your wallet won't work, even if you use two.

Using Your Cell Phone

Your cell phone works in Canada, but it's expensive. Whether you're accepting an incoming call or placing a call it will cost about sixty or seventy cents a minute, unless you've sorted out some sort of Canadian plan with your service provider.

Getting Paid

Bands like to be paid in American money rather than Canadian because the currency exchange always charges a commission.

Yvonne Matsell: "An agent may demand that the band be paid in U.S. dollars, but clubs prefer to pay in local currency as it means not having to go through the bank and ordering U.S. currency beforehand. Then there's all the math involved with transferring how much came in at the door into U.S. funds. It gets very complicated.

"Another thing a band has to do is file a tax waiver from the Canadian tax revenue office. This again must be done in sufficient time before they play. This must be done by their manager or agent and does not involve the club booker. The club booker will receive notification prior to the show if the band has been waived. If not, the band is subject to a 17 percent withholding tax after they have played their show. Most bands will be waived, but if they are in a higher paying category then they will end up having to pay."

Publicity

Yvonne Matsell: "I would suggest young bands hire a publicist for their Canadian shows, as the club is taking a BIG chance in booking new and unknown acts and runs the risk of losing a lot of money. If the club owner loses his shirt, then there's less chance of being re-booked in the future."

8. Life on the Road

Two hours of rock. Twenty-two hours of everything else.

All the life that isn't a rock show still exists while you're on the road. You'll want to take care of yourself. You want to get along with each other. You'll have to do your laundry. You may get sick. You may develop attractions to fans or each other. Holidays are celebrated. You'll want to stay in touch with your home and see some of the country you are traveling.

TOUR PROFILE: ONE WEEK OUT

The first thing you'll do wrong (or right) at the start of your tour is to consume everything offered: alcohol, snacks, conversations, parties. You'll overspend your energy, which is essentially your gold on tour. Will you care? No. Not at first. The adventure and the thrill of being out on the road will give you an incredible amount of energy and optimism. The first week is like being on a fabulous amusement park ride. But then, you'd like it to stop for a moment, and it doesn't. Alcohol and caffeine keep you rolling for a while, but moods start to suffer.

I'm needing some solitude to enjoy the multitude.

You need food and shelter. But that isn't so easy, especially on the early tours. You can't eat when you're hungry. You can't sleep when you're tired.

There's no time, there's no food, there's no bed.

Traveling in a pack day after day, your bandmates may start to annoy you. They can be generous but also mischievous, incredibly fun but also narcissistic. By the end of week one, you may find you aren't as nice as the day you left home, either. You aren't as patient. You aren't as resilient.

"It's not that I don't love you. It's that I know you."

Questions start to be asked: Could this tour have been better planned by monkeys throwing darts at an upside-down map? It zigzags like a W or Star of David tour design. Why did we go this way? Why didn't we go to the hotel first? Why are we leaving so early? Why is there no deli tray? Why is there no more beer? Why did we leave from this airport? Why are these people in our dressing room? Why do you hate me? Why am I here?

Management Problems and Solutions

By the end of week one, you'll know what's going well and what's not going so well on your tour. The following is a list of some of the most common problems that affect the mood and well-being of a tour.

- Drive times and directions are never accurate, so there's no time for a warm meal, a stop at the hotel before sound check, or some personal time.
- Hotels aren't ready. You're all standing in a hotel lobby after an overnight drive and realize that no one has bothered to call ahead to arrange an early check-in. (No, you don't want to go to breakfast. No, you don't want to see the cathedral. You just want to take a hot shower and have a nap in a bed that isn't moving and is long enough for you to straighten out your legs.)
- No one is at the club when you arrive, much less ready for the band.
- There's no deli tray or it arrives late, so you buy lunch with your own money day after day.

If things are consistently falling apart, talk to your tour manager. It may be poor planning on the part of the at-home management. Or, it may be that your tour manager has too much to do and is overwhelmed. Offer to share the burden. Ask if you can help.

"If you don't like something, it would be helpful to include a suggestion how it could be changed."–Keith, our first tour manager

Perhaps you have no tour manager. If it's just the band, everyone needs to pitch in. Divide out the duties–someone does hotels, someone settles the show, someone is in charge of merch. Each band member is responsible for something.

"A well-run band is a democracy with a king."

Interpersonal Problems and Solutions:

There are five basic personal infractions that occur on many tours:

- Diva behavior–avoiding work, arriving late, having no manners
- Not respecting personal space of others–talking all the time, being a know-it-all, leaving your stuff all over
- Overplaying or forgetting your parts during the show
- Overindulging in alcohol or drugs
- Hitting on a bandmate

One solution, of course, is to ignore the problem. If it persists, make light of it. If it gets worse, sarcasm may set in, which solves nothing. Here are some suggestions to resolve interpersonal problems on the road:

LET IT GO. Don't try to change your bandmate. If your guitar player is the loud American in a quiet restaurant in Ireland or puts his cowboy boots on the furniture in a nice Italian restaurant, there's nothing you can do. You can't be responsible for your bandmate's behavior. If you find yourself thinking, "People just shouldn't act like that," well, they do. Don't fight it. "Susan, it takes all kinds," Alejandro once told me. Put this on a laminate.

TAKE A BREAK. Maybe you're worn out and need to break from the rapid pace of tour. You can choose to spend some time alone, veer off from the big posse, and walk away from the cacophony for a little while. You might call it an early night or just take an afternoon for yourself. You can miss an adventure or two.

Whatever you do at home when you get out of sorts, if possible, do that on the road. If you can do this, you'll be better able to do what it takes to coexist with others on the tour.

SCHEDULE A DAY OFF. Often a day off is actually a drive day. But even that is useful to the emotional and physical health of everyone on tour. A true day off is blissfully boring. You wake up in a city. You do not need to gather or do anything on time. There is no performance that night, no radio during the day. You can just do nothing. You can sleep and sleep if you want to. You can watch movies and order room service. It's your day off to recover however you please.

One day at a Virginia Beach hotel on a Charlie Sexton tour I opened up the guest services book. Who wouldn't want to go on a boat ride to see the dolphins at sunset? I knocked on my friends' hotel room door and found five guys staring at the TV. "Hey, who wants to take a boat ride to see the dolphins?" "We're watching *Star Trek* here." I convinced them to come with me.

Author Note: If you arrive in town the night before your show, you can usually get in free at the venue you'll be playing tomorrow.

If you've been thinking you'd like the privacy of your own room, now's the day to make it happen. Ask your roommate if he wants to split the cost of another room with you and you'll each have your own space.

> "I'm going to take an air bath today under a cabana by the pool."–Phoenix Hotel, San Francisco

BE GOOD TO EACH OTHER. You can buy little presents for bandmates. If the drummer says he loves fancy socks, pick up a pair as a present and leave them in his bunk. Buy everyone a little fingernail clipper in the shape of a guitar from a shop in Nashville. Buy a round of drinks. Arrive at sound check with coffee. Order a pizza for everyone after the show.

> I'm sick with some French flu I caught on the plane and I guess I'm home-sick, too. Santa arrives at the hotel lobby and it makes me weepy. They buy me presents from the convenience store, pretending they haven't seen me cry.

Let a bandmate know you're listening to him onstage. Tell him when he plays a great solo or surprises you with an unexpected melody. These things go a long way on a long tour.

Don't be the one who always throws a ten-dollar bill on the dinner table as you excuse yourself to make a phone call. You're probably not leaving enough, and someone has to cover for you. Are you the guy who asks to borrow a pen every day? Or asks what time it is all the time? We'll be happy to help you, but then we won't be.

CHECK YOUR ALCOHOL AND DRUG INTAKE. Partying is not the prime reason you're out on tour. Yes, it's fun to have fun, but not at the expense of every show on the back half of the tour. If the party becomes more important to you than the music, you'll begin to have a serious problem with your bandmates. If all you've got to give onstage is a five-day hangover, you don't have much. If you're ragged, you'll play ragged. If you're half-there, you'll play half-there. If you're too worn out to play well, remember the songs, and keep your mood and attitude together, you may be taking the party further than anyone else and not realizing it.

> "I think there's quite a bit to be said for the chemical goodness. But be cool. It doesn't take long for that to turn real sour."–Mark

One morning a bandmate was telling a story of the night before. He looked at my blank expression and said, "You have no memory of this, do you?" I didn't. That's when I implemented a two-shot limit.

THE TALKING CURE. If a problem continues between you and a bandmate that some time, a present, a compliment, or buying breakfast won't solve, you may have to talk about it. Talking it over sounds so practical in real life. On the road, where everyone's skin is so thin it's about to break and their support system is 800 miles away, it's tough.

But if you don't talk, you'll complain or gossip–poor methods of communication. Complainers influence everyone. It will affect the mood and morale of the tour.

Gossip has broken up more than one friendship or band. It's dealing in half-truths. So if you find yourself talking about someone, imagine that person in his bunk eavesdropping on you. He probably is. So instead, make the choice to try and work this out with the person and not the whole band.

In the event you choose to not nip this in the bud, and the problem doesn't go away. the tension could escalate to the point of wanting to haul off and hit each other. It's amazing how mad we can get at bandmates. We have to remember we aren't on this tour for the rest of our lives. They aren't our lovers (usually). But we are some sort of family on the road, and it's important to not allow our feelings to fester.

Don't be afraid to tell someone if something they are doing is bothering you. They may not be aware of it. There are two realities.

> "Everyone has their version of the truth. The truth is: the truth moves around."–Peggy Firestone

Author Note: If you want to avoid conflict with a bandmate entirely, you can ask your tour manager to intervene. A difficult bandmate can then be mad at the tour manager (part of the job description) and not you. Good cop, bad cop.

ILLNESS

There's an emotional adjustment at the beginning of every tour that rolls into the physical. Someone gets a headache and has to leave the dinner table. Someone has a stomachache and wonders if they should go to the hospital. Your digestion that is flawless every other day of the year will stop the first twenty-four hours of a tour.

Amazingly, with all the weird hours, weird food, and weird sleep, there's not a lot of show-stopping illness on a tour. You kind of hold it together and don't get really sick until you arrive home. Even if you feel something coming on, the adrenaline and sweating during a show may burn the potential cold, fever, or flu right out of you.

> "You're made of the same stuff as the rest of us."–Alejandro. I'm loading the van this morning. Twenty degrees, wind, wet hair, and a sore throat.

Prevention

On the road, you are going to challenge your body's health with lack of sleep, lack of exercise, constant stimulation, alcohol, smoke, and bad food. What can you do to remind your body to stay healthy?

First, do whatever you do at home to stay healthy. Nothing fancy. It works for you at home; it should work on tour.

Wash your hands often. You don't know exactly what has touched that doorknob, the handle of a half-and-half carafe at a coffee shop, dollar bills, or television remotes.

Choose to drink water. Take liter bottles of water from the dressing room and always have two in your bunk. Never drink tap water. The Cirque du Soleil performers are advised to drink bottled water as they travel from town to town because their intestinal tract may not be familiar with local water and they might become ill.

Dr. Andrew Pasminski, chiropractic physician and naprapathic specialist, on staying healthy on the road:

"If I was going to take one thing on the road, I'd take vitamin C. It's a good strong antioxidant. You can eat oranges or drink orange juice, but you can't drink 1,000 to 2,000 milligrams a day.

"With all that smoke or stagnant air, vitamin C helps the lungs. It helps the respiratory cycle. Vitamin C also helps maintain the collagen of the body. It helps the skin tone and maintains your eye muscles. And it prevents scurvy. People would have scurvy on the boat trips. I imagine that's a lot like tour. Scurvy makes your legs bow. It weakens your bones. Vitamin C helps the elasticity of the tissue. You can stand straight, and your posture is better.

"You also want to maintain the environment of your GI (gastrointestinal) tract. It's very important for maintaining your health. Apples are good. Nuts are good. Less bread. When you're sitting a lot on the road your bowel gets backed up, so I think fruit fiber is excellent. What goes in, if it hangs around too much, you get headaches. By maintaining better colon health you'll have fewer problems.

"If you're going to drink [alcohol], make sure the drinks are of a better quality. Coffee has a lot of pesticides. If you make organic coffee with pure distilled water you have a nice brew and it's not as acidic. Pure Kona coffee from Hawaii has minimal acid."

Getting Medical Help

There's an odd discontent when someone leaves the tour to get medical help. Will the tour end? Will they die? When will we see them again? There's much curiosity about the circumstances of their departure and joy when they return. Frank had to stay behind in Paris to get a cyst removed. Joey went to the hospital with an infected spider bite on his leg. We've had a tech hospitalized for appendicitis when he was actually constipated. (When he returned, he took such teasing he had to switch buses.)

INJURY

Tour is hazardous. Not like war, but still perilous enough for an under-slept musician to trip, fall, or bump into something. Backstage can be fairly dark with uneven stairs to navigate. Our thoughts may be on the show we're about to play or the show we have just played, but not on the stairs. More than once I've almost stepped off the stage while looking for the stairs. (I've only seen one person actually step off of a stage like that. It was a conductor gesturing to musicians in an orchestra pit when he stepped into the darkness. His fall was interrupted by a lighting tarp hung loosely over the pit.)

Often the tour injury isn't connected to the show but to leisure-time activities. Dave Max almost drowned swimming in the Pacific Ocean. El John was hit by a car and badly hurt while crossing the street in St. Louis before sound check. There are dangers of drinking in a moving tour bus. Foreheads have been bumped, arms have been bruised. Take your time in your hotel room. You may be moving quickly to get to lobby call on time. Or after the show, you may be a little tipsy and the lights may be out. A corner of a wall or the edge of a stainless-steel shelf may not be placed where you expect it, and suddenly you've banged your head again.

DRUG ABUSE

If someone in the band or crew is abusing cocaine or heroin, you've got a tricky problem to solve. You won't be sure what is going on with this person. They may hide it well. At first you just think they're all wound up. Or in the case of heroin, you just think they're really tired and look like they need some time in the sun. An addict is not safe for the tour. If they are driving the van, it's definitely not safe. If they are looking to buy some drugs in the next city, they may be arrested and miss the show.

> "It starts out fun. The line becomes blurry. By the time you cross the line it's way back there when you think it's still way up there."–Mark

Of course drugs are fun. Why else do them? "Drugs work for you in the beginning and drugs work against you at the end," the saying goes. You may think you're just doing it now and then with your friends, but hard drugs are dangerous to mess around with. No one expects to become an addict. At some point, the high becomes a whole lot more interesting to you than your day, your tour, your friends, and your music.

> "You keep doing it to find that first feeling again, but you will never feel like that again."–Ex-junkie

Heroin is a big rock myth of a drug. It's no badge of anything. It doesn't make you play as great nor be as great as Jimi Hendrix, John Coltrane, or Miles Davis. To those watching or living or playing with you while you're high, you just seem gone.

> "I wish I had met her before she did heroin, because she never came all the way back."

If more than one person on more than one occasion has noticed the monitor engineer nodding off at the soundboard, it's time to talk with him. If more than one show has been less than stellar as the bass player slurs through chord changes, whoever is running this road show needs to talk with him. He will deny, deny, deny, deny. Still, let him know what everyone is observing. It gives him a chance to pull it together. If you still notice it happening, there's not much to be done but fire him until he proves he can handle himself on the road.

Heroin is a bit of Russian roulette. Because you won't know the quality and makeup of the dose you are getting, you might overdose. On the road? In your bunk? In your hotel room? Who is going to find you in time to give you CPR? What happens when 911 gets called and the police come, too? And if you die, someone is going to have to call your mom . . .

Do you want to be a drug casualty? Even if you don't die, you'll be thought of as sort of dumb and be sort of avoided. It's a myth that if you clean up your life you'll having nothing left to write or play.

"Life will still be hard if you're not high, depressed, fucked up."–Jon Dee

QUITTING OR BEING FIRED

If someone has a drug problem on the road he may be fired. A tech who refuses to do the work he was hired to do and is threatening to quit may also be fired. If you've slept with a bandmate's girlfriend you'll probably be fired. Maybe the lead singer's new girlfriend doesn't like you. You may be fired.

> "We have a saying in German: 'Don't try and stop a traveler.' It means if someone wants to go, you let them go."–Heinz

Maybe your home life is a wreck and you need to quit the tour and go home. Maybe the lead singer is not very nice at all and there's been a dramatic mutiny. Maybe you feel invisible, anonymous, unhappy, and unable to rock with your band mates. You'll want to quit. Usually, though, everyone just hopes it all sort of works out for the next few weeks and no one quits and no one is fired.

> "It's better to quit the devil than be fired by the devil"–Luke

But then it happens. You were in and now you're out. Maybe you were fired before you could quit. It hurts like the end of a relationship because it is. You may be told over breakfast or with a phone call.

> "Window or aisle?"–Tour manager's infamous firing of the junky bass player over breakfast.

You may read in the paper that the band is playing Thursday and you weren't told. Navigate this with self-respect. Fans will take sides. Things will be said that are not true. The press is no place to air any of the problems. Yet, when you read you left "to have a solo career" it feels like the public lie that it is. You know there's a story or two, rich with sex, money, or deceit, causing the demise of most kingdoms, relationships, and rock bands. Keep it quiet. No one cares as much as you do.

HOW TO KEEP THE HOME FIRES BURNING

(If you read that as "home fries," go get breakfast and maybe a nap before you continue reading.) The road can become a complete life. It's easy to get caught up in the travel day and performing night and not bother to stay in touch with your home. But the tour will end and you'll be happy to have a home to return to.

> "When you start living on the road and not living at home . . . that's what happened to me."

Calling Home

You promise to stay in touch with those at home and you intend to, but it's often hard to find privacy and a stretch of uninterrupted time for a good call home. Persevere. Some days the conversation feels pretty empty. Some days it will be excruciatingly short. But some days a leisurely message left on an answering is all you need to reconnect.

CELL PHONE. Of course you have a cell phone. If not, get one immediately. With a cell phone, those back home can call you directly, bypassing the front desk clerk or the club production office who will forget to tell you about the call. You can call home from your bunk or from the alley behind the club.

I have no idea what service is best anymore. Everyone complains about whatever carrier they have.

"In my house: no signal. On an island in Maine: signal."

Sign up for a lot of minutes. Out on the road, you'll use your cell phone significantly more than at home. And if you go over your minutes, pay the bill, add more minutes to your plan, and forget it. Every call home keeps it there for you when you return.

Of course, the connection will be lost or cell phone battery will run out at key moments of a conversation. Borrow a phone and call back. Even just to say goodnight. Never let the phone win.

LAND LINE PHONE. Cell phone connections can have an echo or a delay or just sound weird. You may want to talk on a hard-wired phone a few times a week for better reception and conversation.

To pay for these land line calls, you can purchase prepaid calling cards at truck stops for $5 to $20, depending on the amount of time you feel you need. No ugly $300 phone bills upon your return. Often they'll round up minutes used, so for a five-second call you've used up one minute of time.

Tips for a Good Call Home

1. It's not how often, it's the quality of that call. She will know if you are typing on your computer, adding receipts, entertaining those around you. She will also know if you are being fully with her. She knows you. She loves you. She wants u and only u right now. Nothing compares to u, u know. This little tip will save you the forty-five-minute "I need attention" fight.
2. Call once at noon and once at midnight. These can be ten-minute conversations. It seems these are crucial times of day–when you

wake up and when you are thinking about sleep (or someone somewhere is). Make sure you both know if this is a definite call time or an optional call time. You don't want to be in the "You said you'd call, so why didn't you call me?" fight. (One was waiting for the call. One was dealing with a poorly run outdoor festival and didn't get to the hotel until after 3:00 AM and is going to get seventy-five minutes of sleep before joining the pilot and flight crew on the airport shuttle. Can we not fight right now?)

3. It can be helpful to declare the length of the call at the beginning. "This is just a quick call to say hi" or "Okay, now I have some time to talk." This prepares your beloved so she won't be pouring her heart out only for you to interrupt and say, "Oh, that's good. Sorry, I've got to go."

4. The first question you ask is, "How are you?" which is essentially a greeting. Follow this immediately with: "What have you been doing?" This is the actual question. Follow this with excellent listening skills. You may launch into the story of your day only if your beloved is not offering up much in the way of *her* day.

5. If you are hearing monosyllabic answers like the ever-evasive "fine" and the craftily manipulative "not much," be very aware you may be on the way or already entered into the long-distance telephone fight.

6. Divulge early on if you are in a very, very bad mood. And she too must confess to a bad mood. You can't see your beloved's mood coming. You won't have seen them for days and you only have words and tone of voice and attention to communicate. Lots of fights are just misjudged moods and nuance. If one of you actually asks, "What are we fighting about?" there has been a mistake and there should be no fight. But it is time to hang up and try again later.

7. Always declare you wish you were home, even if you have been out having a picnic followed by a roller-coaster ride and a bit of gambling. Your sweet one was having her normal at-home day. Deep down you know you wish you could be there for a moment, for a little touring break, for some tenderness.

> "Do I tell her we've been out paddle boating most of the day and now we're barbecuing salmon having merlot?"–Dave Max

8. Always remind your significant other that the "at home" world is valuable, fascinating, and interesting. She may worry that

Samantha the drummer is more intriguing to you than the fact that she amused herself by feng shui-ing the bedroom. It is your job to tell her she is deeply interesting, amazing, and metaphysically superb. Musician joke: What do you call a musician without a girlfriend? Homeless.

9. If you have to leave a message, leave a good one. Describe what you've looked at today or things you wonder about. It's always a drag if you miss each other, but if a message is all she'll hear of you today, make it one she'll want to play more than once.

"Hey Susquehanna fox, we just drove over the Susquehanna River. It's one of those big wide open East Coast rivers. I just imagine canoes going across it. Probably was an amazing place, like a paradise really—filled with fish, deer in all the forests. Good living."–Voicemail

Send a Text Message

There will be days where the tour is running late and there's no time to relax into a phone call. A text message with a photo of you or a photo of what you are looking at can be sweet (or hot) until you have time to stretch out with each other later.

Send a Postcard

Use your Sharpie and write two big sentences and then *mail* this postcard. Don't wait around for a post office to buy postcard stamps. Use the letter stamp you have in your wallet and mail the postcard today.

Send a Fed-Ex Envelope

Send a handwritten letter. Include little presents in the envelope—some chili powder from Santa Fe, a pinecone, a clipping from a local paper, an interview with Tom Waits. Yes, there is the chance the pinecone will be smashed and the chili powder will leak out of the plastic bag. She will love to receive a package from you containing things you touched and chose for her.

Send an E-mail

Most hotels have Internet access. Ironically, the four-star hotels will charge you while at the less expensive hotels you'll find free wireless. If you weren't able to call last night, you can leave an early morning e-mail message to make up for it. It can be short. It can be intimate and private.

If you don't have a laptop, find an Internet café. Compose your letter offline so your novella doesn't get lost in rebooting or when your time runs out unexpectedly.

Buy Presents

Yes, buy presents. Shirts or tops are good choices because they almost always fit. Pants or dresses often don't. Buy something unique to where you are–an olive wood ring from Greece; a straw hat from Lexington, Kentucky; a silver necklace from Santa Fe. You can mail the present home, but the personal presentation is best. Your very presence on the day you arrive home is all that's needed, but reaching into your suitcase and pulling out a present is a delight. Also, a present can bridge any reacquainting awkwardness the day you arrive home.

Yes, You Have a Family

Call your family now and then, especially when you're in impressive cities. Describe the dinner you had, the monument you saw, the cadets in full uniform on the street in Annapolis, the accents you heard in West Virginia. Perhaps your relatives aren't able to travel and will enjoy hearing tales from somewhere else.

Your family may love or ignore the fact that you're in a touring rock band. If they're not so keen about it, one day something will happen to make your career choice seem a little more valuable in their eyes. It could be something as simple as an article about the band in their local paper or a good review of your record. Maybe you've met someone famous. Maybe they've seen you perform on national TV. You'll no longer be the black sheep. You may have become the family's shining star. During holiday gatherings they may enjoy hearing road stories. They may also want you to perform or do karaoke with them: "C'mon, you're a professional."

ADVENTURES BIG AND SMALL

It's come to this. Drive. Play. Drink. Repeat.

Yes, every tour is different and every day on tour is different, but it's also a lot the same. You drive to the gig, play the show, have a beer or two–day after day. It may be hard to believe, but you may become really bored of the rock club and the rock club after-show party.

We go to the Dungeon and have "Dragon's Blood," but I'm bored. The coolest thing is the gigantic roach crawling across a painting of a demon.

Frank Orrall of Poi dog Pondering and Thievery Corporation told me this about his touring experience:

"The shows are the highlight of the day. I look forward to them. It's what your energy is going toward. The after-show is great. But other than that it's all just sound check and driving time. When you're out there doing the bulk of it, the adventures that happen during the hours in between make it good for me. Everything becomes an adventure. Finding something good to eat becomes an adventure. The fabric of my memory of touring is all the little things that happened that took me by surprise along the way."

If a drive day is scheduled to make it to the next gig, you might include an adventure to break the long drive up a bit. (Do not let anyone call a drive day a day off. It's not a day off so you can lie by the pool and order room service. You will drive and drive.) Since you've got plenty of time, you can stop and do something rather than lie comatose in the front lounge or your bunk.

- Buy a grill. Stop in the desert outside of Las Vegas and have a barbecue.
- Stop the bus by a river. Climb over the barbed wire and swim half-naked in the icy water of a mountain stream. The current will be severe. The water will be mind-numbingly cold.
- Convince the bus driver to let you stop at 5 AM to see the biggest glacier in Canada.

  "It looked bigger in the brochure, I'm going back to my bunk."

- Take the longer route and go see the primitive artist studios in the Southeast. Buy hand-painted license plates from the artist himself at a fraction of the city price.
- Stop for forty-five minutes at any roadside amusement park, go-cart track, or dirt bike rental.

DEALING WITH YOUR LAUNDRY

Seven days into your tour, you'll start looking for a laundromat. Socks can be worn more than one day, but when you start smelling yourself in your own clothes it's time to do your laundry.

"You want coffee, a place to buy a used book, and a place to wash your clothes across the street."

There are four choices in getting your clothes cleaned:

1. The someone-does-it-all-for-you method. Obviously, a fabulous option. Find a laundromat near the club or hotel with "wash, dry, and fold" service. They charge by the pound. It'll cost around $10. Ask when your clothes will be ready for pickup. Will they have your laundry done before the band leaves town?

When you pick it up, everything is fresh smelling, folded, and wrapped. There may be a bleach mark on your favorite shirt and your jeans may have been shrunk, but they did it all for you, it's done, and you're leaving town. Shop for another top and jeans in the next city.

Another way to have someone else do your laundry is to ask a bandmate who has declared he's doing laundry today if he would wash one pair of pants or a few socks for you. He may have room in his load for a few items, and you're set for a few more days.

2. I guess you could do laundry yourself at the laundromat, but only if they don't offer wash and fold service. I guess you could do it on a day off in Santa Fe with your road hook-up, and that might be okay . . .

> I cabbed to the laundromat. Two women came in with eight bags to dry and took up all the dryers. Is it okay if I take dry clothes out of a stopped dryer in this city? I waited and then took the clothes out, sure I would be shot, folding them just to be safe.

3. Do it yourself at the hotel. Everyone on your tour seems to choose the same day to do laundry, so there may be twelve loads of laundry ahead of yours. If you do choose the hotel laundry, you can always take a hot tub while your clothes are in the dryer. This is risking thievery, I know, but no one has ever stolen my clothes from a hotel drier.

4. You might be able to do your laundry at the club. If you are stuck there anyway and they've got a washer and dryer, you might as well do your laundry. These machines usually work well.

BEING A WOMAN IN A BAND ON THE ROAD

I don't like watching an older Asian man walk fifteen paces in front of his wife.

Bands are often men. Stage techs and production guys at the clubs you are visiting are most often men. It's refreshing to meet a woman sound engineer, lighting director, or musician. Often she's been working with a lot of men and is sort of tough and incredibly capable. Here are some practical suggestions for women on the road:

1. Be a woman, because you are. If you want to wear makeup, use hair products, and dress up, then do.

2. Do your part. Know the songs. Know how your gear works. Bring

only what you can carry yourself. If you are going to bring six pairs of boots and all the grooming supplies in your first two bathroom drawers, it's your responsibility to move it all for the next five weeks. Drive the van when it's your turn. Load in and load out until you have crew and even then you can help.

> "They're road worthless. Road worthless. They stand there in front of the bags and don't pick up a thing."

3. Flirting to get something done because you are lazy is manipulative. That said, I'm sure I've flirted to get something done, and there is probably some unspoken fair exchange going on.
4. Count the days between periods *very* accurately and stash tampons in handy places. And if you've just got "a feeling," go check and make sure that a period hasn't started a few days earlier than expected moments before you go onstage. God love Chrissie Hynde for being the first woman I heard speak of periods on tour, in *Rolling Stone.*
5. You'll probably share hotel rooms and backstage dressing rooms with male bandmates. Hopefully you had brothers and this is no big deal.

In a big generalization that is sure to fail me, I've noticed men are more casual than women. They roll with things a bit more. They don't discuss things as much. They say what they mean and often they make it funny. So if you are a woman, take your time to speak clearly, get to the point, and lighten up a bit.

My friend who travels in theater thinks the question "What's it like being a woman on tour?" really means "Do you get hit on?" Okay. Yes. The question "Is she attached?" doesn't mean he wants to get to know you. He wants to sleep with you.

> "Now, if you wanted to get laid tonight you could, right? Now, it's different for guys. We can't. It's what makes men deep down insecure."

If asked for your phone number, ask for his e-mail. If you feel like keeping in touch, you can. But never, ever turn a night at a bar into a long-distance romance, thinking it can survive. It just can't. You fill in the distance with perfection.

Sex? Never with bandmates. That's what ex-boyfriends coming to the show are for (maybe). That's what some of this back, neck, shoulder, foot and hand rub business is all about. (See "Road Romance: Its Prevention and Cure," page 225.)

"Sex in my life has diminished greatly since I've gotten into this 'sex, drugs, and rock 'n' roll' business."–Keith

Author Note: Yes, you'll hear a lot of sexist jokes.

PSYCHOLOGICAL PROFILE: WEEKS TWO AND THREE

I found a used bookstore and opened a copy of *A Life* by Charles Dickens and read: "His childhood had been lost there and all his wanderings were a search for it." Is that what tour is? Is that what playing is?

Remember the first week of tour? It's fun. You get to eat out, never make a bed, drink, and stay up until dawn because there's a party every night. You're just a little roughed up. Nothing a little sleep won't cure.

My emotions are cold and then emotions are full. Sometimes I want emotion to go away.

At week number two you're over the initial shock of tour and start to get in the rhythm of it. It's still a grand time, but you'd like a rest, and a fabulous dinner wouldn't hurt. You stop being sure what day of the week it is. Every night you play seems like a Friday. Every day off seems like a Sunday. You see sides of your bandmates you never knew–panic attacks, surliness, impatience, and also generosity, optimism, and humor.

We were on the bus laughing about a W.O.W. HALL T-shirt across a pair of breasts and as I laughed I burst into tears and everyone got quiet.

By week number three you are nowhere near home and can't even start thinking about it. The lack of privacy, sleep, or touch can start to make you weepy and off balance. Wasn't there an experiment where the monkeys (or was it babies?) who were not touched simply didn't grow and died young? You'd like some unconditional love and attention.

The sign in the elevator said, WHEN LIGHT IS FLASHING, HELP IS ON THE WAY. I watched and waited for that light to flash all the way up to the 8th floor.

ROCK STAR MOMENTS

Rock star moments are silly and indulgent. "You feel like you deserve it for a change," as Robert says. It's a moment of posing with a fan blowing your hair back onstage, or asking someone to do more for you than they should.

"Don't you know who I am?"

Laureline laid on a bench in the dressing room and asked in her French accent, "There is no chocolate here? Doesn't anyone want chocolate?" And a guy working at Joe's Pub went and bought the French girl her chocolate. Max convinced a tech to go out and purchase small fingernail clippers for him. I demanded my tech open the bottle of water for me before placing it by my microphone stand every night. And he did. Every night. Howe and I both booked flights from Seattle to Chicago instead of driving in the van with everyone else. ("No way. I've done the drive. I've seen the country. I'm flying.")

"This is bullshit; I will be in my trailer."–Mark

THE VISIT FROM HOME

At three weeks, fly your sweet one to an interesting city where you will be staying more than one night. I don't care if you think you can tough it out longer than three weeks. You'll begin to think, "Well, we've gone this long already. I'll see her when I get home." If you don't see each other now you can count on phone fights and the incurable lure of road infatuation. The reacquainting when you get home will feel like you are making love to a stranger.

Some bands make a rule of no girlfriends on tour. A rock star told me in a London cab that flying the boyfriend out to the tour will be the demise of the relationship. On tour, the tour *is* your relationship, she said. She is right and I am right. At three weeks, you need a visit with your at-home relationship.

The visit has its awkwardness. You are in the midst of the tour. You need to be two places–on tour and with your loved one. You may feel the tug between wanting to be with the band and wanting to be with your sweet one.

How do you divide yourself during the visit? If I were your tour manager, this would be your visit from home schedule: First, say hello privately. She probably doesn't want to have to hang out with you and the whole band until 4 AM before you get to be alone. Give each other some undivided attention when she arrives. At sound check you give yourself entirely to the band. Then, have dinner with your best friends on tour and your girlfriend. After dinner, rest with your girlfriend. Thirty minutes before the show, turn your full attention to your bandmates and the show you're about to play. After the show you need to come down with your bandmates. As the night goes on, it would be nice to slowly leave the party and share a pillow with your sweetness. Good luck.

If your girlfriend travels with the tour for a few days, her presence will change you so it will change the rhythm of tour. Bandmates probably don't dislike her; although she may not tour well and her visit may be disruptive, it's just that the flow of the tour is altered.

> The lead singer's new girlfriend invited a party to the one hotel room we kept to change and chill before the NY show. They were pleased and rested and smoking, drinking, telling stories, passing dip. We just wanted no party while we showered and ironed semi-clean clothes before the show.

Wise words from the author: After the tour, who will hold your hand when you have a fever? Who will talk you through your dreams and disappointments? In a year, who will care about your deepest self? It may be your lover and it may be a bandmate.

THE HERE-AND-GONE STOP HOME

It does happen that the tour may stop in your hometown for one show or pause for two days at home before going off to Europe or another coast. It's the here-and-gone stop. Careful now, you aren't home for good, so you can't let all that tension, tiredness, and need release like water breaking a dam. You'll have to re-gather yourself before you have had a chance to recover.

If there's no show, just a brief stop, determine four or five things that are "home" to you. Do those, feel those, have those. Order the pizza you love, drink a bottle of red wine on your back porch with your girlfriend or boyfriend, take a hot bath, and sleep in your own sheets. In the morning make your coffee the way you like it and off you go again.

The hometown show mid-tour will be unexpectedly stressful. You'll be in two places at once–home and tour. You'll want to get your car. Please remember your house keys and car keys are in your suitcase under the bus before you take a $20 taxi home. You'll be impatient with urgency trying to find and reconnect with your girlfriend or boyfriend. Returning to the venue for your show, you'll have to find a place to park your car. (Ask the tour manager to save you a parking place.) You'll have a full guest list of people you want to talk with and may not get a chance to. If the bus drives out tonight it's a wrenching goodbye. If you sleep overnight in your own bed, it'll be very hard to gather yourself and your things in the morning.

PLATONIC LOVERS

> "Don't you need tender sometimes?"–Laureline. Yes, I need some tender.

You get closer in a week of traveling together than if you spent six months in the same city. There is a depth of friendship that occurs as your conversations meander deeper: "Why are we living on this planet?" "Can you be in love with two people at the same time?" "If there was an alternate universe what would you improve on?" You share adventures and misadventures. During long hours of travel you tell your stories. And there is a lot of leaning on shoulders and sleeping like pups.

"Has the boyfriend left so it's okay to touch you again?"

This is platonic love, dears. It doesn't seem right for the lover at home out for a visit to see this affection, but it is platonic. Don't confuse yourself.

"I love her. Not like a sister, not like a lover, but other. A musician. Other."

If the lead singer calls you his soul mate, saying, "You're perfect and just the right amount of clumsy," it's a sweet conversation, looking for a little tender. Of course we get a little attracted.

ROAD ROMANCE: ITS PREVENTION AND CURE

Platonic love can easily cross the line into a road romance—an affair with someone in the band, someone in a band you're traveling with, or member of the crew. But can the author make a huge suggestion: do not sleep with these lovely new friends.

"So, what are y'all, the happy loving couple of the tour?"—the bartendress, Long Beach

You know exactly where the flirting becomes more than platonic.

"Why don't you smoke?"
  "It makes me dizzy." And then I held out my fingers to have a puff of his cigarette.

You start having a road language or shortcut slang that only those on the tour understand. You start having shared stories of fun and of difficulties. You accept a little neck rub because your sweet one isn't there to give it. Now add shots of tequila or some absinthe and the cocoon of a bus back lounge . . .

"Well, we were in New Orleans. It always happens in New Orleans. We were down some alley, up against a wall crazy for each other . . ."

The road romance will usually (read: *always*) fail. Even if it is bliss and the best you ever had, when the bus stops at your hometown, it's over, over, over. If your road infatuation is worth it and worth it to you, it can wait. Call them up after a few weeks and go look at amplifiers or record a song together. I've warned you. You're on your own. And you will tempt the fates anyway, won't you?

You may want to keep your road romance a secret from everyone. Those who don't know for sure will try to plot to discover if it's true. You can set up a diversionary tactic such as implying you are sleeping with the bus driver, I suppose. You will be found out.

> "Of course it was the best tour you've ever been on. You were sleeping with your tech."

Perhaps you need more information, dear reader. Imagine this: your friends will suddenly be off getting a bite, seeing a movie, having a look around town without you because they'll think you want to be alone with your dear one, when in actuality you want to be with all your pals doing whatever it is you do on a day off.

Those who are not your closest friends will think you are just having sex, while you may think you're falling in love. If your road romance tells you he would follow another girl to the four corners of the earth, believe him. Even if he gets tender later and asks, "Do you want to come back over here?" Do not believe it if someone tells you they love you on the road. If they still love you when you get home, well isn't that nice?

> "A kiss on the roof does not love make"–Dave Max, Baton Rouge

Most everyone on tour will think you're not doing your work, not giving your full attention and love to the music and the tour. You may feel that love makes you happy, open, and strengthened, but it makes the band feel left out. At a meeting they will say it makes the band "dysfunctional." Now, the band is also dysfunctional when the bass player gets drunk, the drummer holds a grudge, the keyboard player gets snotty, and the guitar player still forgets the damn songs. But a band will try to end the road romance first.

> On a practical note, regarding forbidden love–yes, it *is* possible in a bunk.

> "All I need to see is a show of hands."–tour manager, standing outside a closed bunk curtain, trying to get a late-night bus count

Author's suggestions for preventing road romance:

Option 1: May I suggest staying with the group? Don't veer off with your platonic love.

Option 2: Be mature? Enjoy that sweet attraction without giving in to it. You may become fast friends through time and years. You may find yourselves traveling on a European tour bus ten years from now, drinking red wine, the moon coming up, BBC radio coming on, talking like the good old friends you are, happy to have never crossed that line.

Option 3: If you have a sweet girlfriend or boyfriend back home that knows how to rub your shoulders, kiss your neck, and you share life stories with, have them come out for that week-three visit.

Option 4: If you must sleep with someone, sleep with the crew. Why? Crew can be fired.

> She is hurt. She is angry. She is drunk. Band should never date crew.

If it's too late for my prevention tips, if you have succumbed already, I have one suggestion (and didn't you know I would?). Dare that road romance to work. Move to their hometown or have them move to yours.

> We're all lit up from Christmas lights in front of my house. I think I could fall in love. Tomorrow, he's gone.

I'm sorry, but it will fail. I'm sorry to be cynical, but I can't warn you enough.

> He is gone unless I move there. Big, big, expensive breaking-up calls. We must live in the same city or end this.

The road is another world. It is one long theater production, and you play yourself as a novice rock star. There are no bills to pay, no house to pick up, no wondering what to do today. The tour ends. The romance ends.

> Feeling helpless and bewildered with a casual goodbye. Nobody cried and nobody talked about a future visit. I told him I loved him in the parking lot and he said nothing.

INFIDELITY

(If you read that as high fidelity, you're doing all right. Music is your mistress. You're keeping your focus.) If you have a serious boyfriend or girlfriend back home don't even think of putting your tour in the position of lying for you about your infidelities or road romance. Keep it private. Don't ask your roommate to lie about your whereabouts.

If your marriage was on the rocks before you joined the band (See "The 100 Great Lies of Rock 'n' Roll," page 249), don't play out your own messy drama in the very public arena of a tour. Wait until you get home and be honest and end it.

> "If his wife were here he'd be having orange juice."
> "If his wife were here he'd be having a double."

If you do sleep with someone once, can you keep it to yourself? You don't have to be honest and forthcoming while you're out on the tour. It will be hell for you and your bandmates and the girlfriend or boyfriend back home.

THE LONG-DISTANCE BREAKUP

When will you not be beautiful to me? You must stop being beautiful to me.

If you are breaking up with the person back home, no phone calls after 11 PM. They won't be receptive. Sometimes the touring musician, circus performer, or tour manager is away from home too long for the love to stay. Sometimes there are just too many hours and moments not shared. Sometimes you just have to let it go. Unwrap your arms from the wrong thing. It's already gone.

"She's a Pisces. She understands me."–Breakup, North Hampton

If you are fighting to the point of breaking up, don't invite the girlfriend out on tour at this fractured point in your relationship. It may be great to see each other, but it won't help the bigger problem and you won't have time to sort through it all while you're mid-tour.

Personally, I think the breakup should be forestalled until the tour ends and you can be face-to-face, because then you probably won't break up, unless, of course, there's someone else already in the picture.

RELIGION

God and the devil were taking a walk, talking about religion. The devil says, "Oh, let me organize it."

"What's your religion on the road?" El John once asked me. I said, "Probably the golden rule, or you 'reap what you sow.'" "Mine is food," he said. "I eat something good once a day. And as a body and mind cleansing experience, I try to find the one moment alone. I think that's why you try to choose a hotel with a gym or a pool–so you can get by yourself."

During the long drives and late nights, religion comes up. I have some suggestions:

1. Do not get into a religious disagreement in an enclosed vehicle with eight other people traveling down the highway with four and a half hours left to go.
2. If you want to see the Mormon Tabernacle Choir and are curious about the history of the Mormons, go ahead and look at the

grounds, but don't sign anything or give them your correct address. They will come visit you in your hometown.

3. "If anyone cites Bible passages to support their insupportable idea, just know there are other passages that will support an opposite idea," Bill Carter, our filmmaking and Baptist-raised friend, tells me.

4. Take a St. Christopher medallion with you just to be a safe traveler.

5. Consider the golden rule. It's the law of cause and effect, you reap what you sow, karma . . .

"Oh, what's another lifetime?"

6. You could learn to meditate to empty out your mind. My acupuncturist, Dr. Andy Pasminski, suggested meditation on tour: "Ten minutes of meditation and you'll have less double work. It'll help you remember where your keys are. You'll know where your drumsticks are."

Here's the easiest instruction I ever heard: Take a deep breath and hold it. Breathe in a little more and hold it. Breathe out. Now close your **eyes** and breathe normally. Think only about your breathing. Thoughts will come. Imagine them to be little kids with their hands raised in class urgently wanting to be called on. Notice them and say, "Thank you, you can go," "Thank you, you can go," every time you start thinking. Pretty soon all your fast thoughts will slow down and leave. You feel differently in your own skin. You'll be meditating.

RECEIVING BAD NEWS

It's hard to be away from home when you get bad news. Someone has gotten gravely ill or someone has died. You get the phone call while standing in the front lounge, a long, long, way from home.

"I was on tour in Toronto when I found out my mom had died right before sound check. J‑‑‑‑‑‑‑ went down the street and found a record store and bought me the Hildegard von Bingham, *Feather on the Breath of God* CD. He handed it to me and said it had helped him a lot when his mom had died."

You may leave the tour tomorrow, but this afternoon you may choose to sound check and play the show tonight. You want to be composed and rational. You know we don't live forever. But this is not an easy moment on tour.

I think my mom is dying. I can feel her get airier. I got a phone call from my brother that she has gotten worse, and these songs about death and life that we're playing at sound check make me cry and I can't stop. We drive through old London and I think of all the families that have lived and loved and had babies, and strong fathers and radiant mothers and dinners and then it all ends. Many, many, many, families have died off. I'm looking at the old abandoned stone houses they lived in.

The bad news may stop the tour completely. The tour bus turns around. Death and grave illness are considered acts of God in your performance contract and the gigs will be cancelled.

DEATH

We played Summerfest on Sunday. On Wednesday afternoon Matt was missing. And at 11:35 PM his mom called to say he had died in the truck, the Ryder truck we had used for the show. No one can believe it.

Why does this happen so much? Someone in the band or the crew dies. Is it that hard drugs can be around? Is it because musicians live in less expensive and less safe parts of town? Is it because artists react deeply and emotionally to life and it overwhelms them?

Somebody will die. It might be suicide, a car wreck, or an overdose. It could be your monitor guy, your keyboard player, the lead guitarist, or the singer. He was just alive and now he's not? We can't believe it.

"Everyone dies but no one is dead."–Tibetan saying

Go to the funeral. The power of your presence there is incalculable. Cry if you cry. Laugh if you laugh, because something will make you laugh. Play the music you know he liked through a good sound system. Make a video and project it on the funeral home wall–your bandmate on the bus, backstage, anywhere.

"Only love is left on a day like this. Everything else washes away."

HOLIDAYS

I'm sorry to tell you, you may not be home for Easter, Thanksgiving, Valentine's Day, or your birthday. You may not even know it's a holiday. It was one dismal Easter in Cleveland that I watched a big dirty Easter bunny wave at families as I ate an overcooked egg salad sandwich at a sports bar.

Remember that holidays sometimes include parades. Fourth of July, Memorial Day, St. Patrick's Day, Columbus Day, Veterans Day, Christmas

Parades. You don't want to be stuck in parade traffic on your way in or out of a city. When you advance a show near a holiday, ask the club if there are any street celebrations to avoid.

Mardi Gras parades start weeks before Fat Tuesday and the weekend before was traditionally (pre-Katrina) already raging in the French Quarter. Double-check with the hotel, club, or NewOrleans.com for parade schedules and routes so your tour bus or van won't get stuck on the wrong side of a parade. Make sure your bus driver gets a hotel room far away from street noise so he can get some sleep.

Playing on a holiday, you will never be the headliner. The holiday is the headliner. Your show will be secondary. New Year's Eve—although the pay is good, the night is all about the countdown and champagne, not your band. On Halloween—you'd probably prefer not to play your sensitive songs to penguins, cowboys, witches, goblins, hookers, doctors, robots, etc.

> We had Halloween night off. Walking back from dinner I heard, "Got you, bitch," and a splat as a stupid car peeled off. Someone had egged us, and it hit Hector's leather coat. He rubbed the coat on the grass and picked up a sharp rock to be ready if they circled back around.

WEEKS FOUR AND FIVE

At week number four you're in the back half of the tour. You're sort of adjusted to no sleep, no privacy, a kind of hazy-all-the-time delirium. You start noticing animals, kids, and old people. None of these is very rock. But each softens you on a tour that is hardening a crust around you. You think you could tour forever and the next moment you must buy your own hotel room or you'll go crazy.

> Frank comes out of the shower in a towel with green clay on his face. "My anti-stress mask."

It is at eight days you can begin the countdown home. Why? Because you can call it a week. It's toward the end of a tour that you wonder why it is we do this. We look at the audience; they look at us. Why are they here watching us in a hot and smoky club? Why are we all standing here looking at them?

But something is beginning to happening. You may notice the effects of your national performing, radio interviews and performances, TV shows, and press. You may have created a buzz. It's like a wave gathering up. More fans are showing up at your shows. There's an excitement in the room when you play.

That squealing stuff is happening when Frank sings "Be the One."

If you have been neglecting home, it's time to give it some attention. Otherwise, when you get there who will care? You may not assess your relationship at this time. You've been separated too long and you want some loving attention. Needy has become your invisible friend. Needy does not care about being fair or seeing a bigger picture. Needy wants some attention NOW. Well, you can have all that and much more eight days from now.

9. The End of Your Tour

That last show listed in your tour itinerary may or may not be the end of the tour. You've been easing out the last of your energy so you can make it to the end, but your booking agent might have been offered another (or several) shows and you aren't going home on Thursday after all. You may be two and a half hours from home playing on a college campus at a toga party on the hockey rink. But soon the final night of the tour arrives.

THE LAST NIGHT

It'd be nice if the last show was the pinnacle of the tour, but it almost never is. (The best night happened unexpectedly somewhere mid-tour.) On the last night, the wheels start coming off the tour. The band starts collecting things they've left here and there on the bus or in the van. You can feel everybody getting ready for it all to be over. Friends may arrive and the band is pulled out of its tour groove.

Tomorrow is home. Your body knows it even if your playing is flawless. You let yourself feel how close you are, knowing you don't have to hold it together physically, mentally, and emotionally much longer.

"The last night can make you weak."–Alejandro

If you've got one more night in the hotel, there will be a party room that celebrates until daylight, sharing champagne, leftover anything you've been collecting from deli trays and fans. If you've got a long drive home on the bus, supplies will be gathered–tequila, movies, wine, snacks–and the bus rolls through the night.

> "All I know is I close this door and press 'Chicago.' It's a horizontal elevator and it takes me home. Next floor: Chicago."–Max

EXTENDING YOUR STAY

If your tour ends and you find yourself in a city you like, it may be possible to stay on another day or longer. Staying an extra day is actually an acceptable method of transition from tour to home. It will be weird to watch the bus and your friends drive away and know you will now have to pay for your hotel room and food and decide when and where to go and how to get there. But you get the bonus of some privacy, some relaxing, and some exploring.

> We drive to Hot Springs and finally find a spa open and get massages and soak in mineral tubs. The hot waters seep deep and we all relax and open our eyes. A bath on the inside. I call my roommate and she has evicted me.

THE AFTERMATH

Tour is over. The last show has been played. You've all told each other how much you love each other and what a great time it's been. And then you're home.

Arriving Home

The day arrives and you're at the designated drop-off point/meeting place waiting to be picked up by your loved one. Then there they are, looking like all the stars in the sky landed in their eyes. Or maybe they've overslept and aren't there at all.

> He slept through picking me up at the airport at 10:30 AM. I cab home and he meets me at the front door in his white robe from Morocco, looking like Jesus. The kitchen table is set with champagne in a bucket, candles, and berries. So we drink morning champagne and enjoy talking. Then go to bed.

Every coming home is different. Sometimes the first moments are easy. You walk into your lovely home that you have traveled to in your daydreams.

> I hugged my house I was so happy to be home.

Sometimes you're home but you don't feel at home. This is your girlfriend or boyfriend, but it doesn't feel like your girlfriend or boyfriend just yet.

He looks great. Did we lose it in the two months apart? Maybe I'm afraid his fantasy of me will collapse with the real me.

To the one at home: The first conversations may be all about the characters, plot turns, or intrigue of the movie of tour. Let it all burn off like a fever. It will. And when it does, it may break hard, leaving your loved one depressed, listless, aimless, and out-of-sorts. (See "Prognosis," page 236.)

"I can't keep up with you right when you come home. You're all wound up."

Well, weeks apart can't be sorted out in an hour. This is when presents help. It temporarily moves the attention from the relationship or the housekeeping onto the new dress from Portugal or the fish combs from Greece or the handmade pottery from Annapolis.

My boyfriend is tender. His luggage was lost. And it was the suitcase with the presents and wine.

Perhaps it's time to simply draw a bath with some eucalyptus oil. Wash the plane ride, the bus ride, or the van ride off of your skin. Yes, your love should join you. Then put on some extremely comfortable clothes that hold no memory of the tour and begin the unwinding.

We made a three-dish dinner, drank Veuve champagne, and with the Christmas lights on watched the first snow. Welcome home perfection.

Reentry

"We should definitely all come home and check into a hotel all together and then the next morning go home. And two nights later meet for a band dinner."–Frank

It's hard to know what to do the first day you're home. It's as if you've been dumped out of a speeding van or bus and everything has suddenly stopped. Oh, you have. Now what? On tour everything was so scheduled that you may want to do nothing. But the quiet is so quiet you may want to find all your at-home friends immediately and have a big party. You'd like to rest, but you're too wound up to sleep and you're too tired to get up.

"Do you want to get in my car and drive in a circle around town for an hour tonight?"–Adam, first night home

For weeks your mind has been fighting your body and your body has been fighting your mind. You have been overriding every primal instinct. If you wanted to sleep you may have had to force yourself to stay awake to prepare for a show. If you wanted to eat a hot meal, you couldn't just make it yourself; you had to wait for a dinner stop. When you wanted to sleep with your lover you couldn't. And now you're not sure how to listen and respond to your body again.

Without a tour manager and a day sheet, just exactly what happens at home? The ordinary stuff is there to do, to fix, to pay. But it's not so glamorous. (I have to make the bed?) You're just the "at home" you again. And home has been "off" or on "standby" for weeks. It takes a while for home to turn on, for friends to call, or for a purpose to emerge.

"Out on tour you feel like, 'I'm somebody doing something.'"

Now that you're home you vaguely wonder if you are no one doing nothing. In a word, you're not at your best. You won't make much sense to your sweet one or to yourself. The welcome home fight is almost inevitable. You're tired. The kind of tired where gravity seems stronger than it is. You don't want to hear your boyfriend tease you: "Crabby girl. Crabby girl." You want some care. You want some attention. You want some tenderness. You want your tech. But this is your lover.

Last week all you wanted was to be home. How come you don't feel at home? Last week there were so many things you wanted to do when you got home, but now the list just seems long and overwhelming. How do you get over a tour? I've helped you this far, haven't I? First, let yourself rest. Then slowly, something will interest you. Something will rise up and compel you. One thing at a time you'll reacquaint with home life. The first morning home, fix yourself a perfect cup of coffee and sort your mail. No emergencies there? Then get in the car and go out for breakfast. (Easy now. Remember how to drive? You don't want a welcome home car wreck.) After breakfast, browse the used record store as if you were still on tour.

"Home is just the next stop on the tour."–Matt Fish reentry tip

Then, come home and rest again. Later, make some calls from your front porch and notice how the seasons have changed since you left five weeks ago. Take a look in the refrigerator and make a trip to your favorite grocery store. Look at all the avocados, tortillas, eggs, arugula, red lettuce, fresh mozzarella, vine-ripened tomatoes, salmon, French bread, basil, and olive oil. You can purchase any of these and have them any time you want because they'll be in the great big refrigerator in your kitchen.

At 8 PM grab some of your stashed per diems and walk to the coffee shop to get an Americano. You might run into a friend riding her bicycle who tells you about a cool show tonight. At 10 PM, go see a band and order a beer in a smoky rock club. You'll probably have to pay for it.

I think I can just walk backstage and say hi to the band, but I get stopped by security. My Poi laminate is like Confederate money now.

Unpacking

Your suitcase must be put away out of your sight soon—within twenty-four hours. Here's my tip for easy unpacking: Take things out of your suitcase and place in piles around you, sorting them by their ultimate destination: the laundry pile, the pile of items that go back into the kitchen, the stack that goes to the bathroom closet, the clothes that go in the bedroom, and the questionable stack of maps, receipts, matches or business cards. Then put the suitcase away. As you feel like it, move a stack where it belongs. Soon it's all gone except for the things you don't know what to do with, and you don't really care. Essentially, everything is put away. You are unpacked.

Prognosis

Some have said it takes a week to get over a tour. Some have reported it takes the length of the tour to get over the tour. I think it takes ten days to two weeks to recover. The return to physical and emotional equilibrium can't be hurried.

Let yourself sleep anytime you want. (Call it "watching movies" if you like.) Eat anything that your body is asking for—from a thickly frosted cupcake to fresh juice. Be gentle with yourself. You will feel wide mood swings. Maybe it's time for a short Master Cleanse fast or a massage. The transition is hard for all traveling musicians.

"I used to get home and dial 9 to get an outside line."

"I get home and put up a day sheet."

"I heard the guy in Cheap Trick had an exact replica of a Holiday Inn room built in his house."

"I heard of a guy who built a bus bunk in his bedroom."

Slowly you'll ease into your home life and let the tour leave your muscle memory. You start realizing weekends are for novices and that you might be claustrophobic in a big rock audience. (How do fans do it?) You may be pleased to watch the band you have been opening for play on *Saturday Night Live* or *David Letterman*. Or see a rerun of your own performance.

"Yes, it's a rock star home on a Saturday night doing the dishes."–Dag email

After a few weeks you may start romanticizing about tour and feel a restlessness. You sense correctly that you shouldn't let the band's momentum drop. Let yourself soak up every taste and comfort of home. Because, my dear, in twelve days you'll begin the next tour. But this time you'll be traveling in a counterclockwise direction. And there's still talk of Japan and Australia in the spring.

Epilogue

"It's kinda stupid, kinda fun, kinda weird, kinda wonderful."

Touring shows you the country that truck drivers, gypsies, and pioneers traveled. An immense sunset stretches out before you as you approach Denver. You follow a sunlit river in the Green Mountains, looking down from above the pine trees. You drive through the moon rocks in Nevada and stop to thrift shop in El Paso at noon. You make a dinner stop at dusk in Bliss, Idaho. You survive a snowstorm on a mountain as a bandmate keeps repeating, "This too shall pass. This too shall pass."

You immerse in the slipstream that is tour, and it shapes you, even if you only have a brief moment to explore these one-day destinations. You'll talk to people going about their day: a Cajun who owns the haunted club, a beekeeper, a husband whose wife is fighting cancer, a painter. You'll try a microbrew, read the editorials in the local paper, take a quick run through town noting the name of a café you might have time to go to the next time you're here.

You adorn yourself visibly and invisibly with things collected at each port far from home. Maybe you pick up a mannerism here, a turn of phrase there. You're pleased to wear four necklaces and five rings simply because you remember each afternoon and each city where you purchased them.

Every day aims for the rock show that night—ablaze one moment and almost broken from tenderness the next. Some nights are flat. Don't give up. Someone will tell you it's the best show they've ever seen. Other nights something effortless happens. It all comes together and something bigger than all of us lifts up the entire room. You come off stage and know that you're the best band in America.

The next morning, you're alone, eating blueberry pancakes in Portland, Maine. You sleepily overhear a conversation about your show last night as you read an ad for a rental house in Nova Scotia across the bay and consider renting it.

You carry with you every gig that came before, every county, state, and highway mile, every side trip, every after-show party, each declaration of love, and every sigh of doubt. It's in your muscles. It can't be helped. You may lose your hearing, lose your lover, or lose your home, but what a life you'll have lived—twice the life in half the time.

"I hated it. I loved it. I'll always remember it."

Appendix A: Tips by Musicians for Musicians

DAG JUHLIN—
SONGWRITER, AUTHOR, GUITARIST WITH PDP

You are a lucky person. You are in an elite club that sanctions childish behavior and often rewards it with large sums of money and misguided adulation.

Treat your fans nicely. Enjoy the road. Be polite. Conserve your energy. Face your daily duties with enthusiasm and, if necessary, slightly bemused irony.

Soak up the scenery, good or bad. Try and do things like the locals do. Get some quiet time each day. Do not misplace or lend your tour pass or bus key. Be prompt. Eat as well as you can. Don't abuse yourself or others.

Save some money for your inevitable decline. Accept your youth as passing and your cutting-edge ideas as soon to be passé. The main thing to remember, though, is this: when you get home from tour, please DO NOT write a song about how hard it is.

JACKSON HARING—BOOKING AGENT WITH HIGH ROAD TOURING, FORMER PDP TOUR MANAGER, FORMER MANAGER FOR CAMPER VAN BEETHOVEN

1. Everyone feels like they have to bring out a front-of-house engineer. You have to ask yourself, "Do I want a dog that knows where all the bones are buried or do I want a dog that will dig up the yard?" If you use the club sound person, he knows what channel doesn't work, and it won't freak him out when it happens.
2. Hand the sound engineer some points that are particular to your band. Some things that will suggest how you'd like the overall mix to be, instead of him trying to guess what you sound like.
3. Put together a sensible rider that has some modest or at least commensurate catering. Maybe a stage plot.
4. Not everyone is out to get you, so quit treating people like that. Some people are in it because they like music. They're not trying to steal your nickels and dimes. You can work out the math. If you sell 250 tickets at $10 each, the math isn't that hard. There's not another thousand missing.

JOHN WESLEY HARDING—SONGWRITER AND AUTHOR

1. Don't leave your wallet in the dressing room.
2. Hire someone to do it, if you possibly can.
3. Vital—When you are really hating a gig and it's your worst night ever, remember that someone in the future will come up to you and tell you that it was the best gig they ever saw in their life.
4. You will probably need to be the support act for every one of your support acts at some point in the future. The reverse might not necessarily be true.
5. Always be very open about what everyone is being paid.
6. Keep a diary: www.wesweb.net.

FRANK ORRALL—FOUNDER, POI DOG PONDERING, SINGER AND PERCUSSIONIST WITH THIEVERY CORPORATION

1. Pack light and enjoy being in the tour moment. I used to bring books I'd been meaning to read, a typewriter to capture song ideas, and a four-track to work on songs in my hotel. For all the lugging around, I never really read the books or used the typewriter or four-track.

2. Clothes and laundry–It's hard to find time to do laundry on the road, and you don't want dirty clothes smelling up your clean ones, so synthetic fabrics like nylon and rayon dry really fast. You can wash them after the show in the sink. And they should be dry by morning.

   I used to have a pair of vinyl pants that I used to rinse out after the show and spin around above my head in the parking lot to dry. I hung 'em up in the bay of the bus and they were dry by morning.

   Just bring a few choice stage clothes and wear them all the time. Also, pajamas are beautiful bus wear.

3. Ditch mode–It's fun to be out on the road with your friends. It can also make you crazy; always traveling in a pack. Say you want to go and get something to eat and you ask if anyone else wants to go too. You agree to meet in the lobby in ten minutes. Pretty soon you are waiting in the lobby for a few notorious stragglers. You start to get frustrated. You want to ditch them. BY ALL MEANS, DITCH THEM!

   As long as everyone understands "ditch mode" ("Meet here by this time or we'll be gone."), it works very well. You never get frustrated. You just get on your merry way. The person who is late understands that when they get down to the lobby late and you're gone they know what happened and most likely where you went. It gives you a sense of free movement on the road.

4. "Please ditch me" (the other side of ditch mode). This speaks to the person who wants to be ditched. If you know you are not going to make it to the lobby on time and don't want to rush, you can dillydally, assured that you are not holding anyone up. So much of your time on the road is dictated by a schedule. On your free time, ditch mode gives you a sense of autonomous movement.

5. Van touring–When driving, be thoughtful of other band members trying to sleep. Drive smoothly and at a comfortable speed. There is nothing worse than feeling the van wobble and careen when you are trying to get some much needed rest and visions of head-ons go dancing through your brain. If your bus driver is doing this, ask him to stop. He is working for you.

ALEJANDRO ESCOVEDO—SONGWRITER, ROCKER

(I think he is quoting someone, maybe Keith Richards?)

1. Everyone is a ticket.

2. Be nice. You'll see the same people on the way up as the way down.

3. Spread the wealth.

4. Make the stage your own. Make the stage your home.

LISA LOEB—PERFORMER

The three most important things I have on the road are:

1. Really good Chapstick/lip balm. I make my own little containers of Theraplex ointment.

2. Whatever medicine you need from home. I carry a kit of Rx that my doctors have prescribed, especially for throat/cold/cough and stomach issues, or whatever might ail you on a regular basis.

3. Fruit. Go to grocery stores along the way, or even convenience stores, to buy good food choices to balance out all the pizza you're about to eat.

STEVE LEFT—EUROPEAN TOUR MANAGER FOR GIANT SAND AND CALEXICO

1. On arrival at hotel, always get a card or letter head with hotel's name and address on it and put in some pocket. So whatever state you are in, you have something to show the taxi driver to get you home.

2. On night-liners (overnights), arrange with the bus driver that if anyone gets off the bus at night at a truck stop, they will leave something on his driver's seat. Nothing worse than seeing the bus drive off at 4 AM when you're half-dressed and half-asleep with no money.

3. Watch the drinking/drugs intake. The immune system will be running low, so don't push it to its limit by overindulging. Try and eat fruit and fresh salad and vegetables to help.

4. Work together. You're stuck in this circus together and it runs a lot smoother if everyone pulls their weight. Egos are prone to rearing their ugly heads, and this works wonders to upset your touring party and fuck it up.

HOWE GELB—FOUNDER OF GIANT SAND

Leaving the tour is like leaving the mother ship. Here we are in the ship. But then we leave. Here we are on another planet. We try to fit in, learn the customs and ways of the new culture.

LISA GERMANO—WRITER, SINGER, VIOLINIST

Be able to be alone so you don't need other people to entertain you or put yourself in a position where you are needed to entertain them.

Everyone needs their own space, so make sure you have one.

Take books, diaries, your own coffee, wine, and favorite foods . . . things that make you feel at home anywhere.

Don't have sex with other band members or techs. It takes away from your focus, which should be the music. It's all a weird dream time, and when it's over . . . it's usually real over.

KELLY HOGAN—SINGER

Packing–I always try to pack bulk items (bought for cheaper at K-Mart or Target in advance) that would cost you a kidney to buy at a convenience store in time of dire need–e.g., tampons, AA or 9-volt batteries, aspirin, bottled water, and, uh . . . Jägermeister.

Sleeping–This is the most important part of all for being able to sing well night after night–must be lying-down-type "real" sleep, not sleeping in van while someone drives. I just don't do floors anymore. I never could do them very well (I always get numb "camping butt" that wakes me up), but now I REALLY can't do it, being an old lady. I take earplugs and a mask when I think of it.

"And what does this question mean: What's it like being a girl on the road? Do you have the answer to that one?"

See "bulk tampons/Jägermeister" above. That, and the soundman is condescending sometimes and it makes me homicidal.

CHUCK PROPHET—SINGER, SONGWRITER, AND ELECTRIC GUITARIST

Winston Watson (drummer for Bob Dylan, Warren Zevon, Robyn Hitchcock)'s Five Tips for Maintaining a Healthy, Happy Van:

1. Avoid handicap zones. The harmonically and rhythmically challenged do not qualify. Do not take your road karma lightly.
2. Always travel with a pair of pantyhose and some JB weld (a specialized, high-temperature epoxy). Any shade-tree mechanic worth his salt will tell you that pantyhose makes a good fan belt in a pinch.
3. Pie plates for fuses are not recommended except during certain emergency circumstances. Beer does not operate as antifreeze–Dr. Pepper, on the other hand, will do the trick. (Both antifreeze and

Dr. Pepper share the common ingredient, Propylene glycol.)

4. Any exhaust system can be saved by the proper creative use of a coat hanger

5. There is a right way and a wrong way to pack the van. When in doubt, consult bass player.

ABRA MOORE—SINGER, SONGWRITER, SATELLITE PDP

Hold on to your rituals, whatever your thing is. It's majorly, majorly, majorly important. Try to keep your routine wherever you are, because tour is so chaotic.

Exercise is very, very important. Exercise is good for the lull and depression and the mental and physical. Keep that part balanced. Everything else is so not stable. Ground yourself with the tools you can take with you.

What I learned on tour? I learned that I like my bathroom and my towels and my bathtub.

JON DEE GRAHAM—SONGWRITER, SINGER, GUITARIST

Always, always, always, always remember, it's just a rock show. Because it's just a show. A great show? It's still just a show. A terrible gig? It's still just a show.

And why do we do this? Because we have to.

JUAN CARRERA—TOUR MANAGER

Be hospitable when you first walk into the club. Ask people what they do. Don't be all rock star. Every place functions a little differently.

I always ask, "At the end of the night, how quickly do we have to load out and is there a disco?"

The guy bringing beer all night . . . ask if at the end of the night you can buy a case of water from him. Chances are you won't have to pay, and it's great to have.

Enjoy the buzz of non-sleep as long as everything is going well and nothing crosses that barrier.

Pee stops are quicker if you stop at a rest area instead of a truck stop with shopping. And never, ever stop at a Denny's near a mall.

Don't eat at Denny's ever, even if you think it's going to be good.

What should you *not* bring on tour? Your girlfriend.

Pay per diems weekly; not daily.

Bring a calculator.

"Hey Juan, musicians are onto leave times being a half hour earlier than they need to be."

Well, tour managers are aware that the musicians are aware of that, so leave times are actually an hour before they have to be.

ROBERT CORNELIUS—SINGER, ACTOR, SONGWRITER

Everything that you think you need at home you should take with you. And that includes floss, fingernail clippers, and eyelash curlers and stuff like that. Sewing kit and needle and thread. Just like the stuff your mom would bring; bandages and Advil.

That's what makes a really good rock star. He can cure the hangover after he causes it.

Why tour? Every part of it, I'll never forget.

KENT KESSLER—INTERNATIONAL JAZZ BASSIST

Pack black, polyester clothes.

At about ten days out I always get in a terrible mood. I don't know quite what it is, but it's predictable. I just try to keep quiet and soon it's over.

LAURELINE PRUD'HOMME—SINGER, BASSIST

What is good about tour? In France we have this saying, *"La fuite en avant"*–"You run away toward." On tour, you belong to the world, tasting everything.

TAWNYA LORAE—SINGER, SONGWRITER, ARTIST

Bring Clinique chocolate brown lip gloss.

"What about etiquette, getting lost, no sleep?" Clinique chocolate brown lip gloss.

"But what about bad food, the lure of road romance?" Clinique chocolate brown lip gloss.

DIANA BRUSHKE—MELODY BASS PLAYER, SINGER, SONGWRITER

Have respect for each other. You seem to have more space for yourself if you respect everyone else.

JOEY BURNS—CALEXICO SINGER, GUITARIST

There is an ever-changing balance of frontier and home. You need your home. You need to tour. Each is important.

Road romance: Get over it. Unless you are, as John says, "young, dumb, and full of come." Enjoy the subtleties.

No fast food. Take it from me, never do fast foods. It doesn't matter if anyone says, "They've gotten so much better. They have salads now."

JOHN CONVERTINO—CALEXICO DRUMMER

On tour, your shoes are home.

Interviews: It's always easier one on one. What's tiresome is getting asked the same question over and over.

Always have a towel in the van. You're going to need it.

BOHB BLAIR—SOUND ENGINEER AND TOUR MANAGER FOR CUPCAKES, CHEVELLE, NASH KATO/URGE OVERKILL. CURRENTLY CONCEPTUAL DIRECTOR FOR A CHICAGO-BASED MARKETING AGENCY.

1. Who wants to be the headliner? When you're in the opening band you get to arrive latest for sound check, have more time for the drive between cities, get done earlier, can still drink while the bar, venue, city, is open, score the headlining band's chicks while drinking their beer in the dressing room and sell more merch while the other band is playing. Being the opening band rules. If you can get the headliner to travel your gear with theirs (they frequently will do this to make the load-in and setup of your gear faster and easier), then you've totally got it made and should never leave that tour.

2. Do not get sucked in to trying to keep up with a band in a bus when you are a band in a van. This is evil. That band has a sober (maybe) bus driver and you have your guitar tech who is shooting heroin in his elbow to impress a local. That band can sleep while they travel through the night while you will have to keep telling jokes to said guitar tech for fear of him passing out one minute after you do. Trying to keep up with a band in a bus is difficult business.

3. The road to success is lined with talcum powder. I'm not sure for the ladies, but there is no doubt that a liberal disbursement into

the pants pre-ride can save you from significant discomfort over time.

4. Snacks can be a constant and destructive temptation, especially on a van tour. Not to mention that constant snacking is at odds with your rocker physique. Try this move: create a list of snacks that you really like but that are slightly rare to find in the convenience and truck stop shopping meccas. This list may have to shift regionally to either make items more or less common. Then if you go into a convenience store and they do not have your items, you get nothing.

Appendix B: The 100 Great Lies of Rock 'n' Roll

1. You won't have any trouble finding the place.
2. You can't miss it. We're right up on the corner.
3. Traffic will open up after the tolls.
4. Don't worry, there's lots of parking.
5. The hotel is right by the club.
6. Rooming lists and keys will be waiting for you at the front desk.
7. The rooms will be ready soon.
8. Yes, there is a place to park your bus.
9. Yes, there are showers at the venue.
10. I'm on the other line.
11. I'll call you right back.
12. I think I've got another call—I better take this one.
13. My cell is about to go down.
14. We'll have flyers printed and plastered everywhere.
15. Someone will be there early to let you in.
16. Yeah, we've got loaders.
17. You'll headline.
18. You'll have plenty of time for a sound check.
19. You can share backline with the other bands.
20. Sounds great out front.
21. I checked it myself.
22. I'm sure it will work.
23. Worked the last time I used it.
24. It was working until you got here.
25. That buzz is normal.
26. It's the subwoofers.

27. It'll sound better with people in here.
28. We can fix it in the mix.
29. We'll fix it after sound check.
30. We're doing all we can.
31. I haven't worked here long, but it'll be fine.
32. My girlfriend is a pro at running lights.
33. We'll turn it down if it's too loud.
34. We'll let you know.
35. The band drinks free.
36. It won't affect the performance.
37. Dinner provided promptly at 5 PM.
38. Plenty of places to eat around here.
39. They have great breakfast.
40. We'll definitely check you guys out tonight.
41. Sure you'll get paid if it rains.
42. Tour manager? Looking for him myself.
43. It's all about people needing people, baby; people needing people.
44. Your tickets are at the door.
45. Yeah, they're all roadies. Let 'em in.
46. She'll be backstage after the show.
47. Sounds in tune to me.
48. Of course your mic was on.
49. Lots of industry here tonight.
50. Natalie Merchant, Kiefer Sutherland, and that guy who looks like Ethan Hawke were here.
51. Loved your band!
52. I like your new direction.
53. I think the crowd loved it.
54. I think this marks a turning point.
55. I remember that song.
56. Oh yeah, I saw the whole show.
57. I caught your last song.
58. I tried to come to your show.
59. The place was packed.
60. This is one of Jimi's old Stratocasters.
61. We're going into the studio next month.
62. My last band had a record deal, but we broke up before recording the album.
63. He left to have a solo career.

64. We're all still friends. We had musical differences.
65. I'm really glad to be off the road.
66. Yeah, he cleaned up. He got off the road and cleaned up.
67. Well, it looked crowded, but you're just short of points.
68. Light crowd; well, it was the last episode of [insert any TV show here] tonight.
69. Light crowd; well, school is out.
70. Light crowd; well, school just started.
71. It's a late town.
72. Here's your split; there'll be more once we settle everything
73. My agent will take care of it.
74. We'll just have one beer.
75. Oh have some; it's good!
76. I think we've seen the last of that.
77. Sure I'll sign it. Let me go get a Sharpie.
78. I have no idea where the hotel is, darlin'.
79. My address book was stolen right after I met you.
80. Believe me.
81. I didn't know she was your sister.
82. I didn't know she was your girlfriend.
83. I didn't know she was a man.
84. Your marriage was on the rocks before you joined the band.
85. You remind me of someone I used to go out with.
86. I love you.
87. Yeah, see you at the after-party.
88. We're right behind you.
89. We'll meet you there.
90. Our crew would never do anything like that.
91. Yes, it's in the truck.
92. Yeah, my friends on the rugby team will be there at 2 AM to help you load out.
93. I put it in the van.
94. I didn't forget; I thought you were kidding.
95. Well, what *I* heard was … [anything that follows is a great big lie]
96. Rock 'n' roll keeps you young and kills you early.
97. I'm cool, no problem.
98. It's all good.
99. We'll deal with that at the end of the tour.
100. I'm with the band.

Index